Desert Cities

HISTORY OF THE URBAN ENVIRONMENT

Martin V. Melosi and Joel A. Tarr, Editors

Desert Cities

THE ENVIRONMENTAL HISTORY OF PHOENIX AND TUCSON

Michael F. Logan

UNIVERSITY OF PITTSBURGH PRESS

Published by the University of Pittsburgh Press, Pittsburgh, Pa., 15260
Copyright © 2006, University of Pittsburgh Press
Manufactured in the United States of America
Printed on acid-free paper
10 9 8 7 6 5 4 3 2 1

Library of Congress Cataloging-in-Publication Data

Logan, Michael F., 1950-
  Desert cities : the environmental history of Phoenix and Tucson / Michael F. Logan.
    p. cm. — (History of the urban environment)
  Includes bibliographical references and index.
  ISBN 0-8229-4294-1 (cloth : alk. paper)
  1. Human ecology—Arizona—Phoenix—History. 2. Phoeniz (Ariz.)—History. 3. Human
ecology—Arizona—Tucson—History. 4. Tucson (Ariz)—History. I. Title. II. Series.
  GF504.A6L635 2006
  304.209791—dc22

                                        2006015729

CONTENTS

ILLUSTRATIONS

Maps

Illustrations

Tables

ACKNOWLEDGMENTS

First I thank the members of the University of Pittsburgh Press. Their steadfast support for this project has withstood my own delays and procrastinations, as well as staff changes within the press. Thanks especially go to Cynthia Miller and Niels Aaboe. Much of the time we historians toil in anonymity, particularly in the writing stage of a project, when solitude produces the most notable results. At those times a contract and continued interest by editors at a press can be a source of both motivation and comfort. At every step of the production process the press has provided me with friendly and professional assistance. Most recently Trish Weisman's careful copyediting added clarity and polish to the book. My thanks go to Trish and everyone at the press who worked so diligently to bring the book to print. I also want to thank the press for its continuing commitment to publish books on urban environmental history. Its list of books on this topic includes many noteworthy titles, and I hope my own modest offering adds to its strength in this field.

The Charles Redd Center for Western Studies has provided me with generous support for the research and writing of this book. The center's interest in furthering our understanding of the history and culture of the Mountain West greatly assists scholars working in this field. Its financial assistance has allowed me to travel to Arizona several times for research trips and has given me the opportunity to write and revise the manuscript. My heartfelt thanks go to the center for their support.

The History Department at Oklahoma State University, as well as the College of Arts and Sciences, has provided me with support for writing this book. The college in 2002 granted me a month of summer salary, which greatly assisted in the completion of the early chapters. Michael Larson and his staff of cartographers in the Department of Geography created the eleven maps in the book. I also want to thank Stephen McKeever, vice president for research, for his financial assistance in paying for the maps. The History Department's contribution came primarily in the form of regular and consistent summer research funds. The History Department struggles mightily to generate financial support for faculty research. Given the generally penurious circumstances of higher education nationwide, our department's efforts to support members' research agendas is truly noteworthy. As historians our opportunities to acquire extramural funding are modest. Many departments work to supplement faculty research and conference travel. Our department is no different in this regard except perhaps in the level of support our communal efforts have achieved.

I also owe a debt of gratitude to the scores of scholars who have established the field of urban environmental history as a viable and significant component of academic scholarship. Likewise, I acknowledge the scholars who have studied and analyzed Tucson, Phoenix, and the urban history of the Southwest. I am treading on ground previously traveled by many excellent historians.

Lastly I thank my family for their support during the research and writing of this book. My two sons, Owen and Bryce, were born into this project, so to speak, and have grown to sentient age with Daddy writing about Tucson and Phoenix. My wife, Patti, has also shared the burden of this book. As a historian herself, Patti understands the demands and difficulties of this kind of project. I thank her for her kindness and encouragement.

Although the support for this project has been extremely communal—family and friends, colleagues, editors, and the community of scholars—the responsibility for this book is mine. If errors appear, they are my own. If the book contains insights that inform the reading audience, then the advancement of scholarship achieved by this book is predicated upon the volumes of excellent work that precede it.

Desert Cities

Introduction

DESERT CITIES

URBAN RIVALRY EXISTS in many instances in the United States and around the world. Some examples in the American West include Portland and Seattle, Albuquerque and Santa Fe, Los Angeles and San Francisco. Often one city will lay claim to the cultural high ground, while the other rushes self-confidently toward wealth and prosperity. In Arizona at the turn of the twentieth century, the urban rivals became Phoenix and Tucson after challenges in the late nineteenth century by Prescott and Florence fell away. Although Tucson and Phoenix shared fundamental economic origins founded on irrigated agriculture, they followed independent trajectories that led to their prominence in the state, rival communities shining in stark contrast to one another. It is commonly understood in Arizona that Phoenicians look down their noses at laid-back, small-townish Tucson, and reciprocally minded Tucsonans direct a mild animosity toward bustling, freeway-ridden, besmogged Phoenix. Leaving aside for the moment the issue of how realistic these images may be, I examine the basic question, how is it that such different perceptions of urban communities could develop regarding cities growing up so close to one another and occupying such similar physical settings, within such a brief span of time? Of particular interest to me is the role the physical setting of the two cities played in their development. Both are desert cities, but the constraints of the semiarid environment seem to have played out very differently in the two communities.

Tucson and Phoenix have been admirably studied by historians such as C. L. Sonnichsen and Bradford Luckingham. These two scholars have written urban biographies of the two cities that provide a clear narrative of southwestern urban development. Additional scholars have written many excellent essays, dissertations, and theses on specific topics related to the history of the two cities. Just on the issue of water policy alone, fine scholars such as Karen Smith, Doug Kopel, and Barbara Tellman have offered works of clarity and insight. If such fine books and essays on the two cities exist, then why should I have written this book, and perhaps more to the point, why should you bother to read it? First, the book satisfies a personal curiosity. I was born in Tucson and lived many years there, but I have close friends from Phoenix and have spent quite a bit of time there as well. In short, personal experience has made me aware of both the similarities and differences of the two cities and stimulated a curiosity about the contrasting desert communities. Second, the book offers the general reader, including residents of Tucson and Phoenix, a handy comparison of the two cities. This synthesis saves the reader from having to shuffle the pages of Luckingham's and Sonnichsen's books together. Even if such shuffling could take place, first a page on Phoenix and then a page on Tucson, no clear understanding would develop. The information has to be culled and summarized, and, where possible, an explanation must be offered that explains the differences between the cities. Last, this book serves a more academic purpose. The two cites offer examples of southwestern urban history, having confronted issues of urban growth that face all western cities to one degree or another. The two cities came to different conclusions about their circumstances and strategies for development and so serve as alternative models of urban growth in the semiarid Southwest.

The histories of the two cities describe communities initially traveling similar paths toward prosperity and growth. Irrigated agriculture along intermittent desert rivers was the reason for the communities' existence. Other themes in traditional economic history played out in the two cities. Railroad

development in the 1880s was key to the creation of an industrial infrastructure that propelled the cities' growth in the twentieth century. More recently,
military-industrial enterprises during and after World War II brought new
levels of prosperity and growth to the two communities.

Environmental and cultural factors played significant roles in how these
economic forces played out in the two cities. Traditional models of urban development, often following lines of analysis from economic history, fail to explain completely how the two cities came to embody disparate and contrasting
communities. For example, boosters hotly debated plans and schemes for en-
hancement of water supplies for agriculture at the turn of the twentieth century.
Critical to the debates, decisions, and ultimate construction of some of the
projects was the semiarid environment of central and southern Arizona. At
this juncture in the two cities' urban development, nature's physical parameters played a critical role.

Also critical to urban development were the perceptions of nature's physical constraints. The cultural makeup of the two communities, particularly the
ethnically driven perceptions of the ruling elites, determined the strategies and
mechanisms that would be employed to harness water resources. As it turned
out, Phoenix boosters were more aggressive in transforming their desert environment into an agrarian paradise and eventual metropolis, primarily by securing the federal subsidy of the Salt River Project. Tucson elites, by comparison,
were always more willing to live within the constraints of their natural environment, not without plans and schemes to use the river and reclaim the desert,
but less ambitious and far reaching in their concepts and visions.

The cities have been self-consciously regional since their founding as frontier communities. This is therefore a work of western history. Disciplinary lines
are malleable, however, and so this book is also a work of urban and environmental history. All of these scholarly fields are mutually supportive; none are
mutually exclusive. Discussions about scholarly discipline are of interest to
academics, but I assume they are of little interest to the general reader. On the
other hand, regional identities are grounded in the mind-set of the people and
societies that resided in the two cities. During the Spanish and Mexican eras
the regional orientation of the residents was northern rather than western.
Southern and central Arizona were part of the Pimería Alta, land of the upper
Pimas, and to the Spanish it constituted a remote northern frontier. Settlement came to the region about four generations after the Spanish occupation

of the Rio Grande valley and Santa Fe. With Anglo-American settlement in the nineteenth century, the region's identity shifted from northern to western and more specifically to southwestern. It remained a frontier, however, through its early history and has retained its regional identity even into its postcolonial, modern, and postmodern circumstances. As part of the booming West after World War II, these Sun Belt cities have attracted the attention of noted scholars such as Carl Abbott, Mike Davis, John Findlay, Marc Reisner, and Hal Rothman. Prominent in the scholarly attention to these two cities have been the environmental perspectives concerning water policy.

Because they are desert cities in the semiarid Southwest, water has always been central to the communities' history. Simply stated, without the rivers and the riparian ecosystems supported by the rivers, no permanent, sedentary human society would have developed in the region. Native American, Hispanic, and Anglo cultures have exploited the water supply according to their own concepts of appropriate use. Judgments of ethical propriety toward the natural environment have changed over the centuries, but central to each culture's residence in the valleys have been the politically determined valuation and use of the water resources.

Cities exist within natural settings and display a fundamental aspect of the human relationship with nature. At times urban environments—especially metropolitan expanses—seem to overwhelm nature, as pavement and concrete obscure all but the most tenacious or ephemeral elements of the natural world. But even in these sprawling conglomerations of glass, steel, masonry, and asphalt, nature exists and human society accommodates its presence. In the desert the continuing relationship between human society and nature is evident in the oppressive heat and meager rain that dominate the consciousness of residents and require the constant manipulation of the built environment. Relatively few people lived in these places until air conditioning became available in the twentieth century. Once swamp coolers and refrigeration offered a palliative for the summer heat, human populations soared. The mounting population of permanent residents continued to be augmented by tens of thousands of snow birds, winter residents who scurried home to cooler climes as the heat began to mount in the desert spring, and the whir of air-conditioning compressors became a more or less constant feature of the built environment. The increasing power demands of these desert cities, partly to accommodate the requirements of the air conditioners, had clear environmental outcomes: hydroelectric dams, atomic or coal-fired power generation plants, and freon-based hydrocarbon emissions, just to name a few.

Tucson and Phoenix share many, if not most, of these environmental circumstances. Yet they seem to be such different communities. The following chapters seek to explain both their commonalities and their differences. Viewed separately and from a distance, the cities seem to mirror each other, firmly grounded in their physical settings. Viewed together and more closely, differences of cultural nuance become obvious.

I believe two factors created unique trajectories of growth in the two cities. My thesis posits two causes for difference, one basically natural and environmental, the other cultural and political. First, the Salt River in Phoenix flowed at a rate four and one-half times greater than the Santa Cruz River in Tucson. Quite simply, the larger Salt River provided more opportunity for agricultural development in the age of technology in the early twentieth century. The other factor that contributed to divergence was the cultural and ethnic makeup of the two communities. During a critical juncture in the cities' development at the turn of the twentieth century, the Hispanic nature of Tucson contrasted distinctly with the Anglo nature of Phoenix. Racism and ethnocentrism were rampant then, and Phoenix leaders proclaimed with pride that Phoenix was relatively free of ethnic diversity. In both cities, the ethnic composition of the communities shaped the political initiatives aimed at stimulating economic growth. In this circumstance, Phoenix leaders gained an advantage over Tucson elites in their push to achieve metropolitan status.

Another question concerns the timing of the cities' divergence, and in answering this I provide a minor corrective to the existing scholarship. Those who have studied the two cities have been aware of the outcome of the story, and at times a sort of presentism—the application of contemporary understandings onto a historical narrative—has appeared in the scholarship. Census statistics give a ready indication of the divergence: Phoenix overcame Tucson in population in 1920, according to the census of that year. The assumption has been that the divergence became visible in 1920 and then widened consistently through the following decades. Rather than the 1920s, I have found, the decade of the 1930s was the critical period for the separation between the two cities. At the close of the twenties, the two cities remained close in population and economic position. Optimism reigned in both places, and competitive braggadocio echoed freely. During the Great Depression, however, circumstances in the two cities differed markedly. Phoenix came through the Depression in much better shape than did Tucson, and it used that advantage to increase its superior position in population and economic health through World War II and into the postwar boom.

As a work of western history this book proceeds from the basic position that most westerners have lived in communities ranging from small towns to big cities. This has been true in the Southwest from prehistoric times and arises from the ecological realities of the place. The harsh conditions in the desert required humans to bind together to survive. This applied to the prehistoric Hohokam, and it remains true today. Beyond issues of survival, rising to levels of comfort and prosperity continued and heightened the impetus toward community formation. Within the discipline of history, this focus on settlement patterns and city building in the West remains more than just vaguely Turnerian. Perhaps in the future I will become a partisan in debates about the old and new western history. Right now I simply believe this focus on the urban history of the Southwest to be the most fruitful and rewarding for arriving at an understanding of western society and culture. Most westerners and Arizonans have lived and continue to reside in communities. The best way to get at an understanding of these people is to study their shifting relationship with nature in the desert cities of the Southwest.

Part 1

ORIGINS

PREHISTORY—1890

1

Two Rivers

THE SETTINGS OF the two cities exhibit only slight variations in terrain, vegetation, and annual rainfall and at first glance give little indication that such divergent urban development could take place in the twentieth century. The two cities seem to be situated similarly within desert surroundings. Sunshine is plentiful; rainfall is scant. As Arizona's commissioner of immigration noted in 1889, "The air is dry; bright, sunshiny days the rule; cloudy days the exception."[1] Elevation, ambient temperature, and vegetation differ minimally. On the other hand, minor differences at times proved to be significant. Along the rivers—the Salt River at Phoenix, the Santa Cruz River at Tucson—similar riparian ecosystems marked the water courses close to the rivers, but within the broader ecosystem slight differences occurred. Thirsty vegetation such as cottonwood and willow hugged the stream banks. Mesquite, tapping groundwater up to eighty feet beneath the surface, spread farther from the surface water, at times occurring in thick *bosques* (forests). In the vicinity of the rivers and in the mesquite forests, wildlife flourished. Fertile alluvial soil supported grasses, vines, and lush undergrowth. With greater distance from the rivers, cactus and desert shrubs came to dominate the terrain, along with their indige-nous wildlife species, including desert bighorn sheep, mule deer, and jackrab-bits. It was in these broad valley expanses that the slight differences in the two locations became clear.[2]

Ambitious farmers established the location of the Phoenix settlement, eleven hundred feet above sea level, in the center of the Salt River valley in 1870. At that elevation in the lower Sonoran desert, June high temperatures soar to over 110 degrees. Tucson began as a Spanish presidio in 1775. More than one thousand feet higher than Phoenix (twenty-four hundred feet above sea level) and about 120 miles to the southeast, Tucson enjoys temperatures about ten degrees cooler—still hot and dry, but distinctly less so. Having per-sonally experienced such temperature extremes in both locations, I can attest to the fact that there is a great difference between 110 degrees and 100 degrees, even when accompanied by single-digit humidity. In comparison, the 10-degree difference renders 100 degrees downright pleasant. Phoenix is also drier than Tucson. Phoenix expects about seven inches of rainfall per year. Tucson on average receives twelve inches. Given the semiarid setting, the five additional inches of rain per year in Tucson is significant, although no doubt still insuf-ficient for those who prefer verdant surroundings. The modest additions to annual rainfall make for a more succulent appearance to the desert in Tucson. Palo verde and mesquite trees give modest shade, and various types of cactus abound, saguaro most notably—a national park in Tucson preserves impressive stands. The drier setting of Phoenix prior to urbanization was dominated by spindly clumps of creosote bush, hackberry, and desert broom. More sparsely vegetated, "an arid, forbidding land," Phoenix presented a much less hospitable appearance.[3]

Fitful streams had serviced irrigated agriculture in the desert valleys since prehistoric times. The rivers barely trickled in the dry summer months and conversely raged in destructive floods during seasonal wet cycles. These envi-ronmental factors were critical to future urban development.

At the most basic level, the rivers and their watersheds determined the extent of human society in the region. I am not arguing here for an environ-mentally deterministic explanation of city development. Other factors, ema-nating from human culture, clearly affected the placement and expansion of the two communities. It is important to understand, however, that environ-

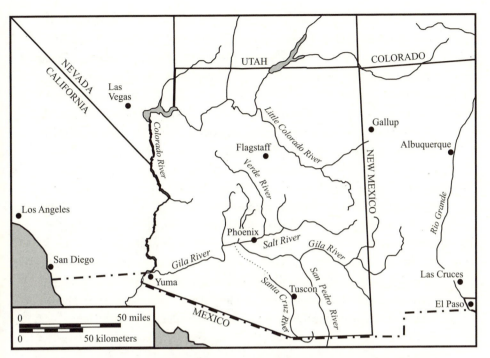

Map 1.1. Arizona and the Southwest. Arizona in its southwestern region, showing the location of urban centers and the rivers that gave rise to the cities of Tucson and Phoenix.

mental factors were often the most dominant in preindustrial societies. Among the industrial societies of the late nineteenth and early twentieth centuries, physical conditions of terrain, climate, and hydrology became more tractable and manageable. With a progressive sense of optimism, residents of the two desert valleys expressed both the certainty and hope that environmental limitations had been swept away by human artifice. Preindustrial societies, on the other hand, lived within natural constraints determined by their environment. The early societies consistently endeavored to stretch nature's limits to the greatest degree possible, or allowable, within their ethical and spiritual concepts of appropriate behavior. But nature set the parameters. What societies do with the parameters depends on their political, social, and cultural guidelines, as well as on their mechanical abilities. At those times when mechanical abilities were limited, or a cultural reverence for nature was heightened, nature exerted a dominating force on the human society.

The Salt River at Phoenix drains a watershed of about 12,700 square miles, while the Santa Cruz River has a watershed of about 8,500 square miles.[4] Given the smaller watershed, the Santa Cruz River flowed at a meager rate of about twenty-five cubic feet per second (cfs) during low-flow periods (measured in the fairly moist year of 1884), while the Salt River's low-flow rate averaged about 116 cfs (averaged from 1889 to 1901).[5] At this basic level, the Salt River could be expected to perform at a rate more than four and one-half times greater than the smaller Santa Cruz. Although this fact did not seem overly significant in 1890, when Tucson still held the lead over Phoenix in population and prosperity, during the subsequent period, in which calls for federal reclamation appeared, the potential usefulness of the Salt River became pivotal.

Rivers spring from their watersheds, which amount to the land mass—mountains, canyons, mesas, valleys—upon which precipitation falls to create the stream. Once engorged, the stream takes on a character of its own, and its personality is formed by the mountains and canyons that gave it birth. The mountains, valleys, and plains through which the river flows determine whether the river trickles, meanders, or rages. To gain an understanding of any river's nature, it is first necessary to grasp the fundamental circumstances of the river's watershed.

Mountains and valleys seem timeless in their physical configurations, but geologists posit with assurance the relative youth or decrepitude of mountain ranges and the rivers flowing through their intervening valleys. In the case of central and southern Arizona, the local mountains began forming about 50 million years ago, supplanting the previous landscape of huge tropical swamps on the margins of ebbing and flowing seas. The seascape had developed about 100 million years ago during the period known as Cretaceous, next most recent to the Jurassic era of dinosaurs. Central and southern Arizona were on the southern and eastern shore of the migrating sea, respectively. Plate tectonics and orogenic episodes of mountain building directed the waters hither and yon. About 60 million years ago, the Sierra Nevada mountains began to arise, creating a barrier to the west that created a huge inland sea. The high mountains to the west also formed an obstacle to rain and storms emanating from the Pacific, creating a rain shadow effect that significantly dried the downwind areas. As the next tens of millions of years ticked off, the range and basin terrain of the American Southwest formed as the inland sea slowly retreated and ultimately disappeared. Mountains rose in sharp, craggy eruptions;

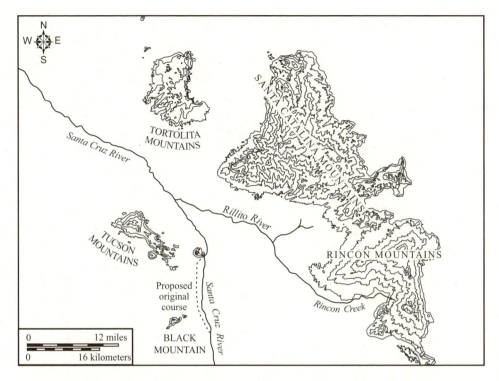

Map 1.2. The Tucson Basin. The basin and its rivers and surrounding mountains and the two courses of the Santa Cruz River are shown.

then erosion proceeded to wear down the uplifted blocks of rock to form the basins and valleys between the peaks. In succeeding events over millions of years, mountains arose, sediment washed down, and the valleys filled with alluvium to depths, in places, of twenty thousand feet. Much more recently, perhaps 1 or 2 million years ago, the valleys so filled with sediment saturated by eons of rain and runoff, that flowing streams and rivers appeared. In both valleys, the subsurface geology indicates the rivers' early history, at times in somewhat surprising fashion.

The Tucson Basin is the middle of three basins in the Santa Cruz River valley. In the far-distant past, the three basins existed independently, runoff forming playa lakes that dried quickly in the bright sunshine. Eventually sedimentation filled the basins to the point that runoff flowed through each basin in succession, creating the protoriver in the Santa Cruz valley 0.7 to 0.25 million years ago.[6] Initially there may have been two rivers. The historical Santa Cruz River flows first to the south into Mexico, then makes a unique U-turn to the north, and reenters the United States near Nogales. The subsurface geology suggests, however, that the original river may have flowed steadily south.[7] In this supposed scenario, the first stream forming in the high basin of the San Raphael Valley would have flowed steadily south in the Magdalena River watershed in Mexico. A second stream would have formed at the head of the middle basin of the Santa Cruz River valley. This stream would have flowed northward through the middle and lower basins of the valley, eventually joining the Gila River system in central Arizona.

Regardless of the geological mystery and the question of two oppositely flowing rivers, the existent Santa Cruz River flows south first and then north. The river enters the Tucson Basin from the south, flowing generally northwest toward its confluence with the Gila River near Phoenix. The distance from Tucson to the river junction is about ninety miles. The topography of the region was described and categorized in 1931 by geologist Nevin Fenneman. The Tucson Basin lies in the Mexican highland section. Most of the lower basin of the Santa Cruz and the Phoenix Basin to the north fall within the lower and drier Sonoran region. The Mexican highland terrain is marked by more succulent cacti species and more varieties of grasses and woody shrubs.[8]

The river in the Tucson Basin was shallow and meandering, hugging the more recent mountains (the result of volcanic extrusions about 1 million years ago) on the western border of the basin.[9] The river's floodplain lay at the foot of low *bajada* (descending) slopes that formed the transition zone from the river to the valley floor. During flood episodes, the river would spread across a mile or more of floodplain framed between the gently terraced uplift to the basin floor. Drainage in the basin flowed generally south to north and east to west. From the eastern side of the basin, moisture and runoff from the surrounding mountains made their way to the river to the west through dozens of minor and major arroyos and stream channels that traversed the mildly rolling terrain.

The Santa Cruz River's broad, shallow valley lacks the sort of rocky narrows favored by turn-of-the-twentieth-century dam builders. On the other hand, the valley—and particularly the Tucson Basin—rests upon thousands of feet of alluvium that contained millions of acre feet of stored water (an acre foot is the amount of water it would take to cover an acre of land one foot deep, or 325,851 gallons). More than twenty thousand feet of silt, sand, and gravel has eroded down from the surrounding mountains.[10] Beneath the sediment is the impermeable bedrock—the ancient roots of the surrounding mountains. On top of the bedrock, and for most of the depth of eroded material, are the most highly compacted (consolidated, in the language of geologists) formations —this is the older alluvium. The permeability of the older alluvium is limited; nonetheless the total volume of stored water is probably quite large because of the huge volume of sediment itself. In general this deep water is inaccessible because of the difficulty and expense of lifting it to the surface. The low permeability of older alluvium causes underground water to move especially slowly through the formations. This results in wells that are slow to recharge. The problem is threefold: the expense of sinking a deep well, the cost of lifting water from such extreme depths, and the slow recharge of especially deep wells.[11]

Resting on the more ancient deposits are the relatively recent (0.7 to 0.25 million years old) sediments known as younger alluvium.[12] The highly permeable younger alluvium, in places more than a thousand feet deep, allows water to move more freely. Difficulty arises, however, when trying to apply our human-driven perceptions underground; we have to adjust, for instance, our concepts of speed and free movement. Geologists tell us that groundwater moves through permeable strata at the relatively quick rate of a little more than two hundred feet per year.[13] That speed translates into the passage of an inch every 3.7 hours. Snails travel faster. Even earthworms munch their way through the earth at a faster rate.

Before extensive groundwater pumping was carried out in the twentieth century, the younger alluvium in the Tucson Basin held about 70 million acre feet of water.[14] This is a staggering amount of water, the result of eons of precipitation and snow melt. The human demand for water since the onset of industrial society has been staggering as well. Since the turn of the twentieth century, groundwater mining has steadily depleted the underground supply, causing the water table in the basin to drop in places several hundred feet. At the turn of the twenty-first century, projected overdraft of the aquifer (the amount of water removed from wells beyond that returned to the aquifer through recharge) was more than 3 million acre feet from 1995 to 2025.[15] Given a supply of 70 million acre feet, an overdraft of 3 million over thirty years may seem somewhat paltry. After all, such rates of withdrawal from the aquifer could stretch into the upcoming centuries. Alarm arises, however, because of the finite quality of the resource. Once the 70 million acre feet are gone, Tucson simply ceases to exist, at least in any form recognizable by current residents of the valley.

The flowing streams and green ribbons of vegetation in the arid South-west have always appeared shocking, if not miraculous. The more typical brown and thorny surroundings are a testament to the prevailing dry conditions. The streams exist only because so much rain and snow falls on the mountainous watersheds. Whereas seven inches or less of rain may fall on the Phoenix Basin each year, over thirty inches will accumulate on the peaks of the upstream mountains.[16] The Salt River benefits from a much more extensive watershed than does the Santa Cruz. Peaks over nine thousand feet overlook the Santa Cruz River valley, but the Salt River in central Arizona emanates from a more general uplift in the terrain. The Salt River's watershed reaches to the east and northeast first to the central mountains and the Mogollon Rim country (three thousand to five thousand feet in elevation) and beyond to the flatter and higher Colorado Plateau (five thousand to six thousand feet in elevation).[17]

The drainage from the high plateau country flows generally to the south-west and west. The Verde River drains extensive territory to the north and joins the Salt River to the northeast of Phoenix. Augmented by the Verde's flow, the Salt River joins the Gila River to the west of Phoenix, near the Gila's confluence with the Santa Cruz River. Continuing west and enlarged by the two tributaries, the Gila joins the Colorado River near Yuma. Compared to the Colorado, the Gila's flow pales, and so the tributary relationship is clear. But upstream the three component parts of the Gila River seem mislabeled, at least as far as volume is concerned. Most diminutive is the Santa Cruz, flowing at a rate less than one-quarter that of the Salt. In second place is the Gila, flowing at a rate typically one-third that of the Salt. According to the volume of the river's flow, maps should be redrawn and the river joining the Colorado near Yuma should be called the Salt.[18] Yet the Gila River is considered the main stem and the other streams, the branches.

The Gila's claim to primacy rests mainly on its length, which surpasses that of the Salt. Another factor is simply the geographic placement of the rivers. Spanish explorers wandered into the region in the late 1600s, traveling gener-ally south to north, encountering first the Santa Cruz and Gila rivers and their Native American inhabitants. No settlements existed on the Salt River, named Salado by the Spanish, and so the Spanish initially showed little interest. Later

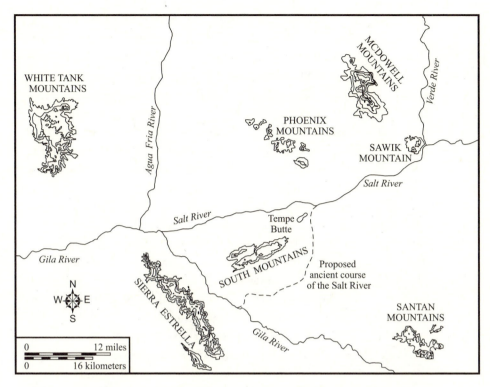

Map 1.3. The Phoenix Basin. The basin and its rivers and mountains, including the ancient course and the suggested underflow of the Salt River, as described by geologist Willis T. Lee in 1904, are shown.

Spanish prospectors discovered gold deposits in the narrow canyons of the Salt River upstream from the Phoenix Basin, but the remoteness of the area from Spanish presidios along with its proximity to Apache realms rendered the Spanish development efforts extremely haphazard. The Salt River was marginal to the Spanish occupation of the region. The Gila, on the other hand, was central to the Spanish. The headwaters of the Gila arise in the mountains of western New Mexico, near the nexus of Spanish colonization in the Rio Grande valley.

Regardless of the hierarchy in labeling, the Salt River's traverse through the central mountains into the Phoenix Basin is significant because the journey required that the river cut its way through several narrow canyons that proved to be more or less perfect dam sites. Not only did the Salt River possess greater volume, it also presented more tractable features to early-twentieth-century engineers. This is not to suggest that Phoenix rose to metropolitan supremacy in the state solely because of the water supply. Rather, the circumstances of the Salt and Santa Cruz rivers provided the baseline parameters for human society in the valleys. Even before the construction of high dams in the early 1900s, the Salt River potentially could support greater human populations. Whether it did so or not was dependent on the human societies themselves. The strategies for water use formulated by the societies in the valley were certainly influenced by the environmental circumstances, but the political decisions regarding the manipulation of water supplies were also subject to a myriad of cultural variables.

The Salt River enters the Phoenix Basin from the east. The basin itself is subdivided into several smaller basins formed by hills and buttes.[19] Examples of the dividing structures are the twin Tempe and Papago buttes and Camelback Mountain. The subbasins (Paradise Valley, for example) are composed of alluvium eroded down from the surrounding hills and mountains. Geologically speaking, the Phoenix Basin is generally only half as deep as the Tucson Basin. The alluvium in the center of the Phoenix Basin is about ten thousand feet thick, whereas sediment in the Tucson Basin extends to depths of twenty thousand feet. The basins share a similar subsurface geology of older and younger alluvium, with stored water resources more readily available closer to the surface. Likewise, the two basins exhibit comparable bajada slope configurations. Prior to urbanization, the Salt River meandered within a floodplain of varying width between gently rising terraces. In places the terraces were shallow—four feet—in other places fifty feet or more. The highest terrace in the Phoenix Basin was the Sawik Terrace, 235 feet above the river.[20]

South Mountain forms the southern boundary of the basin, so named because the river flows from east to west to the north of the mountain. Such geologically determined names seem to be the safest, free of any cultural embellishment that might run afoul of future political correctness and guaranteed of a basic spatial accuracy. Not to dispute the contemporary accuracy of the name, geologists suggest that the Salt River initially flowed on the other side of the mountain. Prior to the most recent sedimentation, an obstructing crystalline ridge ran from the east end of South Mountain to the north through Tempe and Papago buttes, culminating in the Phoenix Mountains. Most of that ridge is now buried under sediment. The buttes near Tempe are a much eroded, visible reminder of the structure. In the past the Salt River was diverted by the ridge, flowing southwest around the eastern end of South Mountain, joining the Gila River much farther upstream and, coincidentally, bypassing completely the future town site of Phoenix. Even after sedimentation had created the historic channel of the river to the north of South Mountain, the ridge continued to block the underflow of groundwater in the aquifer. At the turn of the twentieth century, a large marsh and lake filled the Gila River channel east of South Mountain. The lake seemed unusual, since the Gila River typically was dry for a reach of fifty miles upstream from the lake. U.S. Geological Survey (USGS) hydrologist Willis T. Lee expressed the opinion in 1904 that the lake, six feet deep and four thousand feet long, resulted from the Salt River's underflow.[21] According to Lee, below the surface of the valley the crystalline ridge directed the ooze of groundwater to the south, while aboveground the surface flow trended steadily westward. Eons of surface flow had regularized the channel to the north of South Mountain.

A trickle during the dry seasons and periodic droughts, a flooding torrent during heavy monsoons or El Niño episodes, the perennial stream of the Salt River supported a riparian ecosystem of plants and animals that flourished within the river's pattern of periodic constancy. Its virtue was reliability, even if a somewhat tempestuous nature characterized the flow. Cottonwoods and willows lined the banks, while grasses and mesquite occupied the open spaces between river and bajada slopes. In places where the river's meanders created especially broad open spaces, half-moon-shaped meadows of grass and thick mesquite forests occurred. On the rocky bajada slopes grasses diminished but mesquite persisted, its taproots able to reach water at greater depths.

All manner of wildlife gravitated toward the lush green river channel: six species of hooved animal, including mountain sheep and mule deer; twenty-three types of carnivore, including mountain lions and bobcats; twenty-nine variations of rodent; five types of rabbit; sixteen species of bat; and one insectivore, the vagrant shrew. In addition to the four-legged critters and bats along the river, there were forty-six types of bird, including ducks, herons, doves, swallows, warblers, owls, and hawks. Reptiles and amphibians also inhabited the river's ecosystem.[22]

The first human beings in the valley were ancient hunter-gatherers, venturing into the valley because the river supported the game animals and edible plant life they required for subsistence. At this very basic level, the river made possible human society—it did not create the human society; rather, it determined where humans could live. This became especially true during the Neolithic era, when human beings began developing sedentary lifestyles that required stable and renewable sources for subsistence.

The first humans to happen upon the future town sites of Tucson and Phoenix may have remarked on the pleasant qualities of the setting: gurgling stream, chirping birds, wind in the trees, distant mountain vistas, and many likely campsites for these constantly on the move Paleo-Indian big-game hunters. These nomadic hunters arrived in North America about ten thousand years ago, crossing the frozen Bearing Straits out of Asia at the end of the last ice age. Scholars assume the Paleo-Indians would have quickly spread over the continent since it was their custom to follow the herds of grazing large mammals, and so the hunters soon would have moved into the region of the two river valleys. It can be imagined that these first human residents of the valley arrived by following the Gila River upstream from its confluence with the Colorado. An approach directly from the north would have been blocked by the Grand Canyon. Traveling up the valleys, the Paleo-Indians may have explored each tributary in succession, investigating the headwaters of the Santa Cruz, Salt, and Gila rivers. Whether they considered the Salt to be the tributary or the main stem is subject to pure conjecture.

Many scholars assume that the Paleo-Indians were very efficient hunters, perhaps even rapacious. Soon after arriving, the hunting groups would have depleted the region of its resources, particularly the herds of gregarious animals, and moved on, leaving no trace of their presence other than the occasional stone tool or kill site. Coincidental with the arrival of these first human beings, 70 percent of the large mammal species (adults larger than one hundred pounds) in North America became extinct. Paul Martin refers to this mass extinction of more than one hundred species as Pleistocene overkill.[23]

Clouding the issue of overkill is the roughly concomitant occurrence of fundamental climate change. At the close of the Pleistocene period, glaciers receded and the last ice age came to a close, bringing about much warmer and drier conditions. In central and southern Arizona, extensive grasslands and spruce and juniper forests characterized the region during the earlier, cooler, wetter period. About eight thousand years ago the river valleys took on their current desiccated appearance, prickly brown expanses interrupted by the occasional green ribbon of a river.[24] With the drier conditions, habitats necessary for many of the large mammals shrank and disappeared. The dwindling herds of gregarious animals no doubt migrated north, following the retreating grass-lands and forests. For those scholars focusing on the changing climate, human predation looks much less destructive. The Paleo-Indians may have killed off the last members of a species, but the hunters were not the agents primarily responsible for the extinctions.

Not until about 2000 BCE did sedentary cultures evolve through a reliance on incipient agriculture along streambeds and other likely locations. At that point human presence in the valleys, and on the future town sites of Tucson and Phoenix, became recognizable and verifiable.[25]

Archaeologists have identified habitation sites dating back thousands of years in the two river valleys, but the earliest sites give evidence of periodic abandonment. Not until the development of the Hohokam culture does a human society appear to more or less permanently inhabit the future locations of Tucson and Phoenix. Progenitors of the Hohokam appear in the Early Agri-cultural Period, 1200 BCE to 150 CE, and the Early Ceramic Period, 150 to 650 CE. Archaeologists describe the Hohokam culture as inhabiting the region from about 650 to 1450 CE.

The Hohokam developed extensive agricultural domains with large pop-ulations that used sophisticated methods of crop irrigation. Because of the Hohokam's reliance on the flows of the two rivers, their geographic placement and population ranges provide a baseline comparison between the two river valleys. Unfortunately, the estimates of population and acreage seem to defy any lasting consensus.

One of the first estimates of Hohokam population and acreage came from F. W. Hodge in 1893. Hodge had studied the Hohokam remains along the Salt River as part of the Hemenway expedition in 1887–1888. In his 1893 report, written from his notes taken in the field, Hodge estimated that the Hohokam had "at least 250,000 acres" under cultivation on the Salt River alone. He then went on to estimate their population, despite expressing misgivings about the accuracy of the estimate, "at from 200,000 to 300,000" people.[26]

From 1893 and Hodge's initial estimate, archaeologists have been gener-ally driving the numbers down. The current consensus somewhat tenuously states that at the height of the Hohokam culture, around 1300 CE, as many as thirty thousand Hohokam cultivated thirty thousand to sixty thousand acres along the Salt and Gila rivers near present-day Phoenix.[27] But once again, defy-ing consensus, a recent study increased the estimate of Hohokam population to fifty thousand to two hundred thousand, returning to a high range similar to that which Hodge proposed more than one hundred years ago. Another recent study repeated Hodge's estimate of the Hohokam's cultivated acreage at 250,000.[28]

Despite disagreement about population and acreage, scholars of the Hohokam accept as fact that the center of Hohokam population was along the Gila and Salt rivers, with a peripheral population of Hohokam in the Santa Cruz valley near present-day Tucson. Once again, variations in estimates occur, but the consensus is that the Hohokam in the Santa Cruz River valley cultivated less than ten thousand acres with a population of six thousand to seven thousand.[29] The relative sizes of the prehistoric populations can be taken as evidence of the relative usefulness of the rivers.

At their peak, the Hohokam canals along the Salt and Gila rivers reached a cumulative length of 180 miles; these were the main structures, or trunk lines, some ten feet deep and thirty feet across. As with the expansive estimates of population, some scholars assert a longer cumulative length of the Hohokam canals: three hundred miles of canals on the Salt River alone. Whereas the total length of Hohokam canals along the Salt could have been three hundred miles, it is doubtful that all of those canals were in use at the same time.[30] In addition, there were hundreds of miles of laterals and smaller feeder ditches, thousands of miles in total, with only a small percentage in use at any given time. As to the Tucson Basin, scholars agree that the smaller river and smaller population maintained no such extensive system of canals. Smaller irrigation ditches serviced the fields in the Tucson Basin, but nothing resembling the ten-feet-deep and thirty-feet-across trunk lines on the Salt River.[31]

The Hohokam increased in population and geographic expanse into the 1300s. Slight variations occurred in material culture—for example, in ceramic styles—and in social organization—a trend toward centralizing in fewer, larger communities. Also occurring in the later stages of the Hohokam period were so-called ballcourts, large structures of apparent ceremonial use.

Whether dispersed in dozens of smaller settlements or congregated in a few large communities, the Hohokam lived close to the river. Strung out along the rivers, permanent habitation remained closely linked to the river and its riparian ecosystem. Not until industrial technology arrived in the late nineteenth century did society achieve the ability to move some distance from the river while maintaining access to the river's water supply.

By 1450 the Hohokam mysteriously had disappeared from the archaeo-logical record. Scholars suggest several possible explanations for the collapse of the Hohokam culture. One idea is that warfare drove the people out of their villages. Another possibility is that floods on the rivers irreparably destroyed the extensive irrigation systems (huge floods occurred in the region in the 1300s). In the Tucson Basin, which had no extensive canal system to be de-stroyed by floods, a phenomenon related to floods may have caused the aban-donment of the river. Floods in the Tucson Basin may have caused the river to entrench itself in a deep arroyo, rendering it useless for purposes of intensive agriculture, given the irrigation technology available to the Hohokam. With the river flowing through a channel ten, fifteen, or twenty feet below the intake structures for the irrigating ditches, and no pump technology capable of lifting the necessary volume of water to the fields, intensive agriculture would have become impossible in the Tucson Basin.

Artifacts of the Hohokam culture survived the people's disappearance. Museum shelves display varieties of pottery and other examples of their mate-rial culture. Remnants of the extensive canal system in the Phoenix Basin also survived. The first of the modern canal builders in the 1870s scratched out their irrigation ditches following the outline of the Hohokam system. To these early developers, the ancient canals had stood as a testament to the agricultural possibilities in the desert valley. But since an extensive system of canals had never existed in the Tucson Basin, it might seem that little remained of the Hohokam culture except for the fragile remains of their material culture. As it turns out, the very course of the river may have been the creation of Hohokam engineering. Geologists posit that the first recorded course of the river, as noted by Spanish explorers and map makers, deviates from geologic rationality. This historic river followed the western edge of the basin, closely hugging the foot of the recent volcanic mountains, including Sentinel Peak (A Mountain). Rather, the geologists suggest, a more logical course for the river is a mile or two to the east, following the course of the current arroyo in Tucson.

One scenario that could explain how the river came to follow its illogical western course is that the Hohokam dug a long irrigation canal to the west of the river to service their agricultural fields throughout the basin. The fields would have lain between the river to the east and the irrigation canal to the west. The irrigation canal would have hugged the western limit of the basin at the foot of the recent mountains. To supply water to the canal, the Hohokam would have dug a headcut into the river channel far to the south, drawing water from the river channel upstream near the future site of the San Xavier Mission. Once constructed, this system would have created a vulnerability to floods in the Tucson Basin similar to the vulnerability created by the extensive system of canals in the Phoenix Basin. When severe flooding struck in the 1300s, the headcut in the Santa Cruz River would have eroded away, and the intersected river would have surged down the irrigation canal, destroying all the fields and structures in its path and leaving the original river bed to the east high and dry. This illogical historic river lasted into the late nineteenth century when once again structures built in the river bed, including a headcut, began a process of erosion and arroyoization that created the current, geologically logical, entrenched river channel in Tucson.

Exhibiting a clear engineering ability, and a highly effective development ethos, the Hohokam reached population levels not matched in the river valley until the early decades of the industrial twentieth century. To achieve these population levels the Hohokam maximized the productive capacity of the rivers in the two valleys. Perhaps it was that maximization, stretching resources to their limit, that created the ultimate vulnerability that caused the culture to collapse. Whatever the cause, by 1450 the Hohokam culture was gone in both river valleys.[32] The rivers remained, even if in somewhat altered fashion.

Dos Rios

No source of subsistence in the semiarid region could be ignored or forgotten for long. Pima Indians—so named by the Spanish—occupied the region when the Europeans first arrived in the sixteenth century. The Pimas considered themselves to be the descendants of the ancient Hohokam, inhabiting many of the same village locations along the desert rivers. However, no permanent Indian settlements existed on the Salt River when the Spanish arrived, and only a few small villages perched beside the Gila. By far the largest native population was in the Santa Cruz River valley and the Tucson Basin specifically—a complete reversal of the center-periphery relationship during the Hohokam period.[1]

The Pimas farmed in a manner similar, it is assumed, to the Hohokam, although without the use of grandiose irrigation systems. The Pima canals were much smaller and localized, effective, but incapable of matching the Hohokam's level of intensive agriculture. They lived in permanent villages, however, and proved themselves to be amenable to the inroads of Spanish missionaries.

Typically the Spanish placed their missions and presidios at the site of pre-existing Indian villages. Later the Pimas allied themselves with the Spanish against the marauding Apaches.[2]

The first Spanish explorer in the vicinity of the Tucson Basin or Salt River valley—within a hundred miles or so—was Coronado, who in 1540 traveled north out of Mexico in search of the seven cities of Cíbola. Although Coronado failed to locate the fabled cities of gold, other Spanish missionaries and settlers followed, eventually establishing the center of the colonial regime in the Rio Grande valley far to the east. The governor, Don Pedro de Peralta, established the capital at Santa Fe in 1609. By 1670, about the time the Spanish belatedly directed their attention toward southern Arizona, the Spanish population in the vicinity of Santa Fe was twenty-eight hundred.[3]

First came ranchers, grazing cattle in northern Sonora and spreading into the upper Santa Cruz River valley. Quickly after came the missionaries; the most famous was Father Eusebio Francisco Kino. Traveling extensively throughout the upper land of the Pimas—Pimería Alta—Kino rode a circuit to the Indian villages, either establishing semiregular *visitas* or permanent missions. In 1697, Kino and his traveling companion Juan Mateo Manje reported that in the Tucson Basin 758 Indians were living in 177 houses at the village of San Agustín, later known as El Pueblito, on the west side of the river at the foot of Sentinel Peak. The presidio of Tucson would later be established near the village, but on the east side of the river. No Pimas occupied permanent settlements near the future site of Phoenix, although Kino visited the Pima villages on the Gila River and so may have traveled along the Salt River at some time.[4] At the very least the Spanish named the river, Rio Salado, having noticed the salty and bitter taste of the water, chock-full of minerals, which the Spanish later discovered to include gold.

From the arrival of a permanent Spanish presence in the region, another eighty years passed until the local military commander Hugo O'Connor established the Spanish presidio of Tucson in 1775. During the intervening decades and generations, the sadly typical story of the Spanish conquest took place. Less warfare than cultural exchange, the negative image of the conquest results from the unequal nature of the transaction. Examples of the cultural hegemony that persists to this day are the Spanish place names in the region, including the names of the rivers central to this narrative: the Rio Salado and the Rio Santa Cruz (earlier known as the Rio Santa María Soamca). The Spanish mission and presidio nearest to the river's headwaters was Santa Cruz. The river soon took on the name of its first village, geographically speaking. The Spanish named the people as well: the Pima, living in cohesive villages near the rivers, and the Papago (so-called bean eaters), living in less densely situated village settings, at times some distance from the rivers.

Perhaps the most visible and prominent example of Spanish material culture is the church at San Xavier. Constructed over fourteen years at a cost of three hundred thousand pesos and completed in 1797, the church presents a remarkable example of Baroque art and religious expression plopped down in the midst of a prickly desert on the far northern frontier of New Spain. It came to be known as the White Dove of the Desert; its crisply white-washed exterior walls were visible from miles away.[5] The restored church still inspires awe among visitors in the early twenty-first century. One can only imagine the power of the edifice and the force of its religious iconography at the turn of the nineteenth century.

The Spanish brought Christianity and European culture to the native populations, but they also brought European diseases. Lacking immunities to common European diseases, the native populations suffered terrifying losses from their first contact with Europeans or their material goods. Periodic epidemics swept through the villages, at times leaving only a handful of survivors.[6] The Spanish also brought domesticated livestock and ranching techniques, both a boon and a curse to the Indians. Grazing cattle often trampled native fields and placed serious demands on the region's limited water supplies. In Arizona most often the Indians initially welcomed the Spanish missionaries, but the difficult cultural transitions often led to anger and conflict. Eventually and tragically, the precontact native cultures dwindled. In the Tucson Basin the Pima population dwindled to nothing, but the Papagos persisted, perhaps because of their dispersed settlement locations. Along the Gila River, the Pima villages survived, threatened more by the marauding Apaches than by the distantly colonizing Spanish.[7]

Raiding Apaches entered the region in the 1700s after Comanches pushed them out of the southern plains. Initially the conflict was limited to New Mexico, as the newcomers battled with the indigenous people and the colonizing Spanish in the Rio Grande valley. By midcentury, raids in New Mexico spread into southern and central Arizona, plaguing both the Spanish settlements and the sedentary Pimas. Losses mounted, causing settlers to leave their ranchos and mines to congregate primarily around the presidio at Tubac, thirty miles south of the Tucson Basin. As the warfare with the Apaches became intractable, the colonial government tried to devise a more effective defense. To that end orders went out in 1768 for Indian laborers to commence the construction of a defensive breastwork near the village at San Agustín. This was the first step in the creation of a military presidio at Tucson. The fort was constructed on the east side of the river, opposite the Indian village on the west side. Then in 1775 the military transferred the garrison at Tubac to the new northern outpost.[8]

The year of Tucson's birth is normally given as 1775, and this is fair enough if one considers the beginnings of the city to be contained in a physical structure, the remnants of which are now buried under the contemporary downtown.[9] But if one thinks of a city as a community of residents, a polity, a culture, or simply a collection of families, then Tucson's history goes back much further. In terms of permanent and consistent residence, Tucson's history is as deep as the Pima culture. From the time when the first Indian returned to live and farm in the river valley after the disappearance of the Hohokam— when that was exactly, no one can say for sure: 1490? 1520? 1550?—the community of Tucson came into existence. It has been inhabited ever since, first as an Indian community for about two hundred years. When the Spanish arrived, the social milieu became more complicated. The community became a mixed settlement of Pima, Papago, pacified Apache, and Spanish. Anglos arrived in the nineteenth century, adding another layer of complexity. No single analogy can adequately describe Tucson through its early history: melting pot, tossed salad, or seething cauldron. At times harmonious, in other moments riven by contention, the aggregate parts of the community have always seemed to shift in a dynamic flux between consensus and conflict, peace and controversy, prosperity and poverty. This is the Old Pueblo.

A handy snapshot of the multicultural community appeared in 1804. Presidio commanders had been ordered by King Carlos IV to conduct surveys of the empire's holdings. In Tucson the commander was José de Zúñiga, and he reported on the community's population and agricultural production. The total population in the vicinity of the presidio was 1,014, which included 300 Spanish and 714 others of native or mixed race. The Spanish racial categorization made distinctions between purebloods and mestizos. The gradations give an indication of the at times uneasy relationship between the European and native population. The Spanish intermarried with the Indians, but social status most often related to the presumed or asserted closeness to European ancestry.

Agricultural production was impressive in the presidio: 2,800 *fanegas* (bushels) of wheat and 600 *fanegas* of corn.[10] The civilian residents of the presidio also produced "beans and other vegetables [that] sell at four and a half pesos a bushel." The local Indians produced cotton "for their own use." Zúñiga also reported huge livestock herds: 3,500 cattle, 2,500 sheep, 1,200 horses, 120 mules, and 30 burros.[11]

The 1804 census took place at a high point in Tucson's colonial history. Two factors affected Tucson's conditions most centrally. First was the water supply in the Santa Cruz River. During drought conditions, agricultural production and livestock herds shrank, placing great pressures on the human population. The first time history records a complaint about insufficient water in the vicinity of Tucson is 1761. A drought was in full swing when Father Manuel de Aguirre stated that there was "plenty of land for everyone, but not enough water to sustain the existing Spanish and Indian population."[12] Conversely, the early 1800s were moist, and sufficient water flowed down the Santa Cruz to support impressive levels of agricultural production. Zúñiga's report made reference to the region's water supply and spoke specifically of the variations in rainfall amounts:

> The rivers of the region include the Santa Catalina [Rillito], five miles from the presidio, which arises from a hot spring and enjoys a steady flow for ten miles in a northwesterly direction, but only in the rainy seasons. It is thirty three feet wide near its headwaters. Our major river, however, is the Santa María Soamca [Santa Cruz], which arises ninety-five miles to the southeast from a spring near the presidio of Santa Cruz. From its origin it flows past the Santa Cruz presidio. . . . When rainfall is only average or below, it flows aboveground to a point some five miles north of Tubac and goes underground all the way to San Xavier del Bac. Only during years of exceptionally heavy rainfall does it water the flat land between Tubac and San Xavier.[13]

The flatland constitutes the geological transition from the upper basin, which ends north of Tubac, and the middle basin of the river valley, which begins near San Xavier. Extensive deposits of sediment—both older and younger alluvium—lie beneath the flatland. Eons of rain, snow melt, and thunder bursts had thoroughly charged the aquifer, completely saturating that section of the deep-storage reservoir. In dry cycles, as Zúñiga reported, the river "goes underground." But a drought, no matter how severe, would not affect the water held in subsurface storage. Rather, the drought would dry out the surface of the river bed, as if the surface of a huge sponge had dried out, while the interior remained saturated. Whether wet cycle or dry, rising bedrock occurring near

Martinez Butte brought the river back to the surface. The geological formation that forms the southern boundary of the middle basin is that rising bedrock.

The other factor affecting circumstances in Tucson was the level of warfare with the Apaches. When warfare was intense and when Apache raids were frequent, conditions in the presidio and nearby villages declined. During times of relative peace, such as the early 1800s, conditions improved, population increased, and agricultural production expanded. The Spanish had instituted a new peace policy in 1786—the *establicimientos de paz*—which greatly reduced Apache raiding.[14] Ranchos expanded, mining activity spread, and a meager but steady trade into Sonora accompanied the peaceful conditions of the early 1800s. The relative stability in the society and the expanding prosperity allowed by the peace with the Apaches lasted into the 1820s and the advent of Mexican independence.

Mexico achieved its freedom from Spanish colonial control in 1821. A clear victory for nationalist aspirations, the onset of republican rule in Mexico had somewhat unexpected results on the northern frontier. Peace with the Apaches had been obtained by royal payments to the warlike Apaches. The payments could be considered bribes or tribute, but whatever the connotation, with independence came fiscal crisis, and the peace payments came to an end. Residual effects of the peace policy lasted a few years, but open warfare soon resumed. Clashes became brutal, reaching legendary extremes of enmity. Once again residents abandoned ranches and mines and congregated in the presidios for protection. As the regional population concentrated in a few localities, most prominently Tucson, pressures mounted on the government to provide support. Against the Apaches, however, the republican government seemed powerless. Livestock herds shrank, mines fell into disrepair, and the beleaguered presidio populations huddled within the safety of the walls.

Into this situation walked the first Americans in the region. Fur-trapping mountain men entered Arizona during the winter of 1825, traveling down the Gila River out of New Mexico. Their path perhaps validated the labeling of the Gila as the main stem of the river system. The political center of the northern territories during the Spanish and Mexican eras was New Mexico, specifically Santa Fe. The headwaters of the Gila are in New Mexico, and the trappers entered the region following the river downstream to the west and south. Given that path, every confluence along the river would be labeled a tributary, even if, in the Salt River's case, the tributary carried more water than the river.

Beaver had been noted on the region's rivers by Jesuit missionaries in the 1700s, and the first group of trappers in 1825, led by James Ohio Pattie, found conditions favorable for profitable trapping. After the initial success in 1825, three or four groups of trappers arrived the next autumn and winter, 1826. These mountain men trapped beaver on the Gila, San Francisco, and San Pedro rivers. The trappers were on friendly terms with the sedentary Pimas, and one group of three trappers made the trek to Tucson in December 1826 to report to the local officials about their presence and activities (as required by Mexican regulations). Percolating in the background, however, was the increasing hostility with the Apaches. A group of trappers working on the Salt River near present-day Phoenix was attacked by Indians—presumably Apaches—in January 1827. All but three men were killed, and trapping came to an end on the Mexican frontier.[15]

As conditions worsened on the northern frontier, another survey of conditions appeared. In 1831 the Mexican government chartered a national bank to stimulate development on the frontier. One of the first actions of the bank was to request a census and survey of conditions in the targeted areas. Since the survey was not explicitly an action of the national or state government, presidio officials did not gather the information; rather, a prominent merchant in Tucson, Teodoro Ramírez, made the report. Ramírez's survey indicated relative stability in population (about one thousand residents in and around Tucson, similar to the population reported by Zúñiga in 1804) but severely restricted economic activity, due clearly to the fear of Apache depredations. For example, Ramírez noted, "The land is fertile by nature for every kind of agriculture because of the fullness of its river" but "sheep raising is not established because of the danger of the Apache enemy." The reader should keep in mind that in 1804, Commander Zúñiga reported a sheep herd in Tucson of twenty-five hundred. Also notable in the Ramírez report is a reference to the Rio Salado, not as a center of agriculture but rather as the location of potential mines. "There are deposits of virgin gold in the vicinity of these tribes [Pinal Apaches] next to the Rio Salado. If the government of the Direccion undertook to find them (which the enemy impedes) they could very well be uncovered and through these treasures, they could promote new settlements."[16]

During the Spanish and Mexican periods, the northernmost community on the Arizona frontier was Tucson; no mission or presidio ever graced the banks of the Gila or Salt river. This is not to say, however, that the Spanish and Mexicans were ignorant of the potential usefulness of the central Arizona rivers, including the Salt River. Hispanic missionaries, soldiers, ranchers, and miners traveled through the area and knew of the river's presence. The problem was in its remoteness from any presidio, and conversely, its proximity to the mountain domains of the Apaches. The clearest example of the inhibiting effect caused by Apache warfare on development on the northern frontier was the inability by the Spanish or Mexicans to establish the Salt River valley as a center of agriculture and mining.

The federal government in Mexico City was powerless to achieve either victory or peace with the Apaches. In 1834, however, the state government of Sonora attempted to mount a serious offensive against the hostile Indians. The state organized groups of citizens, including many former soldiers, into military units and waged large-scale actions throughout the region. One attack followed a group of Pinal Apaches far up the Salt River to the narrows of Salt River Canyon. The offensive, however, failed to achieve any lasting resolution of the warfare. The Apaches were neither defeated nor cowed.

During the next decade, conditions in Tucson and the other presidios declined into a desultory routine of survival against hardship. From about one thousand residents in 1831, the population declined to about five hundred by the time American soldiers arrived in 1846 during the Mexican War. Agricultural pursuits near Tucson continued in the ancient pattern: irrigated agriculture in the floodplain near the town. But work on the fields was done constantly with one eye on the hillsides, and only the foolishly courageous would venture outside the presidio walls alone. Likewise, presidio residents pastured small herds of livestock during the day, and then brought them inside the presidio walls to be guarded at night. Cattle ranching became impossible. Isolated vaqueros were easy prey for the Apache warriors, resulting in herds going wild, as the Mexican cowboys lost the ability to undertake the normal castrating of young steers. By the time American soldiers and sojourners arrived in the region in the next decade, herds of wild cattle roamed the Santa Cruz River valley. The prevalence of aggressive young bulls caused the Americans to hunt the cattle like buffalo.[17]

The inability of the Mexican or Sonoran governments to control the Apaches was one reason American acquisition of Mexico's northern frontier came so easily during the Mexican-American War of 1846–1848. Twenty years of warfare with the Apaches had exhausted the Mexican soldiers, impoverished the national and state governments, and discouraged and depressed the settlers and citizens. No local resistance confronted the Americans when they arrived in Tucson in December 1846. Presidio commander Antonio Comadurán had taken the troops of the military garrison at Tucson twelve miles to the south to wait at the Mission San Xavier del Bac as the Mormon Battalion of about five hundred troops passed through Tucson on its way to California. Of the estimated five hundred residents of Tucson in 1846, about one hundred Tucsonenses (Mexican Tucsonans) remained in the town to greet the American soldiers. Some offered gifts of water, perhaps the most friendly act a desert resident can tender.[18]

The Mormon soldiers rested in Tucson for one day, watering their livestock, trading with residents, and generally gearing up for the last leg of their journey to California. Most prominent in the accounts of the settlement contained in the journals of the American soldiers is the wide variety of goods available for trade. Although the Apache depredations had reduced production in the community, variety in agricultural commodities remained. For example, the soldiers traded for three bushels of salt and lesser quantities of beans, quinces, pomegranates, and tobacco. They also acquired some portion of two thousand bushels of wheat, along with flour and meal (it is assumed this was corn meal). As one soldier, Henry W. Bigler, remarked, "It looked good to see young green wheat patches and fruit trees, and to see hogs and fowls running about, and it was music to our ears to hear the crowing of the cocks."[19]

The Mormon Battalion was the only group of American soldiers to travel through the region during the war. No combat between American and Mexican troops interrupted the depressing routine of Apache raids and penurious conditions. With the end of the war, however, more Americans began traveling through the region, and conditions started to change. The war ended in 1848 with the Treaty of Guadalupe Hidalgo, which established the new boundary between Mexico and the United States at the Gila River. Thus Tucson and the Santa Cruz River remained in Mexico, but the accepted southern route to California—the Gila Trail—included the 210-mile-reach of the Santa Cruz River. Tucson became a trading post and market center for caravans of sojourners, especially the groups of Forty-niners scurrying along the trail to hoped-for riches in the California gold fields.

Many of the Forty-niners traveling on the Gila Trail also kept journals, and Tucson is mentioned in most of them. The descriptions are generally less than glowing. Typical is the report made by John E. Durivage, a journalist dispatched by the New Orleans *Daily Picayune*. Durivage referred to Tucson as "a miserable old place, garrisoned by about one hundred men."[20] The constant harassment by the Apaches continued to limit agricultural production. But since the Apaches generally left the Forty-niner caravans unmolested, most Americans failed to recognize the constraints under which local residents worked. Pejorative accounts resulted. The depressed conditions were blamed on the Hispanic residents' supposed cultural traits: laziness, defeatism, superstition. Ethnocentric descriptions are common in the Forty-niner accounts.[21]

Trade was clearly on the minds of the residents and visitors. As the New Orleans reporter explained, "The camp has been filled all day with Mexican women and Indians, all eager to traffic and anxious to buy needles and thread. A few good purchases of mule flesh were made." The group of Americans also acquired flour and corn, and noted that the mission gardens at San Xavier and near Tucson "were well stocked with fruit. The whole valley is exceedingly fertile."[22] The analysis of latent fecundity also contributed to the ethnocentric descriptions. Most Anglos failed to recognize that locals had long since come to understand that production of large surpluses only encouraged the Apaches to come down out of the mountains to take it. Maintaining an appearance of poverty served as an effective strategy to avoid Apache raids.[23]

Despite the Apache threat, however, the steady stream of travelers stirred commercial activity to life. In part, the incentive to engage in trade and to commit time, labor, and capital to that pursuit was the result of the obvious sellers' market. Forty-niners and other migrants were clearly at the mercy of local residents, far from any established marketplace or center of commerce. Tucsonenses in particular developed a reputation for difficult bargaining.[24] A wide variety of goods could be had, depending on a cycle of seasonal availability— but at high prices. Wheat and corn surpluses could be stored for some time and portioned out bit by bit. Fruit and vegetables, on the other hand, were consumed and sold as they became ripe: peaches, pears, and quinces in the spring; apples, grapes, pomegranates, and wild cherries later in the summer; beans, peas, squash, and pumpkins in the autumn. Occasionally other luxury goods were available: for example, cakes of sugar and tobacco.[25]

Following the war, growing prosperity through trade with the Forty-niner caravans and other Americans had started to shift the regional identity of Tucson from the northern frontier of Mexico to the southwestern frontier of the United States. The Old Pueblo was falling into the orbit of the growing American empire. The increasing connection to American commerce convinced many residents that their future would be better served as part of the

American republic. In 1853, the United States negotiated, practically at gun-point, the Gadsden Purchase, which added territory south of the Gila River, including Tucson, to the United States. It was this treaty, negotiated primarily to acquire the rich grasslands of the Mesilla Valley and secure a favorable route for railroad construction, that dissected the Santa Cruz River twice, creating the unique quality of beginning within the United States, flowing out into Mexico, then returning to the United States after making its trademark U-turn. For residents of the presidio at Tucson, the Gadsden Purchase required that a choice be made: remain in Tucson and accept American sovereignty, or leave the community and resettle across the new border in Sonora, perhaps at the old presidio of Santa Cruz.

Most chose to stay. As American soldiers raised the U.S. flag at the old presidio, excited Tucsonenses commenced a fiesta. As one account relates, "The Mexicans had confidence in the Americans and most of those who were not soldiers stayed."[26] In another report, Americans seemed a deliverance from heaven:

> I have often heard my mother say that the coming of the Americans then [sic] the U.S. took over this country was a Godsend to Tucson, for the Indians had killed off many of the Mexicans and the poor were being ground down by the rich. The day the troops took possession there was lots of excitement. They raised the flag on the wall and the people welcomed them with a fiesta and they were all on good terms. We felt alive after the Americans took possession and times were more profitable. . . . I have heard my mother say how remarkably quiet everything was. Of course everyone carried guns and a good many things were settled that way, but as a whole things were orderly.[27]

Clearly, the decades of travail in the community had left their mark. Isolated from the centers of Mexican culture and political power, many Tucson residents found their ties to Mexico stretched to the breaking point. But as James Officer observed, "Not all the residents of Tucson welcomed the transition." Mexican troops, of course, led the procession out of the community when the change in sovereignty took place on March 10, 1856. The troops from Tucson were heading for Imuris in Sonora; the former Tubac soldiers had already been trans-ferred to Santa Cruz. A few settlers, acting on their loyalty to Mexico, or per-haps on their distrust of the Americans, joined the migration south. Unusual weather greeted the procession. Spring is usually dry in the region, rains falling most typically during the winter or summer seasons. The travelers were perhaps ill prepared for the heavy March rainstorm. Some may have described the showers as desultory; others may have looked at the precipitation with more optimism. Unexpected rain in a dry region is most often welcomed, except perhaps if you are trying to make progress along a dirt-to-mud wagon road.[28]

As the Hispanic era closed in the history of the region, the Santa Cruz River valley remained the center of human society in Arizona. The Salt River valley had no town or settlements, no ranches or mines occupied or worked. It seemed that as long as the Apaches remained free in the nearby mountains, the Salt River's potential would never be tapped or developed.

Tucson's long history through the Hispanic period became a fact that shaped its future development. In the early years of Anglo settlement, Hispanic Tucsonenses continued to hold prominent positions in the community, as both political and business leaders. Even as Anglos began to take control of the local economy and government, the large and vibrant Hispanic community served to mitigate against the most onerous forms of racism and ethnocentrism. On the other hand, Tucson's multiethnic character would prove to be a liability during the debate over the location of the territorial capital.

Likewise, but in an inverse circumstance, Phoenix's lack of history through the Hispanic period also shaped its growth and development. The artifacts of the Hohokam culture remained in Phoenix, recognized and acknowledged by the first Anglo settlers in the Salt River valley. Missing was everything in between the Hohokam and the contemporary mid-nineteenth-century culture. Phoenix became a southwestern town without a Hispanic past, unique in a region so culturally dominated by Spanish and Mexican society. Phoenix boosters later used the white nature of Phoenix as a selling device, pronouncing with pride the town's Anglo qualities. Phoenix became a "modern" town, as one promotion proclaimed, "Peopled by a progressive, American class, on every side are to be noted evidences of thrift and enterprise. Here are none of the sleepy, semi-Mexican features of the more ancient towns of the Southwest."[29]

Urban rivalry lay far in the future when Anglos first arrived in the region in the 1850s. Phoenix did not exist. But the next decades would see the return of settlement to the Salt River valley, and in the ensuing years, rivalry would arise. With the competition between the communities far in the future, the presence of Hispanic traditions in one place but not another was inconsequential. The consequences of this difference would arise at the turn of the twentieth century.

Indian Rings, Ditches,
and Railroads

ANGLO SETTLERS BEGAN arriving in Arizona in the weeks before the change
of sovereignty in 1856. Whereas the social history of Anglo Arizona began in
the 1850s, the political history of the territory commenced in 1863, when
Arizona achieved separate territorial status from New Mexico. Tucson's rival
at that time was the mining district in the vicinity of Prescott. Phoenix still did
not exist as the decade of the 1860s began. The first territorial government met
at Navajo Springs, east of Prescott, in late 1863, "amidst a general rejoicing,
the firing of guns, and addresses."[1] A small gold rush was under way, which
may have accounted for some of the rejoicing. The rush had lured several
hundred miners to the region, and so the commander of the U.S. Army in the
territory, General James H. Carleton, established Fort Whipple in October
1864, explicitly to protect the mines and the workers. It was also Carleton's
task to pick the location for the territorial capital. Expressing suspicion of se-
cessionist sentiment in Tucson, as well as displaying an anti-Mexican animus,

Carleton first placed the capital at Fort Whipple, then a few months later moved it twenty-two miles to the south to Prescott.[2]

Carleton's decision did not go without criticism. Tucson could claim to be the only town of significance in the territory, and other established, albeit smaller, communities also asserted their right to be designated the territorial capital. Given that the territorial legislature had fewer than twenty members, lobbying and deal making took on personal qualities and voting majorities required constant maintenance. In the first meeting of the legislature in Prescott, efforts arose to place the permanent capital elsewhere. Prescott held on to the capital for three years through a series of very narrow, 9-8 votes.[3]

Tucson's Mexican character as well as its geographical location became issues in the political debate over the placement of the territorial capital. As was common at the time, the territorial legislature met during the autumn or winter months, when agricultural pursuits typically went into hiatus. Unfortunately for Arizona delegates, Prescott's elevation and northern location made for chilly falls and occasionally icy winters. Partly because of the weather, and reflecting the wheeling and dealing among delegates, the legislature voted in 1867 to move the capital to Tucson. As might be expected, Prescott boosters cried foul and protested the move. In the criticism of the legislature's decision, the Prescott newspaper referred to Tucson's Hispanic nature and proximity to Mexico. The incensed Prescott editor advised "white tradesmen and laborers" to stay away from Tucson. "In fact, Tucson is no place for a poor white man, as all the work is done by runaway peons from Sonora, who arrive there by the hundred in destitute condition, and who will almost work for board."[4]

The Prescott editor's wrath not withstanding, the capital moved to Tucson in 1867 and stayed there ten years. Legislatures continued to argue over the dissemination of public largess, including the boon to local business that accrued from hosting the capital. No doubt legislators found the balmy winters in Tucson a welcome change from the brisk Prescott climate, although others probably found the indigenous Mexican culture disconcerting.

Tucson was the largest and oldest town in the territory. Tubac could claim greater age but could not claim continual occupation. Both had served as Spanish presidios, but Tubac had been abandoned on more than one occasion during the Apache wars. Only Tucson could claim continual inhabitance since its founding in 1775.

Anglo settlers began arriving in the months and weeks preceding American sovereignty in March 1856. Solomon Warner arrived in February, within days purchasing several plots of land inside the old presidio. Warner and his partner, Mark Aldrich, established the first mercantile store in Tucson on the land Warner had purchased. Aldrich soon became the largest landowner in the community, as well as the first mayor.[5] Solomon Warner later diversified his holdings by constructing a small dam and flour mill along the Santa Cruz River just west of the town. Samuel Hughes also arrived in Tucson in the 1850s and began a long career as a developer and businessman. In twenty years, by the mid-1870s, Hughes had become "the largest single landowner."[6] Tucson remained culturally Hispanic, however. Many of the early Anglo settlers married Hispanic women and conducted business in Sonora. Even though the political connections in Arizona now flowed east, west, and north, the commercial ties in Tucson remained primarily local, regional, and southern into Mexico.

The interest in prospecting and the development of mining in the Santa Cruz River valley contributed to the regional nature of Tucson's economy. Mines in the Santa Rita Mountains to the south of Tucson opened in the late 1850s as Americans brought capital to the effort, plus an enthusiasm not yet quelled by incessant Apache raids. Exemplifying the boom was the Sonora Mining Company, lead by Charles Poston. The company occupied the old Tubac presidio and began prospecting and development activities in southern Arizona in 1856. Poston had arrived in the earliest days of American sovereignty. Other Anglo entrepreneurs continued to arrive in Tucson in the next year on the first stage line to service the area. The San Antonio and San Diego line established the first regular service in 1857. The line quickly failed but was just as quickly replaced by the Butterfield line, which with great difficulty, and yet successfully, maintained a system of depots and way stations stretching twenty-eight hundred miles from St. Louis and Memphis to California.[7]

The stagecoaches carried passengers and mail, generating modest profits for the company. More prosperous were the freighting endeavors operating out of Tucson. Solomon Warner was an early freighter, hauling trade goods and sundries across the desert from the boat docks on the Colorado River at Yuma to Tucson and other distant outposts on the frontier. Three companies soon became fixtures in Tucson, accounting for much of the town's prosperity and growth: Tully, Ochoa and Company; Lord and Williams; and E. N. Fish and Company.[8]

Apache raids plagued the freighters, and the Indians targeted miners and ranchers as well. During the gold rush days of the Forty-niners, Apaches tended to ignore the Anglo caravans, but with the Americans' increased presence and acquisitive nature through the 1850s, conflicts started to intensify. The warfare began in earnest in 1861 when the Apache leader Cochise commenced attacking ranchers, miners, and Butterfield stagecoaches.[9]

The increase in Apache warfare coincided with the outbreak of the Civil War. The U.S. military established Camp Lowell in Tucson in 1862 more in response to Civil War policies than the Apache raids. California volunteers supporting the Union occupied the town in May, confiscating houses and other property belonging to Southern sympathizers. Over the next two years, the army post came to occupy all vacant housing in the community, including the most dilapidated adobe structures. The army briefly abandoned the post in September 1864, then reoccupied it the following year. The military declared it a permanent military post in 1866 with the official designation Camp Lowell. In addition to reactivating the post in 1865, the army had established a supply depot in Tucson. To house the personnel and material goods associated with the post and depot, the army occupied thirteen buildings, including several houses formerly owned by Confederate proponents. The army had acquired possession of five of the buildings, but rented the other eight. The total monthly rent was $278, a considerable sum in those days, but as one inspector remarked in 1866, "much less than it would cost to build new quarters."[10]

As the U.S. Army increased its presence in the region, especially after the Civil War ended in 1865, freighters benefited from at least a modicum of military protection; they also gained new business as government contracts to freighters and local producers stimulated the economy throughout the territory. The connection between Indian warfare and the local economy became clear. The army was there to protect settlers from the Apaches, and quite simply, soldiers and their livestock had to be fed. Whether hauling freight or producing grain and foodstuffs for the commercial market, the largest and most consistent customer in the region was the U.S. Army. Army generals clearly understood that buying locally made much more sense than transporting supplies overland over great distances from installations in Kansas or Nebraska.[11]

Merchants profiting from the military trade came to be associated with an Indian Ring. Although current scholars such as Darlis Miller question the existence of the ring, many at the time would have sworn to its existence. General James F. Rusling made perhaps the first reference to corruption among government contractors in 1866: "The year before [1865], these Indians [Pimas farming near the future town site of Phoenix along the Gila River] had raised and sold a surplus of barley, beans, etc. The most of this was bought by Indian traders, located at Maricopa Wells and Pimo [sic] villages, at from one to two cents per pound, coin, in trade; and then resold to the government, for the use of troops in Arizona, at from six to seven cents per pound, coin, in cash. This is a specimen of the way in which the old Indian Ring fleeced both the Indians and the government."[12]

Whether stemming from an entrepreneurial cabal or simply a like-minded association of tradesmen profiting from a common opportunity, the appearance of corruption was clear. Supposedly, the operation of the ring had two goals: first, to take advantage of government largess by overcharging or otherwise feathering accounts, and second, to maintain the army's presence by publicizing the need for military protection, and if necessary, inciting the Apaches to continue their warfare. According to the theory of collusion and conspiracy, the one thing the ring could not abide was peace. As warfare with the Apaches stretched into the 1870s, Generals John M. Schofield and George Crook explicitly blamed greedy contractors for prolonging the warfare to preserve their lucrative contracts.[13]

Running contrary to the ring's interests were the operations of Indian agents and army officers seeking to establish peaceful relations with the Apaches. A major step in that direction occurred in the spring of 1871, when a group of peace-seeking Apaches settled near the army outpost at Camp Grant and commenced farming along the San Pedro River. Two interpretations of the Apache move appeared. Many Tucson residents looked cynically at the Apache promises of peace, considering the Apache move to within fifty miles of Tucson a clear threat to the community and region. On the other hand, army officials, including the commander at Camp Grant, Lieutenant Royal E. Whitman, took a more optimistic view of the Apache overtures, welcoming the Indians to the camp and encouraging their apparent willingness to engage in sedentary agrarian pursuits. Not coincidentally, the Apaches had found a ready market for their production of hay and cord wood, which they sold to the army post at Camp Grant.[14]

Initially the Tucson newspaper expressed approval of the army's peaceful treatment of the Indians, but after a series of Apache raids in March and April, the newspaper's tone decidedly shifted: "Indians sweeping up and down the Santa Cruz River Valley in large force . . ." The newspaper's editor criticized the army for feeding the "murderers" with "supplies purchased with the people's money." Tucson residents formed a Committee of Public Safety in early April and sent a delegation led by William S. Oury to speak with the military commander, General George Stoneman. The army commander maintained the view that the raids were being conducted by Apaches other than those encamped near Camp Grant. Stoneman's position emanated from the reports of Lieutenant Whitman, the Camp Grant commander. Whitman counted heads every two or three days at the camp for the purpose of distributing supplies. By mid-April the Indian encampment had grown to almost five hundred men, women, and children. The raiding party in southern Arizona had been described as containing nearly one hundred warriors. The lieutenant maintained that no force of that size could have left Camp Grant without his knowledge, and so the raiding Indians must have come from elsewhere. Tucsonans maintained that the trails of the raiding parties always led back to the Camp Grant vicinity, and they reported seeing stolen livestock, as well as clothes, boots, and jewelry, recently acquired from the murdered settlers among the Indians at Camp Grant.[15]

Claiming the need for preemptive action because of the army's perceived complacence, on April 28, 1871, a group of civilians from the Tucson area (six Anglos, forty-eight Mexicans, and ninety-four O'odham) attacked the Indian settlement at Camp Grant, killing 144 Apaches. Most of the victims were women, children, and the old. Young Apache men had been mostly absent. One of the leaders of the attack was William Oury, at the time one of the few truly bilingual Tucson residents; he later claimed that the lack of young warriors validated the need for the preemptive strike. The army claimed that the missing young men had been off hunting, but Oury maintained that the young men had been raiding settlements, and would have continued the depredations without the civilians' attack on their home base at Camp Grant. The Tucson newspaper proudly reported the attack by sending letters to the state's newspapers. The *Arizona Miner* in Prescott published the "Letter from Tucson" eight days after the massacre. The letter described the attack, "in which an outraged populace flew to arms and partly avenged the wrongs of ten years by the slaughter of 125 Indians. . . . In my last letter [not published by the *Arizona Miner*] I stated that 60 Indians were killed in the attack at Camp Grant; but I am very much pleased to correct that statement, since the correction compels me to make a better showing."[16]

The Camp Grant massacre and subsequent investigation and trial provide examples of both the assertion and denial of the conspiratorial Indian Ring. Since Tucson was the biggest town and the center of commerce for most of the territory, the conspiracy to many was locally based: not just an Indian ring, but specifically a Tucson ring. Although Darlis Miller has disproved the existence of widespread, premeditated collusion or corruption, the appearance of such activity was plain to many military commanders, who came to feel that civilians had thwarted any possibility of peaceful relations with the Apaches. General John Schofield explicitly blamed the Camp Grant massacre on Tucson-based contractors and their friends, who considered the Apache pastoralists an economic and commercial threat. Since war had become the economic basis for the territory, contractors had acquired a vested interest in prolonging the warfare. As Schofield explained, "It is worthy of remark that these Indians paid for a large part of the rations issued to them by supplying hay and wood to the military posts, that before paid to contractors, and that the contractors, their employees, and customers thus lost the profits theretofore realized. It has been suggested that this may explain the Camp Grant massacre, hereafter referred to."[17]

Partly as the result of the army's insistence, the federal attorney for the territory put one of the participants, Sidney DeLong, on trial in Tucson for murder. DeLong stood as the lone defendant, but the verdict in his trial would be applied to all of the raiders. The prosecution and defense built their cases over five days of testimony starting on December 6, 1871. The government's case was based on the Indians' presence at Camp Grant as prisoners of war, under the protection of the U.S. Army. The defense claimed justifiable action—the defendants considered the attack on the Indian camp to be correct and honorable—and so there was no effort to deny or disprove their participation in the attack. Judge John Titus presided over the trial. His sympathies clearly appeared in his hour-long instruction to the jury at the close of testimony. First, it was clear that the accused had the right to take action: "The Government of the United States owes its Papago, Mexican and American residents in Arizona protection from Apache spoliation and assault. If such spoliation and assault are persistently carried on and not prevented by the government, then the sufferers have a right to protect themselves and to employ force enough for the purpose." It was also clear to the judge that the Apaches had no legal claim to the protection of the army: "If the Apache nation continued to depre-date against the others, then it forfeits the right of protection from the United States."[18]

The jury deliberated for nineteen minutes. The only surprise in the not guilty verdict was that it had taken the jurors so long to render the decision. All were acquitted, but the trial centered Arizonans' eyes on the capital. The Tucson ring became a topic of conversation throughout the territory. The Prescott newspaper explicitly addressed the ring as the trial proceeded in December 1871: "Gentlemen of the Indian Ring, all that Arizonans ask of you is to be honest toward the Government of which we are a part, and to be faithful to yourselves rather than indulgent of your pockets. Here to fore you have been dishonest and faithless, and we have suffered in consequence."[19]

The Apache wars continued to rage, and controversy dogged the army's efforts. Not the least of the problems was the certainty of army leaders that civil-ian intrigues—the Tucson ring—repeatedly thwarted their efforts. In another case of civilian interference, the army also quarreled with the Indian Bureau; at issue was the concentration policy that resulted in the creation of the San Carlos Reservation along the upper Gila River in 1874. Prior to concentration, the army maintained several Apache reservations, including Camp Apache in the White Mountains. The army acquired supplies for the smaller reservations through its local network of contractors, which in the case of Camp Apache meant that supply contracts went to the nearest merchants and producers in New Mexico. Army commanders considered the concentration of Apache tribes at San Carlos to be doubly wrong. First, it uprooted Apache tribes from their traditional locales, and second, it placed the Indians at the mercy of the greedy, Tucson-based contractors, who exercised undue influence on the agents employed by the Indian Bureau. General George Crook expressed his disgust over the policy in his memoirs: "In the Spring of 1874 the Indians on the Verde reservation were removed to San Carlos in the interest of some persons at Tucson, who were on the inside of the Ring. . . . Their removal was one of those cruel things that greed has so often inflicted on the Indian."[20] Army commanders continued to rail against the San Carlos Reservation in the coming years. Charges of corruption and greed surfaced in the 1877 report of the military commander in Arizona, Colonel August V. Kautz. The colonel declared that the concentration of Indians at San Carlos "has been brought about because it was necessary to get more Indians together in order to make it pay to furnish supplies to them. As long as the true number of Indians was unknown, the agent reported such number of Indians as suited his purpose."[21]

In part the controversy indicated a bureaucratic conflict: the War Department argued for control over Indian policy in the name of honest and economical administration, while the Indian Bureau in the Department of Interior advocated a peace policy aimed at Christianization and acculturation. As Colonel Kautz stated in 1877, "I have no hesitation in saying that the Indians at San Carlos are not making any progress toward civilization. I think a close investigation will demonstrate that they are going backward. They are less capable of sustaining themselves now than before. . . . The so-called peace-policy is a chimera that has been created to secure the support of religious and humanitarian societies to the present system of caring for Indians, by that class of persons interested in contracts and furnishing supplies to Indians, who believe it would be against their interests to have the disbursements fall into the hands of the War Department." Later in his report, Kautz made his argument for transferring the Indian Bureau out of the Department of Interior and into the War Department. The army's accusations of corruption among contractors allied with the Indian Bureau may have been exaggerated so as to bolster the army's claim in the bureaucratic struggle over control of the Indians. Clear, however, is the role of civilian contracts in the formulation of the conspiracy theory about the Indian Ring.[22]

The Tucson press inserted itself into the controversy by supporting concentration as militarily desirable, even though the military commanders opposed the policy. The Tucson press also supported the policy by criticizing an outspoken opponent. Tom Jeffords had achieved notoriety as an effective Indian agent primarily because of his personal friendship with the Chiricahua leader Cochise. Cochise had died in June 1874, shifting the nominal leadership of the Chiricahua Apaches to Geronimo. Jeffords had attempted to maintain his influence and effectiveness during the transition, in part by opposing the move of Chiricahua Apaches to the flatland portion of the San Carlos Reservation designated for their placement by the Indian Bureau. As it turned out, Geronimo's ascendancy signified twelve more years of warfare, not peace. The Tucson press could claim that Jeffords had lost his effectiveness, given Geronimo's refusal to move his people to San Carlos. Jeffords was fired in May 1876; he maintained that it was the concentration policy that was ineffective, not his actions as agent. By then Geronimo was on the loose, raiding into Arizona from his mountain camps in northern Mexico.[23]

In the mid-1870s, Tucson remained the capital of the territory and the center of a growing commercial enterprise. It was also clearly a multicultural place. Anglos had arrived and gone into business, but Hispanic residents also conducted business and assumed leadership positions in the community. Historians James Officer and Thomas Sheridan have noted that Tucson became something of a haven for Hispanic culture in the Southwest. As other communities co-opted Mexicans' land holdings and businesses, Tucson maintained a clear connection with its Mexican ties. The commercial links to the south lasted through the 1870s. With the arrival of the Southern Pacific Railroad in 1880, however, commercial ties with Texas to the east and California to the west increased and deepened, while ties to the south weakened. Specifically, Anglo suppliers started refusing to accept dobe dollars, referring to pesos, which many merchants in Tucson used as the accepted local currency. With the collapse of the marketability of the peso, many Tucson businessmen with ties to Mexico went broke. The shift to the almighty dollar in Tucson pushed the community firmly into the east-west commercial nexus and brought to a close the days of a prominent southern trade capable of contributing greatly to the prosperity of the community.[24]

Commercial ties with Mexico waned as eastern American connections deepened, but the southern ties also diminished because of increasing suspicion in Mexico of American imperialistic designs—the notorious filibusters. One of the most prominent Hispanic businessmen in Tucson was Leopoldo Carrillo. In 1875, Carrillo traveled to Caborca in Mexico to buy stock for his ranches in Arizona and to collect a twenty-five-hundred-dollar debt. Once he arrived in Caborca, Mexican authorities arrested him, as he later explained, because he had renounced his Mexican citizenship and was thought to be fomenting rebellion against the Mexican government. Carillo's wife came up with the required fifteen-thousand-dollar ransom, and Carillo was released at the

Arizona border. As historian James Barney recounts, Carillo knelt and kissed the ground once on American soil, saying, "Gracias a Dios que estoy otra ves en los Estados Unidos!" (thanks to God I am once again in the United States).[25]

With Tucson at the center of the campaigns and debates over Indian policy and with the persistence of Hispanic leadership and influence in the community, perhaps not surprisingly, a move to return the capital to Prescott arose during the eighth session of the legislature in 1875. Supporters of Tucson's claim beat back the attempt. The ninth session started in January 1877, and Tucson's delegates struggled again to hold on to the status, patronage, and business advantage that came with the capital. But this time they lost. Delegate votes shifted, perhaps because of cynicism over the Tucson ring or perhaps reflecting a growing anti-Mexican sentiment. The evidence for prejudice is circumstantial. After the capital returned to Prescott in 1877, Hispanic representation at the legislature dwindled. Prominent and numerous prior to 1877, Mexican American delegates became scarce afterward. The center of economic power remained in Tucson for another decade or so, but the shift of political power to the north was clear. The capital remained in Prescott for twelve years until Phoenix snagged the prize in 1889.[26]

A few months after Tucson lost the capital, news came that Geronimo had been captured. The main proponent of concentration had become John Clum, the agent in charge of San Carlos. Clum's credibility received a great boost when he captured Geronimo in 1877 and escorted him to the reservation. Geronimo's stay at San Carlos would be brief, but at least for a time the Apaches seemed quiescent.[27] Peace was a mixed blessing, however. Surely no sane individual desired a continuation of the violence and bloodshed, but a cessation of warfare would bring a reduction of military spending, and so peace, although much desired, would also bring a diminution in the commercial possibilities in Tucson. The future of the Old Pueblo in 1877 could be judged bright or gloomy, depending on your means of livelihood and perception of peace.

AT ABOUT THE same time in 1867 that delegates at the territorial legislature voted initially to move the capital to Tucson, ambitious farmers started gouging ditches in the desert of the Phoenix Basin, often following the outlines and remnants of old Hohokam canals. Within three years the settlement had grown to three hundred people and the land under cultivation had expanded to twelve hundred acres. Credit for starting the resurgence of agriculture in the basin goes

Fig. 3.1. Jack Swilling (CP RD 40: courtesy Dorothy Robinson Photographs, Arizona Collection, Arizona State University Libraries). Credited with returning agriculture to the Salt River Basin in 1868, Jack Swilling was one of the founders of Phoenix. A southerner by birth, Swilling struck a very western pose in this early photograph.

to Jack W. Swilling. In 1868 he completed the first of the new irrigation canals in the valley, known as the Swilling ditch.[28]

The return of agriculture to the Salt River valley was due to developments elsewhere. First, Henry Wickenburg had discovered gold and established the Vulture Mine in 1863; soon a town bearing his name had sprung up near the mine fifty miles northwest of the future Phoenix town site. Simply put, the min-ers, workers, and draft animals in Wickenburg needed to eat, and so agricultural efforts expanded because of the urban market. Second, U.S. Army troops estab-lished camps to protect the mining operations from raiding Indians. Specifically, the cavalry units at Camp McDowell, established in 1865 on the Verde River seven miles north of the Verde's confluence with the Salt, provided a market for hay. Historians Geoffrey Mawn and Earl Zarbin have discussed the cloudy origins of agriculture in the valley, and it remains unclear whether Swilling began farming along the Salt River under a specific contract with the army or out of a general awareness of the commercial possibilities. Undeniably, by 1867 military activity and the mining boom had created a burgeoning commercial market for agricultural production.[29]

Although debating the specific motivation, scholars agree that Swilling es-tablished the first irrigation ditch in the valley in 1868, following the outlines of ancient Hohokam canals. Settlers could not miss the indications of earlier occupancy. In addition to the canals, partially obscured by erosion and infill, Hohokam habitation sites dotted the region near the river. Included among the ruins were mounds of trash rising as high as forty feet above the valley surface.[30]

Swilling and his partners in the Swilling Irrigating and Canal Company, perhaps twenty men, began digging near Tempe and Papago buttes, on the north side of the river, in late December 1867. After excavating only an eighth of a mile, the men abandoned the location. They had hit a solid rock barrier, probably the crystalline structure that diverted subterranean water south to the Gila River, as later noted by hydrologist Willis T. Lee. Stymied in their first effort, the partners moved three miles downstream and commenced again. This time they succeeded in completing the ditch, later known as the Salt River Valley Canal, on March 12, 1868.

A correspondent to the Prescott newspaper reported in early April 1868 that the little canal supplied enough water to irrigate four thousand acres and that the agricultural enterprise in the valley was destined for great profits. The reporter also noted the direct correlation between the Salt River valley farms and the commercial market in Wickenburg. The Vulture Mining Company and its subsidiaries "consumed $6,000 worth of corn and barley per month, the money always being paid in gold bullion, upon its delivery." Swilling's initial crop was one hundred acres of wheat, barley, and corn. By July the *Arizona Miner* reported that "wheat and barley had all been harvested and shipped to Wickenburg, where it was being sold at 8 cents per pound. The corn crop was growing nicely."[31] The next year, April 1869, Swilling had seven hundred acres planted in barley and another one hundred acres in wheat.[32]

When farming had begun in March 1868, only five families inhabited the valley. One was Swilling's. Four years earlier, at thirty-four years of age, Swilling had married Trinidad Escalante, twenty, of Tucson. The practice of Anglo settlers marrying Hispanic women had become commonplace in Tucson, and Swilling's marriage represented this phenomenon in the earliest settlement of the Phoenix Basin. The couple had their first child in 1865, a daughter named after Swilling's birth state, Georgia (although a Southerner by birth, Swilling had sided with the Union at the outset of the Civil War). Three years later, just as Swilling was beginning to grow crops in the Phoenix Basin, Trinidad Swilling gave birth to another daughter, Matilda. By the time of the 1870 census, Swilling's children were five and two years of age. The household also included two Apache captives, Mariana, thirteen, and Gavilan, ten.[33]

By the end of April 1868, news of the opportunity in the Phoenix Basin had spread. The community was part of Yavapai County; as part of his normal duties, the sheriff, A. J. Moore, paid occasional visits. In late April the sheriff noted that crops in the Salt River Valley "looked splendid and immigrants were arriving nearly every day from Texas and California. Messrs. Swilling, Freeman and the balance of the settlers were enjoying good health and [were] well satisfied."[34] Two months later, in June 1868, Swilling was appointed inspector of the Phoenix Precinct during the territorial elections, and by late 1868 Swilling was postmaster of the nascent community. He also had begun construction of his house. Although a transplanted Georgian, Swilling did not erect a porticoed structure reminiscent of the antebellum South. No doubt he aspired to a position of influence in the community he had helped create, but Swilling was also thoroughly acculturated to the Southwest, and so he built a huge adobe home purely in the Mexican style. The walls required ninety-six thousand adobes, and the house eventually became known as Swilling's Castle.

Fig. 3.2. Swilling's Castle (FP MC-H 243, View 1: courtesy McClintock-Halseth Photograph Collection, Arizona Historical Foundation). Fully acculturated to his surroundings, Swilling built a large adobe house in the traditional southwestern fashion—later known as Swilling's Castle—near the head of his canal. The ruins of the house survived into the 1920s.

By 1870 prospects for the community were improving. Phoenix's geographic position in the center of the state placed it within relatively easy reach of several military posts and mines. Centrally located at the intersection of multiple wagon roads, Phoenix seemed poised on the verge of great prosperity. Accordingly, Swilling implemented plans to begin cultivating fruit trees in the valley, obtaining "several wagon loads" of seedlings from California, according to a "letter from Phoenix" appearing in the Prescott, Arizona, newspaper in August. Water was plentiful indeed. As the newspaper correspondent observed, "Willow and cottonwoods have been planted for fences and shade, and they have grown rapidly. Some already make a secure fence, and all give some shelter from the sun and beauty to the landscape." Notice of the construction of the first well appeared as an afterthought. The well was sixteen feet deep and had "a large supply of delicious water." But the correspondent continued immediately with the reminder, "At present the ditches supply nearly every demand of man, beast and crop."[35]

The town of Phoenix began to take shape in 1870. About three hundred residents lived in the vicinity of the town site. Swilling and his miner/freighter friend Fred Henry had come up with the Phoenix name for the original settlement in 1867, a specific reference to the resumption of agriculture on the ruins of an ancient civilization.[36] As one of the initial founders of the community, Swilling apparently expected that the town site would be established near his own property and the head of the original irrigation ditch. Political wrangling, however, determined the exact location of the town site some distance from Swilling's property. Although Swilling was disappointed by the location of the town site, his name stuck.

When established by the territorial government in October 1870, Phoenix remained part of Yavapai County. On February 14, 1871, the territorial legislature formed Maricopa County and called for an election to determine the county seat on May 1, 1871. The two main contestants for the center of county government were Phoenix and Mill City. Mill City received 150 votes, but Phoenix carried the election with 212.[37]

The election to establish the county seat in Phoenix took place only a few days after the Camp Grant massacre. The two events seem worlds apart. Tucson was a community of more than three thousand residents, more than ten times the size of the just-beginning Phoenix. Tucson's economy was diverse and prospering, still centered largely on agriculture along the river west of town but also enjoying a vibrant commerce based on merchant and freighting activity all over the territory. Phoenix was single-mindedly agrarian and would remain so for decades. Most importantly, Tucson was old. As an established community it would be one hundred years old at mid-decade, but as a location of human settlement its history stretched back continually for centuries. Even if one looked at its most pressing political concern in 1871—its conflict with the Apaches—this was a problem faced by the community in Tucson for at least two hundred years. And Tucson was undeniably bicultural, Anglo and Hispanic. Initially Phoenix shared in this Arizona style of ethnic partnership, as represented by the Swilling household and a bicultural group of businessmen that included Hispanics such as Jesus Otero and Miguel Lauro Peralta.[38] In another example of biculturalism in Phoenix, the 1870 census showed the community to be almost evenly split between Anglo and Hispanic residents. The ethnic makeup of the business elite and the general population would change, however. By the end of the decade, Phoenix became an Anglo community explicitly antipathetic to Mexican residents.

Fig. 3.3. Phoenix Canal Digging (Arizona Historical Society/Tucson, AHS no. 49819). This photograph shows a team at work gouging an irrigation ditch in the Phoenix Basin. Early canals followed the outlines and traces left by ancient Hohokam canals. The desert landscape, so inauspicious in its dry appearance, flowered with agricultural production when water became available in the first Swilling Ditch in 1868. Cultivation quickly spread throughout the basin as canal construction continued through the 1870s and 1880s.

Phoenix grew at a remarkable rate through the 1870s primarily because of the expansion of agriculture. Canals proliferated in the valley—Swilling's merely had been the first—bringing more and more land under cultivation. Swilling's Salt River Canal stretched nineteen miles and first opened in 1868. The Maricopa Canal ran twenty-six miles and also opened in 1868. Three canals on the south side of the river opened in 1871. One more on the south side and another one on the north side opened in 1878. By 1897, twelve canals delivered Salt River water to more than thirty thousand acres in the valley.[39]

The expansion of agriculture in the valley drew the attention of new set-tlers. One of the most significant was Charles Trumbull Hayden, a merchant and freighter from Tucson who had arrived in the territory in 1858. Hayden established the community of Tempe in 1871, building a flour mill and run-ning a ferry at the crossing of the Salt River near the butte later bearing the name of the community. Hayden had first called the settlement Butte City, but early pioneer Darrell Duppa had suggested the name Tempe, after the Vale of Tempe in Greece. Other settlers attracted to the agrarian possibilities in the valley were Mormons. The first settlements established in 1877 failed, but the Mormon community at Mesa persevered and eventually prospered. The com-

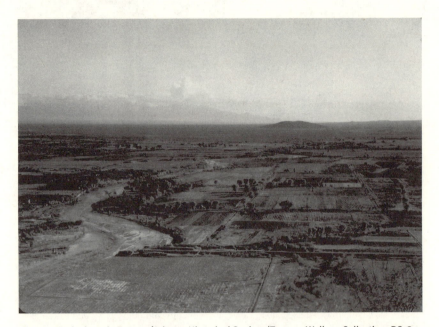

Fig. 3.4. Agriculture in Tucson (Arizona Historical Society/Tucson, Wallace Collection, PC180-524). This photograph looking south from Sentinel Peak (A Mountain) in Tucson shows a pattern of irrigated agriculture that stretched back to the beginning of recorded history. The stability of such agricultural production depended on the flow of the Santa Cruz River and expanded or contracted according to the supply of water meandering by the farmers' fields. This continuum of agriculture in the Tucson Basin gave city leaders a feeling of optimism and confidence in their superior position as Phoenix canal builders began scratching their ditches into the sandy soil in the Salt River valley.

pletion of the Mormon temple in Mesa in 1927 established the city as the center of Mormonism in Arizona.[40]

As agriculture expanded in the 1870s and Phoenix grew in size and infrastructure, anti-Mexican animus mounted as well. Trees lining the broad streets benefited from the ample irrigation water, but Anglos began to exclusively occupy the notable residences. An observer in 1872 noted the changing appearance of the community and remarked with approval on the changing ethnic nature of the community:

> Lately hundreds of ornamental trees have been set out, which, in a few years, will give the town the appearance of a forest city and will add to its beauty and comfort. When it has become the capital of the Territory, which it will, un-

doubtedly, at no very distant day, and when the iron horse steams through our country on the Texas Pacific road, Salt River Valley will be the garden of the Pacific Slope and Phoenix the most important town. The Indian is now a nuisance and the Sonoran a decided annoyance, but both are sure to disappear before civilization as snow before the noonday sun.[41]

In 1873 another report echoed the ethnocentric sentiment: "Every house in town is crowded with its human dwellers and even that part of it occupied by the Mexicans is being encroached upon by whites."[42] By 1877 Mexicans still constituted about half the population of Phoenix, but they were almost exclusively restricted to living and working in the agricultural areas. One of the new canals in the 1870s was called the Mexican Ditch, and it served only Mexican users. Some Mexican residents owned land, but many more worked as agricultural workers, toiling in the fields and building and maintaining canals that served other landowners.[43]

The first newspaper in the valley, the *Salt River Herald*, began publishing in January 1878. Later that year Phoenix residents built the community's first public school: an adobe structure covered with stucco. But adobe structures were becoming problematic, as Bradford Luckingham explains, "As soon as possible, buildings of fired brick, wood, and stone, including schools and churches, replaced the Mexican adobe structures constructed in the early years, in order to give the town more of an 'American' look. Adobe was considered too 'Mexican' for most Anglos."[44] As one observer explained in 1879, expressing a clear class consciousness, "We find that the older residents of Phoenix begin to put on style and discard adobe in favor of brick as a building material, and in fact few, except those who are poor and unpretentious as ourselves, talk or think of adobe."[45] In perhaps the best example of this transformation, residents raised the funds to replace the first school with an imposing two-story structure of fired brick, creating in the process one of the "chief adornments" of the town.[46]

Back in Tucson residents still smarted from the loss of the territorial capital. One effort to recover from the loss of political patronage centered on getting the army headquarters for the territory moved from Prescott to Tucson so as to maintain control over the dwindling military contracts. In the meantime, Tucson-based freighters and merchants continued to bid on contracts during the interlude of peace that followed John Clum's capture of Geronimo in 1877.

The freedom from Apache warfare lasted less than four years. In 1881 Geronimo fled the reservation, fearing that government concern over the Ghost Dance phenomenon would cause his arrest and imprisonment. The Ghost Dance was a religious movement that spread from tribe to tribe with promises of bringing back buffalo and resurrecting dead warriors. The dancers also fore-saw the disappearance of all whites. General Crook returned to Arizona in 1882 to lead the effort to track down the Apaches. After a long campaign, during which Crook gained permission to chase Geronimo's group into their moun-tain hideouts in northern Mexico, the Apaches agreed to return to San Carlos in February 1884. The Indians only stayed on the reservation for three months. In May 1884, Geronimo was on the run again. General Crook negotiated an-other surrender in March 1886, but before the Apaches had reached San Carlos, word arrived that Crook's superiors in Washington had refused to approve his negotiated settlement. Fearing betrayal, Geronimo once again fled back into the mountains in Mexico. Also at work in this episode was one of the most notorious examples of civilian interference. Bob Tribolett was a merchant who traded, among other things, mescal to the Indians. Rumors circulated that it was Tribolett who warned the Apaches of the government's duplicity, inciting Geronimo to flee back into the mountains. General Crook, and other officers, became convinced that Tribolett was either a member or a tool of the Indian Ring. Whether this was true or not, undeniable was the fact that Geronimo's flight prolonged the need for substantial supplies provided by civilian contractors. To the army, any action by a trader that seemed to delay or impede the resolution of warfare with the Apaches was suspicious, to say the least.[47]

The Indian campaigns had resumed in 1881. At that time many Tucsonans may have presumed that multiplying opportunities for government supply con-tracts would contribute to the community's prosperity. After 1880, however, the Southern Pacific Railroad garnered much of the army supply traffic, and most of the freighting operations in Tucson went out of business. These busi-ness failures were compounded by the collapse of the commerce in pesos. The ebb and flow of business in Tucson was not new, but now the decline of com-merce in the community could be judged in relation to the fortunes of another community over the horizon to the north. By the early 1880s Phoenix busi-nessmen had begun to see themselves as the rightful economic and political leaders of the territory. One can almost hear the sense of superiority as a

Phoenix newspaper observed the business failures in Tucson in 1883: "The failure of the extensive mercantile houses of W. Zeckendorf, Tucson, is the third assignment made by the principal firms of that city within the past 18 months—Lord and Williams and the White House being the other two. The business foundations of the ancient and honorable must be a little 'shaky' or else the manner of carrying on business there is loose. At all events, these failures do not give the coming metropolis a very good name."[48]

General Nelson Miles replaced Crook. After a massive campaign pitting 5,000 U.S. Army troops against 42 Apaches, Geronimo surrendered in September 1886. This latest warfare had lasted five years, but during that time all of the prominent freighting companies and presumed conspirators of the Indian Ring went bankrupt. In the future, any economic benefit gained by military operations in the region would be most likely acquired by the Southern Pacific Railroad, headquartered in California, and only tangentially benefit the community of Tucson.

While the Indian campaigns continued around Tucson, Phoenix entrepreneurs, not at all concerned with an Apache menace, had been dutifully multiplying and extending irrigation canals, placing more and more land under the plow. The biggest effort was organized by William J. Murphy. Murphy arrived in the Salt River valley in 1883 after working as a contractor on the construction of the Santa Fe Railroad in northern Arizona. His project in the vicinity of Phoenix was the Arizona Canal, the longest and most extensive irrigation system yet to be constructed. The canal grew to forty miles in length and required a large dam and headgate structure on the river. To finance the project, Murphy sold bonds in Chicago and New York and even traveled to England to raise money. To convince investors, Murphy boasted about the valley's climate and resources, including its mild winters and twelve-month growing season, starting the process of advertising the region's benefits to potential residents in the Midwest and beyond. Murphy also acquired large tracts of land that would be serviced by the canal, standing to profit from both the canal's construction and its use.[49]

With more arable land came more people, including entrepreneurial veterinarian Alexander John Chandler. With links to investment capital in Detroit, Chandler arrived in the valley in 1887 and began the acquisition of land for his Chandler Ranch. He also developed the Consolidated Canal Company, whose canal grew to forty-one miles in length and controlled most of the Salt River water serving land south of the river. With secure water supplies through his canal, by 1900 Chandler had developed several thousand acres. He also added a hydroelectric power facility to his canal system, which provided the power necessary for groundwater pumping to augment the river water.[50] Over the next few years, Chandler acquired eighteen thousand acres south of Phoenix but within the future Salt River Project area. This proved to be significant in later years, when Chandler profited from the federally subsidized water system.

Other settlers arrived in the 1880s, including groups of farmers emigrating from the Midwest. These groups established towns at the outset. One group came from Ohio and located in the far western valley at Buckeye. Another group, from Peoria, Illinois, established Peoria, Arizona, in the northwest valley in 1888. These groups set the precedent for later groups, including religious communities, that established themselves in the valley.[51]

As farm communities proliferated throughout the valley, the city of Phoenix continued to expand with brick and stone structures along a grid pattern of wide thoroughfares. Phoenix delegates had lobbied for and won from the territorial legislature the territory's insane asylum. Tempe had received the territorial normal school, and Florence received the territorial prison. Tucson was considered the loser in the patronage game, gaining the least desired public institution—the university—with its relatively small staff and meager annual appropriations (twenty-five thousand dollars versus one hundred thousand dollars for the insane asylum).[52] Fresh from their patronage success, Phoenix boosters set their sights on a bigger prize: the territorial capital. Included in the new buildings going up in the booming town was a county courthouse and government center that was much larger than required by the current Maricopa County offices. So commodious was the new county building, Phoenix boosters began fostering the idea that the territorial capital could easily fit into the new office space. Phoenix businessmen had donated the land for the county building and had contributed to the expense of its construction. They were also rumored to be dispensing "boodle" to territorial delegates, buying votes to secure the transfer of the capital.

The Prescott newspaper published complaints to no avail: "So it appears that the residents of Phenix [sic] and Salt River Valley, not content with a just share of public institutions, are plotting for the capital also. They form a part of the body politic whose numbers are not confined to Salt River Valley, that have become notorious for their assault upon wholesome laws, and for the corrupt measures that they have endeavored to enact by the infamous use of money to bribe legislators." To the Prescott editor, Phoenix boosters exhibited "voracious greed" and traveled with a "boodle sack" with which to bribe.[53] Phoenix businessmen clearly had invested large sums of money in the effort to attract the capital to Phoenix. At the very least, the gift of land for the county building and the monetary support for the construction serve as examples of this investment.

As a point of comparison, Tucson businessmen had donated the building to house the territorial legislature during its ten-year stay from 1867 to 1877: a former warehouse, made of adobe. Behind the territorial capitol was the army depot's corral, with all of its characteristic sounds and smells. By no stretch of the imagination could the Tucson facility be considered luxurious. Phoenix boosters, on the other hand, offered legislators an impressive new building constructed of stone. Boodle sack or not, Phoenix businessmen had invested in their community's future. The private expenditures paid off in 1889, when the legislature voted to move the capital to Phoenix.

In 1870, Tucson was the territorial capital and clearly the leading community in the territory. By 1890, Phoenix was the territorial capital, and the position of leadership in the territory was contested. Few of the territory's residents in 1870 would have predicted the future rivalry of the two communities.

The developing rivalry was due to the timing of the Apache campaigns and to the communities' respective geography. General Crook's first Indian campaign in Arizona had been against the Pinal Apaches in the early 1870s. After pacifying these mountain Apaches, Crook had then moved on to the southern region to control the Chiricahua Apaches. It had been the Pinal Apaches who were in a position to threaten the new town of Phoenix, and having that threat removed first proved to be a great boon for Phoenix developers.

As it turned out, the campaigns against Geronimo in the south continued for another thirteen years after the Pinal Apaches of central Arizona had ceased warfare. One reason the southern Indians proved to be so difficult to control was the nearness of the Mexican border. The proximity to Mexico both contributed to Tucson's early prosperity through trade networks stretching south and provided Geronimo and his band with secure mountain bases in the Mexican Sierra Madre, initially beyond the reach of American military forces. The continuing warfare contributed to Tucson's prosperity, but it also interfered with developing infrastructure and civic improvements in Tucson. Partly this was because the leading businessmen in Tucson became complacent with the profits to be gained through government contracts, relying on federal largess to secure the town's economic well-being. In retrospect this may seem short-sighted and provincial, but at the time few if any alternatives existed. Only the most cautious and conservative development plans made sense in Tucson while the Apache menace remained. The Apaches had plagued the sedentary residents of the region for hundreds of years. With great and persistent effort, it had taken the weight of the American military more than a decade to finally control the raiding Indians. Since it had taken longer in the south, Phoenix gained the benefit of secure peace earlier than Tucson. For thirteen years Phoenix businessmen could plot the community's future with single-minded determination. During those years, Phoenix gained ground on Tucson.

Part 2

RIVALS

1890—1930

The Duty of Water and
Agrarian Rivalry

AFTER THE POLITICAL wrangling and conspiracy theories about the Indian Ring had died down, and after the railroad made its long-awaited arrival into Arizona, shifting forever the trade routes and commercial links, the two communities settled down to a quiet but intense competition. Elites in both cities pursued their own financial well-being, no doubt considering their own individual success to be a harbinger of good tidings for the broader community. Such hidebound capitalist concepts were commonplace at the turn of the twentieth century. In Tucson and Phoenix, agriculture provided a fundamental basis for prosperity, and so the competition between the two cities focused largely on an agrarian rivalry. By the 1890s, the competition had become explicit, with city leaders eyeing with envy and suspicion developments in each other's community. The rush to metropolitan status in Tucson and Phoenix would be determined initially by the ability of each community to expand agricultural production. The source for this economic development was, of course, the two rivers.

By 1890 the different natures of the two rivers had resulted in different strategies for delivering water to the farmers' fields. Canals were the focus of irrigated agriculture in both places, but the canal systems in the Salt River valley were always larger and more extensive—a circumstance dating back to Hohokam times. In Tucson, a system of irrigation ditches—*acequias* in Spanish —serviced the fields near the town, and in the 1890s, more extensive canals made their appearance. But in Tucson the smaller river soon reached its limit. Before the federal reclamation era began in the early 1900s, canal builders in Tucson had begun digging wells and installing pumps near the heads of their canals so as to augment the modest supply of surface water.[1] This reliance on groundwater became the norm for Tucson farmers, while a reliance on surface water and dam-fed canals became the pattern in Phoenix.

The two methods of agriculture had proven to be fairly equal in their effectiveness. In the Salt River valley, farmers cultivated 35,212 acres. Landowners claimed over 150,000 acres under the plow, but this had more to do with establishing future legal claims to reclaimed or federally subsidized water than with land actually sown with crops.[2] In Pima County in 1890, including the Tucson Basin, farmers worked 31,852 acres.[3] Primarily dam-fed canals provided water to the farmers' fields in the Phoenix Basin, while the surface flow of the stream augmented by groundwater serviced the fields in Tucson.

Farmers along the Salt in the 1890s relied on twelve canal systems that stretched more than 260 miles to the north and south of the river. More than six hundred miles of laterals delivered the water from the main canals to the actual fields.[4] The canal system was extensive, but it remained vulnerable to periodic floods that damaged dams and intake structures. A devastating flood in 1884 caused a newspaper to suggest creating a unified canal system as community property, but nothing came of the call. Other newspapers in Phoenix were always willing to trumpet the rights of private property, and this was the concept that resonated most deeply in the Gilded Age society. Another particularly damaging flood in 1891 rendered the Arizona Canal—forty-seven miles long, potentially servicing fifty-six thousand acres north of Phoenix— useless, since the flood wiped out the main diversion dam. The flood not only destroyed the Arizona Canal's dam but also damaged every other diversion dam on the forty-mile stretch of the Salt River between its confluence with the Verde and its confluence with the Gila.[5]

Another vulnerability that plagued the Phoenix-area farmers was drought, which at times reduced the flow in the river to almost nothing; no matter how extensive the dams and delivery system, farmers' fields went dry. This happened, for example, in the drought year of 1900, when the low flow in the Salt River fell to 45 cfs.[6] Such a circumstance of course affected farmers and residents to the south in the Santa Cruz valley, but agricultural acequias and the municipal water system in Tucson also relied on groundwater, which provided something akin to immunity from "water famine" even during the most severe drought. During a dry spell in 1893, the Tucson newspaper reported that the surface flow of the river was insufficient even "to water a mockingbird," but "thanks to the wells and pumps . . . every part of Tucson is amply supplied with the purest of water."[7]

Tucson boosters at times bridled under the unfavorable comparison with the Phoenix Basin's Salt River, given that the Salt's acknowledged flow was over four times greater than that of the Santa Cruz. But the growing access to groundwater—a secure source even in a prolonged drought—had awakened a rush of optimism. Wells would be "Better than a Canal," as the newspaper crowed in 1891.[8] The hopeful calculus became clear as the proliferation of wells devoted to irrigated agriculture proceeded through the coming years. In 1902, the Tucson newspaper proclaimed the groundwater supply would "equal more than one-half the entire water supply of [the] Salt River Valley."[9] The "more than one-half," combined with the Santa Cruz River's surface flow of 25 cfs (at its most consistent low-flow rate), added up to more than three-quarters of the Salt River's expected volume. Groundwater created a near-parity water supply for Santa Cruz valley farmers and ensured that the Tucson Basin would remain "one of the most fertile and productive valleys in the 'Land of Sunshine and Silver.'"[10]

Agriculture was critical to the economic health of both communities, but Tucson's prosperity also stemmed from its geographical location and lengthy history as the center of a trade network that extended throughout southern Arizona and northern Mexico. Whereas wealth and prosperity in both valleys depended to a large degree on irrigated agriculture, in Tucson it was only a partial dependence, perceived by boosters to be one component of a larger strategy. Phoenix businessmen, on the other hand, understood that any increase in prosperity in the early twentieth century—along with progress toward metropolitan status—would have to adhere to the age-old pattern, achieving an increase in water supplies that could be directed toward agriculture. At this point, the environmental realities that had shaped the style of irrigation along the rivers reasserted itself. In Phoenix, landowners organized the drive toward ever-bigger dams and more extensive canals, as well as the effort to acquire federal reclamation projects. In Tucson farmers sank more and more wells, ever deeper, capped by increasingly sophisticated pump technology, while other Tucson businessmen engaged in trade, merchant activity, and efforts to organize private capital for economic development.

The development of the Salt River Project has been well documented and narrated. One of the remarkable aspects of the story was the consensus among Phoenix landowners and business leaders behind the drive for a high dam on the Salt River. The farmers sometimes argued among themselves, but the disputes generally regarded the distribution of reclaimed water: who would get it, how much, and at what cost. Never debated was fact that the river's flood-water and low-flow trickle should all be stored behind the high dam and then partitioned out with an engineered consistency. In an example of the unified spirit, landowners in the valley lobbied Congress during the debate over passage of the Reclamation Act in 1902, winning an amendment to allow reclaimed water to service private land as well as public land. The amendment was crucial for Phoenix-area farmers. Early discussions about federal reclamation had centered on the goal of developing public land, including areas designated as Indian reservations. In the Salt River valley, however, arable land was almost entirely in private hands by 1900. As examples of the political consensus behind federal reclamation in the Salt River valley, the boosters in Phoenix came up with fifteen hundred dollars and sent scores of lobbyists to Washington to smooth the way for the amended reclamation legislation and subsequent approval of the project for the Salt River.[11]

The Salt River Project was one of the first three projects approved by the secretary of the interior, and it was the first one started. The first one completed, however, was the Truckee-Carson Ditch in Nevada in 1905. That project serviced the home state of the reclamation bill's sponsor, Senator Francis G. Newlands. Tucson and the Santa Cruz River valley never appeared on the Reclamation Bureau's list of potential dam sites, but the big losers at the start of the federal reclamation era were the Pima Indians along the Gila River and the Anglo farmers in the vicinity of Florence, not Tucson. Given Florence's

Fig. 4.1. Tonto Creek dam site on the Salt River (Arizona Historical Society/Tucson, AHS Photo Number 14985). The Reclamation Service built the Salt River Project near Phoenix in part because a nearly perfect dam site occurred at the confluence of Tonto Creek and the Salt River. No such dam site existed along the Santa Cruz River. Agricultural production expanded to more than two hundred thousand acres in Phoenix because of the reclamation project, while acreage under cultivation in Tucson remained stable at about thirty thousand acres.

nearness to the Gila River Indian Reservation, local boosters had assumed that federal reclamation would first serve them by developing the Gila River. The false assumption caused Florence leaders to send only one representative—a minister—to Washington to lobby on behalf of the Gila River project. Whereas the group of Phoenix boosters had arrived in Washington well heeled, the lone Florence delegate carried no boodle sack of cash to distribute to Interior Department administrators.[12]

It is not my intention here to recount the process of building Roosevelt Dam—the first step in the creation of the Salt River Project—seventy miles to the northeast of Phoenix at the confluence of Tonto Creek and the Salt River. But it is important to note the planned extent of the project, since the projections came from the first scientific measures of the river's natural parameters. The USGS cartographers and engineers projected a reservoir of 840,745 acre feet. The surface area of the lake would be 13,459 acres. The flow of water from the reservoir was projected to service 200,000 acres of farm land downstream. In addition, the power generator at the dam would provide electricity to valley residents, including the growing urban area at Phoenix. The fall of water at the dam turning the generators would provide 25,800 horsepower.[13]

Although the generating power of the fall of water could be mathematically determined, the calculation of benefit to be derived from the irrigation project was more problematic. It hinged on the measure of "the duty of water." In part the calculation of water's usefulness and capacity for work was shaped by the turn-of-the-century Progressive faith in scientific knowledge. The reclamation effort itself was part of the Progressive Era's crowning faith in science and engineering. One of the nation's most endemic problems—aridity in the West—could be engineered out of existence. Part of the science behind that effort was based on the discipline of hydrology and the assumption that water's usefulness for irrigation could be mathematically calculated.

Little understood today is the nascent quality of the science behind reclamation at the turn of the century. Surveys of topography, including the mapping of rivers from their point of origin to termination, was well established by 1900. Difficulties in surveying techniques in the mountainous West had been worked out in the California Survey of the 1850s and by Clarence King in his seminal survey of the fortieth parallel in 1867. More problematic was the scientific measurement of the volume in a stream's flow or the volume and movement of underground water.

Congress formed the USGS in 1879 to conduct scientific surveys of the public domain, primarily in the West, with an eye toward the mapping and cataloguing of natural resources. Clarence King was the first director of the agency, followed in 1881 by John Wesley Powell. Under Powell's leadership, the USGS gained authorization to conduct an Irrigation Survey in 1888. Powell organized the effort by dividing the work into separate surveys: the Topographic Survey, "to prepare topographic maps on which the lands susceptible of, or best suited to, irrigation [including] possible reservoir and canal sites" and the Hydraulic Survey, itself divided into two branches: the Hydrographic Survey, to "measure the water supply," and the Engineering Branch, to "locate and design the necessary irrigation structures."[14]

By the time Washington-based scientists and bureaucrats began organizing the USGS surveys, Tucson and Phoenix agriculturalists had a long history of extensive irrigated cultivation. When the Hydrographic Survey commenced operation in 1889, the Salt River valley had more than eight hundred miles of trunk and feeder canals. The science was following on the heels of a great deal of practical knowledge.

First priority for the Hydrographic Survey was the acquisition of accurate measurements of stream flow: stream gaging. Advances in the mechanisms of stream gaging made the results of measurement more accurate but also required engineering skill in their placement and maintenance. Accordingly, the director of the Hydrographic Survey, C. E. Dutton, picked ten young men to study stream-gaging techniques at a camp chosen by USGS director Powell, at Embudo, New Mexico. The ten young employees, including Frederick Haynes Newell, spent five months at the camp gaining practical and experimental knowledge. Newell had obtained a bachelor's degree from the Massachusetts Institute of Technology (MIT) in mining engineering, and after working for a couple of years, had returned to MIT for graduate work in geology. After meeting John Wesley Powell at MIT after a speech in 1885, Newell asked the USGS director for a job. Powell responded with an invitation for Newell to join the group at Embudo in the winter of 1888. Of the ten students of stream gaging at the camp, only Newell received a permanent position with the survey.[15]

The first locations extensively studied by the Irrigation Survey were in Arizona, because of the state's aridity and the likelihood that the Gila, Salt, and Verde rivers would provide good irrigation sites. The Santa Cruz River was not included in the gaging efforts of 1889. One might wonder why the southern river was left out of the study, but no explanation exists in the USGS documents. It could be that the river was deemed too small to bother with, or it may simply have been a recognition that the river's flow had already been measured with satisfactory accuracy. Tucson's own water engineer had measured the flow in 1884, reporting a low-flow rate of 25 cfs. Work on the three central Arizona rivers began promptly in 1889 with efforts to establish stream-gaging stations in the rivers. Floods hampered the initial effort, and the first station went into the Gila in August. Efforts on the Salt and Verde were hap-hazard, also thwarted by periodic floods.[16]

The Irrigation Survey and the work of the Hydrographic Branch ended in 1890 because of budget cuts as Congress retrenched in the face of a deepen-ing depression. Newell and four other employees of the Hydrographic Branch found work in the Topographic Survey and so stayed on the USGS payroll; all others were laid off.[17]

Stream-gaging work, so critical to the development of reclamation plans in the Salt River valley, did not resume until 1894. Budgets were still low, but the survey managed to make per diem payments of five dollars a day for the work. Newell at this time hired Arthur Powell Davis to organize the stream gaging in the West. Davis was a nephew of the former USGS director Powell (John Wesley Powell had resigned in 1894 because of health concerns as well as frustration over congressional wheeling and dealing). Powell's nephew Davis had been working in the Topographic Branch since 1884. Newell brought him over to the Hydrographic Branch in August 1894, and Davis immediately began traveling throughout the West hiring resident hydrographers to conduct per diem stream gaging. In late 1895, Davis began surveying the Gila River Indian Reservation for reservoir sites. Congress had made a special appropriation for the work on the Gila River Indian Reservation, and it was out of this expanded effort in central Arizona that the surveys for the future Salt River Project com-menced. In 1895, however, it seemed that the Gila River was the main focus of the surveys, reflecting the common reading of the politics of federal recla-mation, that as a national policy it should only be directed toward public land.

Accurate stream gaging in the 1890s was a matter of technical expertise and congressional appropriations. The scientific understanding of groundwater was another matter entirely. This scientific discipline was just being invented in the 1890s. Unlike the nebulous understanding of underground water, an understanding of the characteristics of flowing surface water was well estab-lished by the end of the nineteenth century, although not without its tradi-tional and folklorish concepts. As Todd Shallat explains in *Structures in the Stream*, scientific understandings from Europe, going back at least as far as the experiments by Daniel Bernouli in fluid dynamics, crossed the Atlantic during the American Revolution. Confusing the issue of scientific certainty was the amateur tradition in the United States, boosted by the success of the Erie Canal. Amateur engineers of the homegrown variety had built the 363-mile canal from

Albany to Buffalo, New York, completed in 1825. Debates about surface water hydraulics lasted into the 1830s before the European-based understandings of the Corps of Engineers won out.[18]

Despite the long history of contested theories about surface water hydraulics, the discipline was well established in the United States by the time Powell formed the Hydrography Branch in 1888. Groundwater studies, however, were just developing. The Hydrographic Branch first began compiling well logs in 1891 from Wheeling, West Virginia, and made more collections of data on the plains in 1893 and 1894. Newell devoted twenty thousand dollars out of his budget in 1895 for groundwater studies.[19] The conceptual problem facing Newell was that few systematic studies of groundwater existed. Geologists and mining engineers had the greatest experience with groundwater, but their studies had been individualistic and haphazard. For example, groundwater in mines—wet mines—was most often thought of as a nuisance and bother, not a subject for scientific study per se. The goal was simply to get the water out of the way so that mining operations could take place. Significantly for later agricultural pursuits, pump technology developed, partly motivated by the need in wet mines to continually remove large quantities of water out of deep mine shafts. Within the Hydrographic Branch, however, Newell recognized that an understanding of groundwater was of importance for the semiarid West. Partly this awareness developed during the drought years of the 1890s, when surface flow in the rivers dwindled to a trickle. Newell got the opportunity to do something about this concern after the passage of the Reclamation Act in 1902. As USGS historian Follansbee recounted,

> The requests for information regarding wells and ground water had become so numerous by the first year of the Hydrographic Branch and the work of previous years had shown such need for specialization in future investigations, that the Division of Hydrology was organized on January 1, 1903. The use of the term hydrology with special reference to groundwater is peculiar to the Survey. The use originated through the fact that a study of geology is requisite to the determination of groundwater, and to that determination was given the term hydro-geology, which was contracted to hydrology.[20]

The Hydrographic Branch was formed in 1888, its first collection of data on groundwater occurred in 1891, and the scientific discipline of hydrology got its name in 1903. Of course a practical understanding of groundwater predated these developments in the USGS, but commonsense knowledge about groundwater often suffered from incomplete or erroneous assumptions. Examples of this flawed common understanding appear in two 1902 Tucson newspaper articles proclaiming that "artesian" wells served the valley. On May 1 the newspaper reported,

> The Underflow—Of the Santa Cruz has been Tapped and is Flowing Handsomely. Some years ago the Alison brothers opened an irrigating canal on the west side of the Santa Cruz valley with its source of supply at what is known as Warner's Lake at the east base of Sentinel Peak, southwest of Tucson. To increase the water supply at the head of the canal the Alison brothers put down several drain pump three-inch pipe [sic] to the depth of from ten to fifteen feet, resulting in several flowing wells, increasing greatly their water supply. It was noticed that in every instance one or two stratas [sic] of hard substance had to be penetrated to reach the underflow, which would rise up and flow out of the pipes some inches above the surface. It was believed then and recent events would seem to confirm this opinion. There is good reason to believe that at depth a large and permanent supply of artesian water can be obtained.[21]

The article went on to explain other farmers' efforts to tap the artesian supply: "They have employed an experienced well borer, James C. Fulton, to do the work. Mr. Fulton has had a long experience in boring for artesian water and oil. He believe [sic] the probabilities for a large supply of artesian water in the Santa Cruz valley in the vicinity he has set his stakes is good."[22] Another article trumpeted the success of the efforts in July. This was the article quoted above for its favorable comparison with the Salt River Valley:

> Water! Water!—Another Artesian Well Spouts Forth Volumes of Water. The artesian water question has been determined in San [sic] Cruz valley. Yesterday Captain Fulton, the manager for General L. H. Manning, struck the fifth flow of water, this about three quarters of a mile up the valley from the first well opened. The flow was struck at twelve feet. . . . General Manning is very much elated over the wonderful success which has resulted from Captain Fulton's work. He feels confident that he has struck a subterranean river, and the flow would seem to warrant the belief. He predicts that he will during the next six months develop 4,000 miner's inches through the artesian wells. This will equal more than one-half the entire water supply of Salt River valley.
>
> One of the interesting features of these wells is not one of them has depreciated in flow since developed, yet this is our very dryest [sic] season.[23]

Eventually an understanding developed in Tucson about the difference between artesian flow and groundwater existing in a deep-storage aquifer. But that understanding was unavailable to the newspaper editor in 1902. The understanding was only tenuously held by the engineers and scientists. The seminal essay on groundwater by T. C. Chamberlain had not appeared until 1885, six years after the formation of the USGS. Given Captain Fulton's "long experience" and his erroneous description of the flow as artesian, it would seem that his knowledge of wells and groundwater was more practically than academically derived. Chamberlain had described seven criteria for determining an artesian flow in 1885. Specifically, the seven factors served to differentiate between artesian water and water stored in an aquifer. Given Captain Fulton's mistake, it would seem that he was unaware of Chamberlain's seven criteria.[24]

Even within the more highly developed discipline of surface water hydraulics, the language of the science remained grounded in a traditional lexicon. Running water was live and capable of doing work: its duty. This concept of the duty of water represents a vestige of traditional, amateur tradition among American hydraulic engineers. An effort to define the duty of water—ultimately unsuccessful—appeared in the 1900 Census of Agriculture: "The investigation of the duty of water is one of the most complicated problems of irrigation, on account of the diversity of conditions and the difficulty of procuring facts. . . . The duty of water is quoted at from 30 to 600 acres or more to the second-foot. For convenience the unit of 100 acres to the second-foot has been considered as indicating careful irrigating, although in the more southwestern portion of the arid region this would be considered low, and in the northern part, high."[25]

Scientific measures resulting in mathematic certainty cannot be based on convenience, just as a range from thirty to six hundred cannot be arbitrarily set at one hundred, with any expectation of scientific accuracy. But such was the circumstance of hydrological studies in the early 1900s. Scientists and engineers spoke with authority and confidence, offering clear solutions based on technological improvements. Even if we quibble with their concepts and definitions today, it is undeniable that the engineers spoke with a scientific authority accepted by their contemporary audience. When Arthur Powell Davis offered a USGS-certified scientific measure of the benefit to be gained from the Salt River Project as two hundred thousand acres irrigated, no one was inclined to haggle. It could be clearly seen that the Salt River Project would greatly increase the area under cultivation in the valley, but as the project began, no one could say with complete accuracy how much land that would be.

Developers and speculators in both communities well knew that any increase in water supplies, if it could be delivered to where it was needed, would turn worthless desert land into valuable agricultural fields. The profit potential was clear, and increasingly it became obvious that greater opportunities for wealth were to be found in the Phoenix Basin than in the Tucson Basin.

In Phoenix perhaps the best example of an agrarian land developer was Dr. Alexander J. Chandler. When the Interior Department approved the Salt River Project, Chandler owned eighteen thousand acres south of the river and the Consolidated Canal Company serving those fields. The first example of a federal subsidy beneficial to Chandler came in 1909, when the federal government purchased all the valley's canal systems so as to systematize and regularize the delivery of a stable and abundant water supply. The Progressive Era optimism shone brightly with the assumption that only through engineering skill could desert scrub be turned consistently into verdant green crops. Chandler's land development plans included continued agricultural production as well as the residential subdivision of his ranch, which commenced in 1911. The next year Chandler established a town site that took his name and later built a noted resort hotel that served as the headquarters for his land sales and tourist promotions.[26]

The simple reason that Tucson never built a dam or acquired a reservoir to service agriculture in the Santa Cruz River valley was that there was no similar site in the vicinity of the Tucson basin such as Phoenicians enjoyed at the Tonto Creek dam site. The only proposal to build a dam and reservoir near Tucson contemporaneously with the Salt River Project targeted Sabino Canyon. Located about a dozen miles to the northeast of Tucson, Sabino Creek flowed out of the Santa Catalina Mountains down a narrow, picturesque canyon to its confluence with Rillito Creek, a tributary of the Santa Cruz River. In 1912 a group of businessmen proposed to build a dam in Sabino Canyon to provide irrigation water and hydroelectric power to the valley.

Although repeatedly proposed, the storage dam was never built, primarily because the project could never measure up to a reasonable projection of usefulness or profitability. The lake behind the proposed dam (in fact two lakes behind two small dams), would cover 475 acres and contain 32,000 acre feet of water, a far cry from the Roosevelt reservoir's 13,459 acres and 840,745

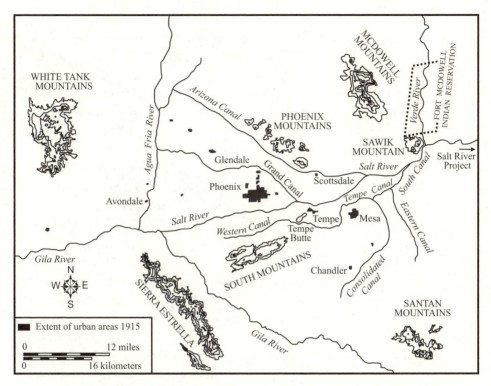

Map 4.1. Phoenix 1915. The Phoenix Basin in 1915, showing surrounding communities and the canal system served by the Salt River Project.

acre feet. The irrigation water would service 20,000 acres, and the fall of the water would provide twenty-seven hundred horsepower for the generators, roughly one-tenth the benefit to be derived from the Salt River Project. The simple debilitating fact of the proposal was that the flow down the canyons was too meager to provide a sufficient benefit from the storage project. The watershed behind the dams was less than thirty square miles, and the low flow down the canyon measured a modest 10 cfs. The projected cost of about $1 million (Roosevelt Dam on the Salt River was projected to cost $3.75 million, but ended up costing $10.28 million) did not equate to any commensurate reward.[27]

Although no storage dam was ever built in Sabino Canyon, another plan for augmenting water supplies for agriculture in Tucson came to fruition in 1913. The developing reliance on groundwater reached its apotheosis in an incredibly grandiose well and pump scheme. It was called the Tucson Farms Crosscut. A series of nineteen wells, connected by a subterranean conduit, stretched a mile across the floodplain of the Santa Cruz River just south, up-stream, from Tucson. It cost $1 million to build—financed by investments drawn from Chicago to Great Britain—and produced a flow of 46 cfs when it first went into operation. This was the type of project that boosters had in mind when they proclaimed that the groundwater beneath the valley would contribute to a water supply akin to parity with the surface flow available in the Salt River. Unfortunately for Tucson farmers, and despite the high hopes, the initial impressive gush from the "flowing wells" soon slackened. Not even the most productive wells could match the Salt River Project's impact on agri-culture and Phoenix's growing prosperity.

The depressing regularity with which the output of wells in Tucson dimin-ished was due to the nature of the aquifer. Early engineers and boosters in Tucson mislabeled the basin's water supply as artesian. Artesian water is groundwater forced to the surface through specific geological circumstances. In Texas, for example, the Edwards Aquifer delivers an artesian-based water supply to San Antonio. Rainfall on the hill country to the north of the city en-ters the Edwards Aquifer. There it trickles and oozes underground to the south and east, making its way toward the coastal plain of the Gulf of Mexico. At the Balcones Escarpment forming the boundary between the hill country to the north and coastal plain to the south, water bubbles up in more than half a dozen artesian springs. The water appears on the surface in the springs at the head of creeks and rivers—including the San Antonio River—because of the pressure of the groundwater within the aquifer behind and above the springs.[28]

Tucson instead rested on a deep-storage formation. In the Tucson Basin rising bedrock and a saturated floodplain caused surface water to appear, rather than bubbling springs caused by water pressure from an up-slope aquifer. At the turn of the century, during the first flush of excitement over spewing wells, Tucson boosters described the "underflow" in the aquifer and the presence of a "subterranean river."[29] The declarations were more hopeful than real. The groundwater in Tucson was relatively motionless (oozing about two hundred feet a year), under no pressure to appear except where bedrock, or a saturated aquifer, brought it to the surface as streams and marshes.[30]

The surface flow of the river in the Tucson Basin required a saturated flood-plain of younger alluvium, with the water table extending from the surface of the streambed to the depth of bedrock. Given the extent of the available ground-water, wells became an easy proposition. Even if the surface flow diminished or disappeared during a drought, plentiful groundwater rested just beneath the surface. Once sunk into the aquifer, however, a local depletion of the water table would occur in a so-called cone of depression. The proliferation of wells throughout the basin caused a general lowering of the water table, resulting in a drying river and earlier shallow wells diminishing in output. From depths of twelve to twenty feet in 1902, wells in the basin by 1920 required drilling to one hundred feet.

Farmers in the Phoenix Basin also sank wells to provide irrigation water for their crops. But tapping the aquifer—likewise a storage rather than arte-sian groundwater supply—was never the sole or primary strategy in the val-ley. The surface flow of the Salt River was big enough to satisfy the demands of agriculture at the turn of the century. The problem was regularizing the flow and controlling the disastrous floods. In addition, digging wells and in-stalling pumps relied on private capital, whereas dam construction came with the prospect of a huge federal subsidy.

By 1920 the two strategies were entrenched. The Santa Cruz valley in the vicinity of Tucson supported 365 pumped wells that delivered 576,234 gal-lons per minute. That groundwater serviced 33,019 acres. Fewer wells sup-plied farmers along the Salt, at about one-fifth the rate as in the Santa Cruz valley (150,874 gallons per minute). On the other hand, Salt River farmers held a wide lead over Tucson Basin farmers in the water held in storage reser-voirs. Eleven reservoirs on the Salt and its tributaries contained more than 1.3 million acre feet. Twenty-six reservoirs on the Santa Cruz contained a paltry 392 acre feet, averaging about 15 acre feet per pond. In the Phoenix Basin, the yield from the groundwater, combined with the water held in storage and de-livered through canals, serviced 247,260 acres. Agricultural production in the Tucson Basin had remained fairly constant from 1890 to 1920, while during the same period agricultural production in the Phoenix Basin had quadrupled.[31]

The great expansion of agriculture around Phoenix spawned the estab-lishment of more farm towns. During the 1870s and 1880s, communities had sprung up at Tempe, Mesa, Buckeye, and Peoria. The process continued in the 1890s. A religious society settled the Ideal Temperance Colony of Glen-dale in 1892. Seventy families from the Church of the Brethren, or Dunkards, created the pacifist community in the northwest valley. In 1895 the Santa Fe

Railroad constructed its branchline from Prescott to Phoenix through Glendale. Primarily as a result of the additional railroad connection, Glendale grew in prosperity in the early twentieth century. Also in 1892, Avondale was established in the western valley along the Agua Fria River; settlers first called the community Coldwater Crossing.[32]

The expansion of agriculture continued in the early twentieth century. More farm towns came into being: Tolleson and Gilbert in 1910 and 1912, respectively.[33] Contributing to the expansion of agriculture was the increasing demand for cotton during World War I, which created a profit potential recognized by industrial conglomerates. One example of this agribusiness was the twelve-thousand-acre cotton farm west of Phoenix developed by the Goodyear Rubber Company. Similar developments in corporate farming occurred in Tucson. The Tucson Farms Company financed and constructed the Crosscut, and other corporations acquired large land holdings during the cotton boom of World War I. Edwin R. Post initiated one such project along the Santa Cruz River north of Tucson. Post, an heir to the Post cereal fortune, developed the land by drilling ten wells capped with powerful pumps.[34]

Corporate owners as well as speculative entrepreneurs stretched the definition of farmer to resemble its meaning in the plantation system of the antebellum South: the landowners did little of the actual work. A few managers and many laborers did the work of cultivation. In the Salt River valley several communities sprang up to house the workers of the large agricultural enterprises. The Goodyear Company established Litchfield Park in 1917. Other towns, such as El Mirage and Surprise, sprang up in the succeeding years. South of Tucson, workers in the cotton farms occupied the village of Continental. As geographer Malcolm Comeaux explains, "Many such towns began as migrant camps, mostly for Mexican Americans, and then slowly developed into towns, or colonias."[35]

As Tucson and Phoenix grew in population and size, municipal water systems developed in sophistication and extent. Initially residents provided their own water, either by digging wells or tapping the flow of a nearby canal. By the 1890s, however, the clear need developed in both communities for a system of engineered works. In Tucson, the system had arisen in a fairly straightforward way. A private company developed a water source in 1882 by capturing a spring six miles south and upstream from the town. The water company augmented the supply of water by excavating a head cut at the source of the spring, deepening the opening and collecting more water. A system of mains delivered the water from the head cut to the city. Water pressure came from the gravity produced by the gradual down slope over the six miles from the source.

In Phoenix the municipal water supply developed in an ad hoc manner, often emanating from the water source provided by the private canal companies. The canals delivered water to the farmers' fields and to any houses or businesses on the land serviced by the canals. A separate system derived from city-owned well water served city residents outside the canal companies' domain. The engineering of the city water system was simple, but the administration of the utility was complicated because of the multiple administrative structures controlling water supplies in the Phoenix Basin. The city water system in Phoenix always had to compete with the canal companies. This continued to be the case after the Salt River Project replaced the earlier canal systems with one gigantic water works. The city water system serviced the town and its residents, but as Phoenix expanded into former agricultural land in the early twentieth century, the new city residents continued to receive their water from the Salt River Project. Because of this dual administrative structure, the municipal water system in Phoenix expanded as Phoenix grew, but not in a uniform or cohesive manner.[36]

The problems for the water companies varied in the two cities. In Tucson the difficulties from the start were volume and water pressure. As the town grew in population, demand continued to increase as the volume from the head cut remained constant; as the physical size of the town increased, the old gravity feed through a single main became inadequate. The solutions were straightforward: additional sources of water provided by wells tapping the aquifer and a growing system of mains with water pressure provided by increasingly sophisticated pump technology. The political history of water policy in Tucson centers on these twin issues: supply and water pressure. Often the arguments and debates focus on the taxes and fees necessary to maintain the system, with cheap domestic water a cornerstone of civic leaders' development strategy.

Phoenix citizens faced the same difficulties of supply and water pressure, but they also faced the additional problem of taste. Even when the Phoenix Water Company provided customers with adequate supplies and constant pressure, complaints still came in over its salty and bitter taste. The river had been appropriately named by the Spanish: Rio Salado. The solution for the taste problem in Phoenix was to find a source of water outside the Salt River Valley.

Fortunately for Phoenix leaders, the Verde River provided an abundant source of good-tasting water only forty miles away. After much debate, litigation, and wrangling, Phoenix completed the Verde River pipeline in 1922. For a cost of $1.5 million, Phoenix received 15 million gallons a day of sweet-tasting river water. The taste problem solved, at least temporarily, the city returned to the more endemic problems of supply and pressure. Within nine years of its completion, the Verde pipeline had to be expanded to double its size and delivery capacity; in addition, well fields along the Verde and storage reservoirs in the city had to be constructed—a piecemeal process of expansion that generally occurred in response to immediate emergency situations.[37]

Since Phoenix as a community had started from scratch, the development of its productive capacity and business infrastructure appears at once remarkable and improbable. During the era of agrarian rivalry, populations in both cities expanded and the geographic size of the towns grew as well. Scholars assert that a critical development occurred at this time regarding the specific type and quality of immigration into Phoenix and Tucson. Specifically, Phoenix seemed to attract a higher caliber of immigrant, including several notable representatives of northeastern elite society. In part this assertion is correct, particularly regarding the acquisition of the Salt River Project, which required a unique combination of political influence and financial affluence.

An example of this initiative and immigrant contribution is the founding of the Valley Bank in 1884. The primary figure behind the creation of the bank was William Christy. Christy had migrated to the Salt River valley in the early 1880s after a successful political and business career in Iowa, which included serving as the state treasurer. He arrived in Phoenix as man of means, acquiring large tracts of land in the western valley serviced by the new canals. He turned the land to crops and experimented with new varieties of plants, but agronomy was more an avocation for Christy. His primary activity was directing the Valley Bank, where he excelled. Christy formed the bank in alliance with other prominent landowners in the valley, including William J. Murphy, the developer of the Arizona Canal, and Moses Sherman, schoolteacher, land speculator, and financier.[38]

Christy and other prominent Phoenix business leaders were first drawn to Arizona by the climate and its perceived healthful nature. Christy had first tried Prescott before moving to Phoenix. The warmer climate and agrarian possibilities were more beneficial to Christy's health and his pocketbook, respectively. Year-round growing seasons made the valley a potential agrarian paradise, and the mild winters and generally dry air attracted those who suffered from pulmonary illness. Many of the newcomers were fleeing humid and cold eastern or midwestern locations, in the process bringing ambition and investment capital to Phoenix. The urban development of Phoenix followed this trend primarily in the northeast valley. By 1890 a small community of settlers had established a town site at Orangedale, so named because of the "orange belt of citrus trees" nearby. The setting was striking: craggy mountains nearby speckled with tall saguaros and in the foreground at the foot of Camelback Mountain, a green belt of orange trees serviced by the Arizona Canal. The founder of the community, and first settler, was Winfield Scott, an honorably discharged army chaplain. In 1894 residents agreed to change the town's name to Scottsdale in his honor. Initially agriculture dominated the settlement, but early in the twentieth century Scottsdale and Phoenix attracted the attention of health seekers.[39]

Included in this group of health-seeking immigrants was Whitelaw Reid. Reid spent two winters in Phoenix recuperating after his unsuccessful run at the vice presidency in 1892. Reid's fortune stemmed from his publication of the *New York Tribune*, and his connections within the Republican Party and New York society were extensive. Reid served as a sort of vanguard, opening the eyes of his elite friends to the attributes of the Phoenix Basin. The desert's clean clear air, brilliant sunshine, and pleasant winter temperatures were an easy sell, as long as visitors avoided the brutally hot summers. Another eastern immigrant was John C. Adams, a prominent attorney from New York, also connected to Gotham's elite society. Adams moved to Phoenix for health reasons and became locally notable by founding the Adams Hotel downtown. Occupying a prime location at the corner of Central Avenue and Adams Street, the hotel became the center of elite social life as well as insider political wheeling and dealing. The hotel was four stories high, containing 150 rooms. The accommodations were handsomely furnished, and each floor had an exterior, shaded veranda. Most notable was the roof garden, used by guests and valley residents for parties and dancing. The hotel burned down in 1910, but Adams quickly reconstructed it with imposing brick. As historian Tom Sheridan explains, "The center of political and economic power remained the Adams Hotel, where farmers, cattlemen, and mining executives continued to buy the votes of legislators and run the state."[40]

In the decade from 1910 to 1920, Phoenix gained more than ten thousand more residents than did Tucson. Phoenix also gained the Salt River Project, with the completion of the Roosevelt Dam in 1912. Among the new residents were several affluent elites who came to occupy prominent positions in the community primarily because of their role in securing the approval of the dam project. Benjamin Fowler was central to this effort. Fowler had arrived in Phoenix in late 1899 and immediately took the lead in lobbying the federal government on behalf of Phoenix-area landowners for the Salt River Project. At issue for the lobbyists was an 1898 USGS report that recommended a dam on the San Carlos River upstream from the Gila's confluence with Queen Creek. The resulting reservoir would irrigate one hundred thousand acres, mostly on the Gila River Indian Reservation. The report had proceeded in part from the assumption that federal reclamation would benefit public land, not privately controlled areas. To overcome this assumption and its restriction on federal projects, Fowler first traveled to Washington with fifteen hundred dollars raised by the Salt River Valley Water Storage Committee. Fowler offered the money to the USGS with the stipulation that the "financial assistance" be directed toward a resumption of studies on the Salt River. The USGS gratefully accepted the donation.

Next Fowler organized a group of seven Phoenix landowners to travel to Washington in 1901 to lobby against an appropriation of $1 million for work on the San Carlos site. After successfully blocking that appropriation in Congress, the group began offering revisions to the upcoming Reclamation Act. The lobby successfully amended the legislation to allow federal reclamation to benefit private land, and in return agreed to the stipulation that projects benefiting private landowners be repaid by the beneficiaries. This amendment to the legislation helped groups such as the Phoenix water users, because they could claim to mortgage their land to pay for the projects, but Indians could not. At that time, the federal government did not allow Native Americans to put liens on their reservation land. The financial calculus thus boiled down to a Salt River project that would be financed and paid for by the beneficiaries or a Gila River project that would require general tax revenues from the federal treasury for financing. As a result of the lobbying by Fowler and the other Phoenicians, President Theodore Roosevelt signed the amended Newlands Act in 1902, and the USGS announced that the first major project of federal reclamation would be built on the Salt River. It should also be noted that Dwight Heard participated in the lobbying. Heard was a personal friend of Roosevelt.

Fowler's role was in making sure that all the weight of personal influence and financial persuasion came to bear at the right time in the right place.[41]

Tucson never benefited from a federal reclamation project such as the Salt River Project, although the city received private investment from Chicago, the Northeast, and Great Britain. The Tucson Farms Crosscut, the Post project, and other manifestations of corporate agriculture increased the community's prosperity. Likewise, Tucson gained from immigration that included wealthy and prominent elites, some of whom arrived in Tucson as health seekers gravitating toward the desert scenery. In Tucson, however, the environmental limitations on the expansion of agriculture soon became obvious. It was the Salt River valley's greater potential for prosperity based on agriculture that lured the farmers, speculators, and USGS surveyors. The potential also impressed the midwestern and eastern elites who visited for their health or other recreational pursuits. The new elites did not create the prosperity in Phoenix so much as they exploited an opportunity provided by nature and the federal government to add to their personal wealth and thereby to the community's economic advancement.

Phoenix surpassed Tucson's population for the first time in the 1920 census. Served by two railroads, a growing commercial infrastructure, and an expanding economic base, Phoenix was well positioned to increase its population advantage during the following decades.

Where Winter Never Comes, and
the Mescalian Could Imbibe His Fill

THE PHYSICAL SETTING of the two cities had established the baseline parameters for the extent of agriculture in the two valleys. But as always in the human relationship with nature, culture and the perception of nature's circumstances played a role in the final outcomes. In the case of Tucson and Phoenix, ethnic differences in part created the variations in the development ethos of the two cities. Phoenix became expressly Anglo, anti-Mexican, and antiblack, while Tucson always maintained a large Hispanic population and Mexican component to the community. This is not to say that Tucson was free of racism or ethnocentrism but rather that Phoenix boosters were more aggressive in pushing their Anglo view of nature.

The difference in the two communities was clearly recognizable at the turn of the century. In part the heightened awareness of such cultural delineations was due to the prevalence of Gilded Age biases based on nativistic Social Darwinism and Anglo-Saxon ethnocentrism. References to Anglo-Saxon superiority appeared in booster publications, with the Anglo culture and society equated with modernism. An example is William E. Smythe's *The Conquest of Arid America*, published in 1900. Smythe describes Phoenix as prospering through irrigated agriculture, which stems in his view from the industry of whites: "Tucson and Yuma, though thriving and populous, are Mexican in architecture and habits. . . . But Phoenix is distinctly modern, and almost wholly the offspring of irrigation."[1] The class-driven and ethnocentric view that equated American with Anglo-Saxon further appeared in Smythe's characterization of Arizona's overall population: "The people of Arizona have been drawn from many different sources, and from more than one race, but the pushing American element is distinctly dominant. While there are many of the lower class of Mexicans, they are much less numerous here than in New Mexico, and much less widely diffused over the Territory. The Indians, who are seen everywhere, even in the best settled districts, are now mostly inoffensive, and even industrious in many cases. Like the Mexican peons, they are useful laborers in the simpler agricultural tasks."[2]

In case there is any doubt regarding Smythe's cultural assumptions, he acknowledges in the preface of the book works that influenced his thinking. Most of the titles fall into the category of ethnocentric polemics, including M. Edmund Demolin's *Anglo-Saxon Superiority*.

The white character of Phoenix has long been noted by scholars of the Southwest. As Bradford Luckingham summarizes, "Unlike many other Southwestern towns, Phoenix did not exist through Spanish and Mexican periods. It was founded largely by Anglos, for Anglos, and they were determined to transplant familiar cultural patterns to their new home."[3] An 1891 chamber of commerce publication explicitly stated the commonly held view—among whites—that Anglo culture was superior to the indigenous societies: "Phoenix is a modern town, 'with all the modern improvements.' Peopled by a progressive, American class, on every side are to be noted evidences of thrift and enterprise. Here are none of the sleepy, semi-Mexican features of the more ancient towns of the Southwest, but, in the midst of a valley of wonderful fertility, has risen a city of stately structures, beautiful homes, progressive and vigorous."[4]

To be American was to be modern, progressive, enterprising, and, of course, white. It also meant to be aggressive in economic development, following the hidebound capitalist precept that a community's well-being was based on an individual's increasing prosperity. Another booster publication appeared in 1892, echoing the idea that Phoenix was American and equating that na-

5.1   Population growth in Phoenix and Tucson, 1890–1920

	1890	1900	1910	1920
Tucson	5,150	7,531	13,193	20,292
Phoenix	3,152	5,544	11,134	29,053

Derived from census reports: U.S. Bureau of the Census, *Census of the United States*, Eleventh, 1890, 1:388, 391; Twelfth, 1900, 1:64; Thirteenth, 1910, 2:86; Fourteenth, 1920, 1:82, 180

tionalistic label with an aggressive and enterprising nature: "Phoenix, the capital of Arizona, is the largest town in the Territory, and the most important commercially and in every way. It is thoroughly American and its citizens are live and go-ahead people full of push and enterprise. The streets are broad and regularly laid out, business blocks of brick, while most of the recently constructed dwellings are of the same material."[5]

The gung ho bravado in the statement is clear and is erroneous in one particular regard. Tucson was still the larger town in 1892. Phoenix's population would not surpass Tucson's until the 1920 census. In another way, however, the statement correctly identified one of the cultural markers of the American community in Phoenix. Buildings of brick became the hallmark of Phoenix architecture.[6]

By 1920, the Anglo character of Phoenix was clearly established and explicitly acknowledged. No more blatantly racist statement can be found than the introduction to the 1920 City Directory compiled by the Phoenix Chamber of Commerce: "Phoenix a modern town of forty thousand people and the best kind of people, too. A very small percentage of Mexicans, negroes or foreigners."[7] In addition to its racism, the statement is notable for its reference to forty thousand residents. The population of Phoenix was less than thirty thousand at the time, but already Phoenix boosters were including in their calculations the populations of neighboring towns.

As the overall population of the Salt River valley increased, landowners and the commercial elite shunted the declining percentage of Hispanic residents in Phoenix increasingly—almost exclusively by 1920—into agricultural labor. In part, Phoenix surpassed Tucson in population in 1920 because of the migration of Mexican immigrants into central Arizona seeking farm work after the completion of the Roosevelt Dam in 1911. As historian James Officer notes, "With little to offer the immigrants in terms of employment, Tucson regis-

5.2 Hispanic population in Phoenix and Tucson, 1880–1920		
	(%)	
	1880	*1900*	*1920*
Tucson	63.8	54.7	36.8
Phoenix	45.2	14.5	7.9

Thomas E. Sheridan, *Los Tucsonenses: The Mexican Community in Tucson, 1854–1941* (Tucson: University of Arizona Press, 1992), 3.

tered more modest gains than did agricultural and mining communities such as Phoenix and Jerome."[8]

Tucson had more of the people considered troublesome by Phoenix boosters (except as agricultural workers). The percentage of Hispanics in Tucson always surpassed that in Phoenix and included a very visible, although small, Mexican middle class, which mitigated somewhat against the more blatant racism that existed in Phoenix.

This is not to say that Tucson was free of ethnocentrism or that the Anglo elites in Tucson differed in any marked way from their Phoenix contemporaries. Rather, the Hispanic population in Tucson was simply too large and entrenched to be ignored or willed away. In Tucson, class stratification existed, but it was a class system that equated prominence with affluence, and it was a system open to Hispanics. An observer in 1881—compiling information for the city's first directory—noted the "stratification of good society" in Tucson: "It is well known that ladies and gentlemen reside here, who were the recognized ornaments and leaders in the best society of their former places of residence; and with this class, as a natural consequence, all the usages of culture and refinement are in common practice."[9]

To make clear the differences in status between the cultured elites and the troublesome lower classes, the compiler offered a description of Barrio Libre:

This description was given by the Mexican residents to that quarter of the city . . . southward of the business portion of the city, occupied by the Americans. It means Free Zone, and in earlier times was allowed to remain without legal restraints or the presence of a policeman. Here, the Mescalian could imbibe his fill, and either male or female could, in peaceful intoxication, sleep on the sidewalk or in the middle of the streets, with all their ancient rights respected. Fandangoes, monte, chicken fights, broils, and all amusements of the lower class of

Mexicans, were, in this quarter, indulged in without restraint; and to this day much of the old-time regime prevails, although the encroachments of the American element indicate the ultimate doom of the customs in the Barrio Libre. It must be understood that these remarks apply only to the lower class of Mexicans, and not to the cultured Mexican residents of the city, who, for intelligence and enterprise, are foremost among our people.[10]

The ambivalence toward Hispanic culture can be seen in the account of barrio life. Clear stereotypes dominate the observations, but missing is the blanket castigation of all things Mexican. Revelers rest in "peaceful intoxication" wherever they choose, without apparent risk of injury or theft. From the generally disapproving account, one can nonetheless imagine all sorts of joyful entertainments, dancing fandangoes, as well as coarser amusements, taking place in the unrestrained Barrio Libre. The most grievous charges against the barrio are of indolence and profligate behavior—clear stereotypes. It seems the observer thought no work took place in the barrio. But once again, ambivalence intrudes. Enterprise may not have been a virtue of the barrio, but the "cultured Mexican residents" enjoyed that characteristic. In Phoenix, enterprise was purely an Anglo virtue, at least according to the boosters' pronouncements.

Since Tucson began as a completely Hispanic town, ethnic segregation in residential patterns developed slowly. By the turn of the century Anglo residents were congregated near the center of the town and in the Armory Park neighborhood just to the east. Hispanic residents occupied traditional barrio areas generally to the north, west, and south of Armory Park. The population of Tucson increased by more than twelve thousand residents from 1900 to 1920. Many of the new immigrants were Mexicans, including those displaced by the Mexican Revolution in the early 1900s, but most of the new arrivals were Anglos. Anglo arrivals spurred the development of new neighborhoods to the east and north. Sprawl commenced first toward the University of Arizona campus and then over the succeeding decades continued across the basin floor toward the Catalina and Rincon mountains. Mexican immigrants in the early twentieth century tended to settle in established neighborhoods, adding to the vibrance of Hispanic culture in the barrios as the pattern of ethnic segregation solidified.[11]

Segregated residential patterns in Phoenix also stemmed from racist and ethnocentric prejudices, but the direction and manner of the segregation was shaped by the presence of the tempestuous river. The original Anglo settlers established the town site some distance from the river, and the expansion of the city had proceeded generally toward the north and even farther from the river. The irrigated fields were closest to the river, and most of the residents nearby were the agricultural workers who maintained the canals and fields. The 1891 flood affected Phoenix in a manner dictated by the segregated residential pattern. Dikes protected the homes of Anglos while the adobe homes of the Mexican workers melted away in the rush of water. A local newspaper fairly exulted in the destruction of the houses, referring to the adobes as "dreadful mud houses." The goal to replace indigenous adobe with fired brick lay behind this statement. The elites in Phoenix routinely disparaged the Hispanic element of Phoenix at the turn of the century. Mexicans and other minorities remained in those neighborhoods most likely to be flooded, while Anglos on higher ground came to view floods as inconveniences. To Anglos, floods became significant to the degree they interrupted agricultural pursuits or commerce downtown—significant concerns in their own right—but not because their homes and property were subject to damage or destruction.[12]

The development of the tourist industry gives further evidence of the cultural division between the two communities. Tourism developed along several tracks: sanitariums for the health seekers, especially those suffering from tuberculosis; resorts for the affluent winter visitors; and recreational venues, including Wild West shows, dude ranches, and other attractions for the curious.

From the beginning of Anglo settlement, Anglo developers, businessmen, and entrepreneurs had expressed the desire to attract new settlers. A basic measure of the territory's prosperity and future was its population, which had to increase before any thought could be given to statehood. Tourists, on the other hand, were and remain transitory. Some may decide to settle after experiencing the locale, but most are likely to pass through and move on, either back from whence they came or on to another temporary haunt. Health seekers were the first of these temporary residents to become significant in their presence and numbers. They fell into the category of temporary residents because of their chronic illnesses. Their stay was sometimes permanent, but short lived; if they found a cure in the desert air, the health seekers were free to escape the harsh desert conditions and return to family and home or move in search of a new life.

A wide range of respiratory illnesses, from asthma to tuberculosis, were basically untreatable in the late nineteenth century. With little else to offer, doctors prescribed dry air for the "lungers," and many traveled to the West seeking cures for their chronic maladies. Some of the sojourners in Arizona were wealthy and famous—Whitelaw Reid and Harold Bell Wright, for example—others became infamous—the gun-fighting dentist John J. "Doc" Holliday, for example—but most were anonymous and poor. Both Phoenix and Tucson experienced a modest flood of health seekers after railroad connections became secure. In Tucson's case the boom was delayed somewhat by the continuing Apache warfare. Phoenix not only gained the advantage of two railroad connections but also obtained something of a head start in the sanitarium business because of its earlier freedom from Indian warfare. The Tucson newspaper referred to the health seekers and Tucson's role "as the sanitarium of the Southwest" in 1888, but the pronouncement expressed more hope for the future than current reality. Tucson's role was potential, not yet fully realized.[13]

Accommodations for the new residents varied widely. Affluent tuberculars and consumptives found luxurious accommodations in the two cities. Phoenix had the Desert Inn Sanitarium on "100 acres of beautiful grounds" six miles east of town. The facility was open from October to June and advertised itself as "especially suited to benefit incipient bronchial and pulmonary cases, and convalescents for la grippe, pneumonia, and other extremely debilitating diseases." The inn cared for guests with a medical staff and provided recreational activities that included golf and tennis, as well as croquet and horseback riding. Room and board cost twenty dollars per week.[14]

In the vicinity of Tucson, wealthy convalescents patronized two resorts near Oracle. The hotels were within a quarter mile of each other and advertised themselves as year-round establishments. Oracle, on the northern shoulder of the Catalina Mountains at an elevation of forty-five hundred feet, was two thousand feet higher and much cooler than Tucson. The first of the establishments to cater to convalescents was Arcadia. E. S. Dodge had established a cattle ranch there in 1881, but soon found that "courteous hospitality" paid better than stock raising. He and his wife expanded their ranch house and constructed several cottages nearby so that, as an observer noted in 1897, "his premises are a veritable little village, where now can be found a coterie of wealthy, cultured Easterners, and, judging from their robust appearance, it is difficult to imagine they were ever in delicate health." The nearby Mountain View Hotel offered twelve spacious rooms in a large Victorian building, each room with "outside exposures," and hot and cold running water. The hotel, as its name implied, offered guests majestic views of the nearby Catalina Mountains from its 160-acre perch on the northern foothills.[15]

One of the elite visitors to the area near Tucson was the novelist and playwright Harold Bell Wright. The writer established a camp in the southern foothills of the Catalina Mountains in late 1915 and later recounted his experiences in the essay "Why I Did Not Die." Wright's doctors in California had recommended "a dry, mild climate—and live out of doors," when they found that Wright had come down with tuberculosis. In response to the doctors' recommendation, Wright had said, "That spells Tucson, Arizona." For almost twenty-five years, Wright promoted Tucson as a health-giving location; he also contributed to the city's artistic and charitable efforts.[16]

Less affluent health seekers arrived to less than hospitable circumstances. Many lived in tents or other ramshackle abodes on vacant lots scattered throughout the towns, congregating in coughing slums. One in Tucson came to be known as Tentville. The colony of health seekers grew up among inexpensive rentals and vacant land north of the University of Arizona campus. The community in the early 1900s sprawled about a mile and a half north of the university and about a mile from east to west between Campbell Avenue and North First Avenue. The tents and shacks lined dusty, unpaved streets, and each residence was served by an outhouse; there were no sewers or street lights. Dick Hall was nine years old when he moved to Tentville with his ill mother and older brother in the early 1900s. Hall later remembered the nights as "heartbreaking. . . . As one walked along the dark streets, he heard coughing from every tent. It was truly a place of lost souls and lingering death. Sometimes life was too much to bear and a victim would end it. He was soon replaced, however, by others who hoped for a cure in the dry air and bright sunshine of Arizona. It was a desperate and sometimes heroic gamble which many lost and few won."[17]

Isolation, both geographical and personal, added to the dreariness of the community. Most residents of the tent city were about a mile north of the streetcar stop on University Avenue at the entrance to the campus. If the ill residents could get to the streetcar, they could ride it to medical facilities in the city about three miles away, but the sick most often were too weak to make the walk. As Hall recalled, "A mile was a long way when one walked with only one lung." The residents were also shunned by other, healthy Tucsonans. Common wisdom of the day warned that consumptives were highly contagious. Stricken mothers even refrained from hugging and kissing their children out of fear of infecting them. Tentville was a dreary place indeed.[18]

Other visitors to the two cities were the tourists who visited resort hotels or traveled to Phoenix or Tucson to enjoy the mild winters or engage in western-themed adventures. In the years just prior to World War I, perhaps three thousand visitors traveled to the Salt River Valley during the winter months that served as the peak season for tourism.[19] The growing phenomenon of these affluent escapees from colder climes created a clear business opportunity. First to recognize this in Phoenix in the early 1900s was W. J. Murphy, developer of the Arizona Canal. W. J. and his son Ralph opened the Ingleside Inn on eight hundred acres nine miles to the northeast of the city. The hotel was operating in full swing by 1910. The Ingleside Inn separated itself from the health-seeker establishments by announcing in its advertisements that it was "not a sanatorium . . . and could not receive as guests any persons suffering from communicable diseases." The inn offered guests golf and tennis, horseback riding, target shooting, and automobile excursions.[20]

Often the resort hotels combined the tourism business with land speculation and development: the resort owners sought to lure visitors into buying land and building either permanent or winter homes. The owners of the Ingleside Inn platted a town site near their resort in the hope that a new community would grow up nearby. The Murphys were unsuccessful, but to the south, Alexander Chandler achieved a bit more success. In the years after the federal government bought his Consolidated Canal, the former veterinarian turned his Chandler Ranch into an experiment in land subdivision and urban development. Chandler advertised his planned community nationally and especially in California, where he hoped to lure residents with the prospects of a "better future than California." Railroad excursions brought prospective buyers to the town of Chandler—aspiring to be the Pasadena of Arizona—and to the surrounding countryside. The town was laid out with curved streets and public spaces, conforming to the contemporary vogue of the City Beautiful movement. Chandler also commissioned the construction of the San Marcos Hotel in his community. The hotel, designed by the Los Angeles–based architect Arthur Burnett Benton, opened in the late autumn of 1913, just in time to attract the winter visitors. The hotel soon became a notable winter resort.[21]

Resorts such as the Ingleside Inn and the San Marcos Hotel catered to the wealthiest winter visitors, and the growing prevalence of tourism created a demand for accommodations that could not be met by the two resorts alone. Another resort hotel opened in Scottsdale in 1924. The Jokake Inn prospered initially because of its own charm and the fortunate circumstance that the Ingleside and San Marcus inns had more prospective guests than they could handle. Even with the addition of the Jokake Inn, as many as eight thousand winter visitors were unable to find their desired accommodations during the 1927 tourist season.[22]

The flood of tourists caused other downtown hotels to open during the golden age of tourism in the 1920s. The San Carlos and Westward Ho hotels opened in downtown Phoenix in 1928. The Westward Ho's sixteen stories made it the tallest building in town. Including two restaurants and 350 rooms, the Hotel Westward Ho opened with a flourish on December 15: "The Hotel Westward Ho incorporates all the elegance, luxuriousness and beauty that thought, effort and heavy financial outlay can command. It brings to Phoenix and the state of Arizona rare distinction. The rooms are most elegantly furnished with every modern convenience. Every room is cooled by the best known system of conditioning air."[23]

. In 1929 the Arizona Biltmore opened north of Phoenix, continuing the combined resort–land development enterprise. The hotel occupied two hundred acres, which included both the hotel and the golf course, eight miles north of the city at the base of Squaw Peak "just across the Arizona Canal." The hotel was part of the Bowman-Biltmore chain and was designed by Albert McArthur, a student of Frank Lloyd Wright. McArthur was also the brother of Phoenix businessmen Charles and Warren McArthur. The brothers had come to Phoenix from Chicago and, along with other Phoenix investors, raised the $2.5 million cost of the project. Landscaping was indigenous in the pattern of the earlier Scottsdale resorts, and the natural setting caught the attention of guests and reporters: "It is so completely a part of its surroundings. It belongs to the desert, it belongs in the desert at the foot of Squaw Peak and ragged old Camelback."[24]

In addition to the two hundred acres for the hotel and golf course, another four hundred acres was set aside for subdivision and residential lots. Most notable among the wealthy visitors and potential investors was William Wrigley, Jr. The owner of the Chicago Cubs and mogul of the chewing gum industry had begun visiting Phoenix during the winter. In July 1929 Wrigley both invested in the hotel company and bought a lot nearby. His $1.7 million investment ensured that the hotel would survive the oncoming crash and Depression, and the construction of his mansion next to the hotel set a precedent soon followed by such members of the elite as Louis Swift, Cornelius Vanderbilt, Jr., and George Bartlett.[25]

Tucson's hotel accommodations first moved out of the frontier mode just before the turn of the twentieth century. In pioneer days, hotels were little more than saloons with a few cots available in back rooms. More substantial buildings were erected in the 1870s, such as the Cosmopolitan Hotel in Tucson. The Cosmopolitan advertised itself as the finest hotel in the territory, but guests sometimes offered less than glowing testimonials. One referred to the Cosmopolitan as a so-called hotel. In 1896 accommodations for travelers and tourists enjoyed a marked improvement; that was the year the Cosmopolitan went through renovations, including the addition of electric lights, and was renamed the New Orndorff Hotel. The old Palace Hotel also was remodeled about then and renamed the Occidental. With the opening of the Santa Rita Hotel in 1909, Tucson gained a truly "first-rate downtown hotel" with 180 rooms. Another larger downtown hotel, the Pioneer, opened in 1929 with 250 rooms.[26] In addition to the downtown hotels, resort facilities also started to develop in the 1920s. North of the city in the Catalina foothills, William and Maria Watson owned a 172-acre ranch. The centerpiece of the ranch was a hacienda-style house that boasted spectacular views of the valley and city. The home, constructed in 1912, was the creation of architect Merritt Starkweather. In the 1920s, the Watsons added fifteen cottages and invited guests to visit the ranch and home. Later the resort became known as the Westward Look.[27]

The most prominent resort in Tucson, at least in terms of newspaper headlines, financial consternation, and political wrangling, was the El Conquistador. Designed and constructed in the Spanish mission style and landscaped with native vegetation several miles east of the city, the El Conquistador impressed arrivals with a drive lined with stately saguaros and a grand entrance beneath a copper-domed bell tower more than sixty feet high. It opened in 1928 with a ceremony that included Yaqui dancers and a banquet and ball attended by 250 guests "that lasted well into the morning." The hotel offered seventy rooms, each with a private bath, some with sun porches, and all on the American plan (including all meals), similar to the practice at the Biltmore in Phoenix. The El Conquistador also provided guests with a range of typical vacation-oriented activities: tennis, horseback riding, and golf at the nearby Tucson Country Club eighteen-hole course.[28]

The El Conquistador—locally known as the El Con—never prospered as its original planners and investors hoped. In part the hotel suffered from its own design. One critic stated that the Spanish-style architecture, including its imposing bell tower, made the resort more closely resemble, in outside appearance, a convent. The hotel also suffered from continuing indebtedness and pinched operating budgets.[29]

More prosperous and enduring, the Arizona Inn remains in operation on its original site to this day. Established by Isabella Greenway in 1930, the Arizona Inn provided quiet, gracious, and luxurious accommodations. The manicured grounds ensured privacy in homelike settings, and many of Greenway's guests used the inn as their winter home away from home, staying the entire season. In 1937, Greenway added features to the hotel that included a swimming pool (ubiquitous in Arizona resorts), as well as clay-surfaced tennis courts—the only ones in Arizona for decades.[30] Greenway occupied a position of elite status. Theodore Roosevelt had attended her first wedding to a former lieutenant in T. R.'s Rough Riders. After the death of her first husband, Isabella had married John C. Greenway, another former officer in the Rough Riders and a decorated veteran of World War I. Isabella had also developed a friendship with Eleanor Roosevelt and had served as a bridesmaid in Eleanor's 1905 wedding to Franklin Delano Roosevelt. Isabella Greenway's connection to eastern elites contributed to her hotel's success, just as her connections to the Democratic Party provided her with unique political opportunities. Greenway served as Arizona's first woman congressional representative, elected twice and serving from 1933 to 1936. She left Congress by her own choice, declining to run for a second full term in 1936. The Arizona Inn remained a popular resort for the wealthy and privileged and carefully controlled its image and reputation. It remained virtually unchanged until the 1970s, when air conditioning, additional facilities for banquets and conferences, and year-round operations began.[31]

Accommodations for tourists increased in number through the 1920s. Visitors flocked to the Southwest in part because of the mild winter temperatures that prevail while much of the rest of the country is frozen and blanketed with snow. Golf and tennis could be played, as one advertisement boasted, "in shirt sleeves on Christmas Day."[32] But not all visitors to the two cities were interested in outdoor sports. Other attractions appealed to many tourists, and the boosters in both cities worked tirelessly to keep the allure of their cities clearly in the public eye.

Phoenix took the lead in entertaining tourists with its winter carnival, which started in 1896. Cowboys and Indians were the featured attraction, and by 1899 the venue had an established form. For the first three years the car-nival took place in February, but in 1899 organizers moved it to December—a more attractive schedule for tourists—and renamed the event the Cowboy and Indian Carnival. The week-long festivities included Indian artisans in a program meant to rival Santa Fe's famous crafts at the governor's plaza. As one booster proclaimed, "Besides their games and contests, the Navajo blanket-makers, the Apache basket-weavers and the Pima pottery-makers will be at work every day, on platforms, at the Court House and City Hall plazas."[33] About five hundred Indians participated in the events, most of them traveling the relatively short distance to Phoenix from their respective reservations. Organizers recruited Native American participation by feeding the throng at their campsite near Phoenix Park and granting the participants and their fam-ilies free admission.[34]

The centerpiece of the carnival was the recreation of Old West scenarios. In 1896, the first carnival introduced the basic performance, sans gunfire: "In the morning music was everywhere through the city, as the different bands turned out to add melody to the occasion, and there was a sharp interlude of clattering hoofs as a few hundred cowboys and Indians charged down the Main street and thence with a wild whoop and yell around the city till the casual stranger was reminded of the tales of Red Dog camp when the 'boys' came in from the range. But no pistol shots were fired and the incursion did not possess the element of inebriety usual to such frontier visitations."[35]

Within three years the Old West performances took on more theatrical qualities. Throughout the week, mounted cowboys chased war-painted Indians up and down the city streets, and the participants staged mock battles and massacres with "blood-curdling yells and whoops."[36] One such performance in 1899 took place in the midst of the opening-day parade: "After the cowboy cavalcade passed the reviewing stand there was a break in the parade column, but the clatter of horses' hoofs and weird yells far down the street told that the Indians were coming. In a moment the overland stage came in sight, the horses at full speed, the passengers and guards firing their rifles and revolvers, and close in pursuit 300 Indians, giving forth their hair-raising yells."[37]

In the early 1900s the shows became standardized Wild West adventures. Railroad companies advertised the carnival as part of their tourist appeals. Likewise, organizers continued the process of recruiting Indian participants, who grew in number to more than one thousand. Cowboys chased Indians while other Indians chased stagecoaches, all in the most colorful style possible. One account from 1900 clearly described the evolving nature of performances:

> After the cowboys' parade yesterday morning, the vaqueros presented an act not mentioned in the official program, and which, in its realism, was a truly wild and wooly scene. Firing volley after volley from their revolvers and with a chorus of yells, the cow punchers serenaded the saloons and gambling houses. From one place to another the rollicking horsemen hurried, firing a fusillade in front and one in the rear of every resort. Occasionally a lariat would be brought into play and an unsuspecting bystander dragged from the sidewalk. The fun was all good-natured and did no harm except alarm a few tenerfoot [sic] who thought their time had come and that the town was taken by the fierce-looking band. For an hour the cow punchers continued their fun, much to the delight of the old-timers, to whom it recalled the times when the "shooting up" of an Arizona town was a frequent occurrence, and when the appearance of a band of merry-making cowboys was a signal to duck for cover.[38]

The Cowboy and Indian Carnival lasted until 1905, when Phoenix leaders replaced the chaotic spectacle with the territorial fair. The focus of the fair shifted from creating an exotic lure for tourists to the more staid goal of displaying the agricultural and technological accomplishments of the territory. The carnival became a fair in part because the territorial legislature subsidized the event, providing for the purchase of a permanent site and the construction of exhibit halls. But fair promoters acknowledged the tourist appeal of the former carnivals and expressed a desire to keep the old bandwagon rolling. Instead of a week-long series of war whoops through city streets, however, the Indian presence was reduced to Indian Day. Crafts, rodeo events, and athletic contests between tribes entertained the crowds, but probably without the visceral excitement of the old chase and battle scenes. Also, fewer Native Americans participated in the fairs. Indians received free admission, but the old practice of feeding the Indians at their campsite, which had become something of a tourist attraction in and of itself, came to an end.[39]

Tucson business leaders never organized anything quite like the early carnivals in Phoenix, but they got into the act of organizing a tourist attraction in 1924. The event that served as the linchpin for the tourist pitch was the Tucson rodeo scheduled for February the next year. Several booster organizations contributed to the effort, but the main impetus came from the Arizona Polo Association. Leighton Kramer, a wealthy newcomer to Tucson from Philadelphia, helped organize the Polo Association in December 1924, with the stated goal of turning Arizona in general and Tucson particularly into the "winter capital of Polo." Not surprisingly, Kramer became the president of the Polo Association. He had moved to Tucson in part for his health but also because of his fascination with horsemanship and cowboy culture. To accommodate those interests, he acquired 160 acres about four miles north of town and established his Rancho Santa Catalina, which became the site of Tucson's first tourist-advertised rodeo.[40]

Initially Kramer announced plans to add extensive stables to his ranch. The stables cost ten thousand dollars and were designed "to house a string of polo ponies and saddle horses, and possibly provide accommodations for the mounts of visiting polo teams." As the 1925 event neared, more construction took place. Kramer and the supporters of the rodeo raised the money to build grandstands that could hold as many as three thousand spectators. They also leveled an area for the rodeo events and ringed the arena with a "hog proof" fence.[41]

Kramer and other Polo Association members hoped the Tucson rodeo, called La Fiesta de los Vaqueros, would entertain residents and visitors alike. It would be good for business, but it was also meant to establish the community's identity as a tourist paradise for the national audience. The fiesta would be to Tucson what the Mardi Gras was to New Orleans, the beauty pageant to Atlantic City, and the flower show to Pasadena. Tucson's image, according to Kramer, would be firmly linked to its frontier traditions:

> We extend a cordial invitation to you to come to Tucson for our annual rodeo. Not so many years ago the first pony express came to a sudden halt on our Main street, carrying civilization southwestward. Not so many years ago the first railroad train whistled in. Gone is the past. The hitching post has been removed. A new civilization has put steel and concrete and built a mighty city where only yesterday horses grazed within the memory of living men.
>
> The pioneer spirit lives. Heroic memories never die. The Old Frontier will be revived—at Tucson, February 21, 22, and 23—as a community revival. . . . We are proud to offer this attraction to the people of America—both contestants and spectators—as a reminder of yesterday. Come to Tucson![42]

On February 21, 1925, the first Fiesta de los Vaqueros began with a colorful parade. Cowboys decked out with their fanciest saddles and costumes pa-
raded with Indians in their ancestors' headdresses. Two army bands—one from
Nogales and the other from Fort Huachuca—marched between the mounted
men and women. Included in the parade was the University of Arizona polo
team, resplendent in bright silk tunics and white helmets. Other participants
rolled through the city streets in gleaming automobiles, including the "'buck-
ing flivver' filled with rodeo clowns playing to children in the crowd."[43] After
the parade, the three-day rodeo commenced. Cowboys and cowgirls competed
in all the traditional events, from bull riding to barrel racing. Organizers staged
other events to appeal to the crowds, as Leighton Kramer later explained: "Bull-
dogging from the running board of a Packard car, operated at forty-five miles
an hour, was one of the unusual and spectacular feats attempted during the
Rodeo. Roy Quick, champion bulldogger of the west coast, made a flying leap to
the horns of a long-horn steer, while Mike Hastings, another bulldogger, hazed
the steer along-side the car for his companion to make the leap. The next day
they reversed positions, and Hastings, after a thrilling chase past the grand-
stand, caught the animal and threw it."[44]

Another cowboy attempted the stunt, but with less success. Jimmy Shannon, from Idaho, "overshot his mark and dove clear over the animal's head."
Shannon was rushed to a hospital, where, as the newspaper explained the next
day, "it was found that Shannon was painfully but not seriously hurt."[45]

The first Fiesta de los Vaqueros ended with a Cowboy Dance at the Santa
Rita Hotel. The Tenth Cavalry band played "snappy music," and by all accounts the revelry carried into the wee hours. Champions were crowned (and
paid their prize money), and the organizers of the first fiesta promised that next
year's rodeo would be even better. All agreed that the event was a smashing
success, although at least one later observer criticized the event's "crass hype."[46]

Besides the lovers of golf and tennis and the spectators of the Phoenix carnival and later the Tucson fiesta, a third category of tourist came to experience
the romance of the Wild West at dude ranches. Some were lured to Arizona
after reading Harold Bell Wright novels. Wright's early novel, Shepard of the
Hills had resulted in a tourist boom in the area of the novel's setting in the
Ozark Mountains. Subsequently Wright had moved west, first to Southern California and then to Arizona in 1915. The settings of Wright's novels changed
with his place of residency; he routinely used familiar locales to add verisimili-

tude to his stories. Readers could recognize the places despite the changed names and enjoyed seeking out the locales after reading the novel.[47]

In the 1920s, Wright published several novels set in Arizona, and film producers quickly turned the novels into motion pictures. In October 1923, Wright's novel turned to film *When a Man's a Man* premiered in Tucson. It was an Arizona story, set and filmed around Prescott. During the summer of 1924, two of Wright's stories began filming around Tucson: *A Son of His Father*, northeast of town near Agua Caliente, and *The Mine with the Iron Door*, northwest of the city near Canada del Oro. The movie crews also used locations around the city for film sets: downtown streets, the Tucson railway station, the University of Arizona campus, the Santa Rita Hotel, and the desert terrain outside of town.[48]

Wright's novels soared in popularity in the 1920s, far surpassing in sales and general appeal the Lost Generation novels so often associated with the culture of the 1920s. In part, Wright attracted a mass audience by developing traditional romantic themes, which included in his Arizona books an update of the western genre. The vivid descriptions of terrain and environment lent realism to his stories, a technique Wright shared with other western novelists, such as Zane Grey. Grey also published a western novel in 1923: *Wanderer of the Wasteland*. But whereas Grey set his story in 1878, Wright's 1923 novel was set in contemporary times:

> Of all the stirring tales of this picturesque region of the Santa Catalina, of all the romantic legends and traditions that have come down to us from its shadowy past, none is more filled with the essence of human life and love and hopes and dreams than is the tale of the Mine with the Iron Door.
>
> But this is not a story of those Old Spaniards and padres and Indians and pioneers. It is a story of to-day.[49]

For decades tourists arrived in Tucson and asked hotel staffs and chamber of commerce workers for directions to the mine with the iron door.

Tucson's business leaders understood that the city derived great benefit from its association with popular novels and movies, and Wright's novels were central to the development of Tucson's image as a western locale. Wright dedicated *The Mine with the Iron Door* "To My Friends in the Old Pueblo." It was the kind of publicity money could not buy. Wright received testimonials from businessmen, published in the newspapers. Other groups lauded Wright for his humanitarian contributions, as well as his support of the tourist initiative.

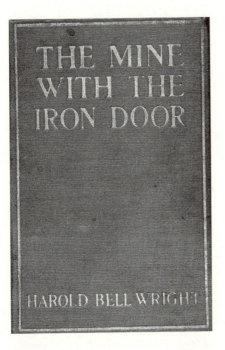

Fig. 5.1. The Mine With the Iron Door.
Harold Bell Wright published his western
romance *The Mine with the Iron Door*
in 1923. Wright set the novel and heroic
western adventures in contemporary
Tucson. Quickly turned into a motion
picture (silent), the novel and movie
fueled tourism to Tucson as a genuinely
western place: the Old Pueblo.

As one note in the newspaper stated, "No city was given more helpful con-
sideration by an author than was Tucson in the novel *The Mine with the Iron
Door*."[50]

Harold Bell Wright built his house eight miles outside of town at the end
of Speedway Boulevard (the intersection of Speedway and Wilmot) about
1920. He built a small shelter—"a tin shack"—on the spot, probably in 1919.
Satisfied with the location and its desert surroundings, he built a large house
and several outbuildings, creating a Spanish-style estate. Included in the buildings were a guest house, garage, and stables. Special features of the main house
"included a large multi-windowed study, a walk-in safe for manuscripts, and a
roof-top patio where Wright could go in the evening to watch the sun set."[51]

With the rising popularity of western novels and movies, more and more
in the 1920s, guests at dude ranches arrived with preconceived notions of what
the West and westerners looked like; they sought authenticity, or at least
verisimilitude, and in many cases expected to do the work of real cowboys. Of
course, ranch managers severely modified work routines to suit the desires
of the middle-class and affluent visitors. An hour or two in the saddle would
suffice, with some rudimentary instruction on roping and wrangling. Guests
might observe and even participate in the branding of cattle, but probably never
saw a young steer castrated. Visitors would often stay at working ranches for
weeks or even months at a time. Part of the illusion was that the work of the
ranch continued regardless of the dudes' presence; the best entrepreneurs in
the business had the ability to make guests feel welcome both for the money
paid and the help rendered—at least initially. When the Dude Ranchers Association formed in 1924, headquartered in Billings, Montana, it required that
all members be "working outfits."[52]

As it turned out, running dudes turned out to be a better business than
running cattle. Starting with the collapse of the open-range cattle business in the
late 1880s, some working outfits shifted to running dudes. As ranches began
to accommodate more and more visitors, the advertising campaigns for dude
ranches appearing in *Sunset* and *Vogue* began to focus more on the splendor of
the natural setting surrounding the ranches than on the representation of authentic cow punching. The transition was most noticeable in the Arizona and
California operations that could offer the appeal of climate and scenery. These
ranches came to resemble modern country clubs more than working cattle
ranches. Swimming pools and tennis courts appeared, as well as fine cuisine

and evening dancing. Gone were the rustic trappings of the chuck wagon and campfire sing-a-long—although some of the old ranch activities continued in one form or another. Horseback riding, for example, remained a mainstay at dude ranch resorts, but the nature of the experience shifted to accommodate more genteel expectations. Rather than providing their visitors with feisty cow ponies that required ear biting to saddle (old hands used methods such as ear biting or a knee to the stomach to get a reluctant horse to accept the saddle), the resort wranglers selected horses that were known for their calm demeanor. The dudes wanted horses to be friendly and receptive to their task; they also wanted a bit of thrill when the animals loped or galloped along the trail. The horses had to work hard, given the crowds cycling through the facilities, and ranches started enacting so-called Horse Sunday—a day or two during the week when the horses rested while guests played tennis or golf, swam, or went fishing.

The transition toward more luxurious dude ranching can be seen in the operation of the Westward Look Resort north of Tucson. The Watson family ranch had started modestly as a guest ranch in the 1920s. By 1940 the ranch had changed hands and become a prosperous dude ranch owned by Bob and Beverly Nason. The Nasons came up with the name Westward Look. The resort maintained its horse stable for the enjoyment of the guests. But rather than chasing cattle through the sagebrush, guests rode along scenic trails through the foothills of the Catalina Mountains. These sedate trail rides only turned into exciting galloping forays when the animals were turned toward home. Sensing water and feed, the cayuses would charge ahead as if in a race to see who could get back to the stable first. In the process guests hung on for dear life and recounted over dinner the thrill of the headlong rush.[53]

Another establishment that made the transition from working cattle ranch to resort was the Flying V Ranch in the foothills of the Catalina Mountains north of Tucson. The Shields family acquired the Flying V Ranch in the early 1900s, and for scenic grandeur the 840 acres abutting Ventana Canyon could not be surpassed. As a dude ranch the Flying V started modestly, with a few guest cabins. Improvements first came in the form of hot and cold running water in the cabins, and later came the addition of entertainment venues such as tennis courts and a polo field. It remained a working ranch into the 1960s, but urban encroachment made it increasingly difficult to continue running cattle along with the dudes.

Edward Dunn spent a month with his family on an Arizona dude ranch in the 1920s and later remembered, "Everyone dressed in western costumes from sombreros to high-heeled boots, and there was much talk of 'wrangling,' 'roping,' and 'rounding up,' despite the fact that there was not a sign of any cattle within fifty miles." One reason cattle became more distant in their presence was the problem of flies—ever present around the munching herds. One sure way to free the guests from the nuisance of flies and the obnoxious smells generated by milling cattle was to remove the herds. Cattle became ornamental on the working dude ranches.[54]

The Dude Ranchers Association formed in 1924 primarily to promote the ranches to tourists. Likewise in the 1920s, chambers of commerce in both Phoenix and Tucson spun off organizations to promote tourism. Tucson boosters had recognized the ability of the winter weather to produce great financial returns as early as 1891, but the effort to attract tourists had remained informal and ad hoc until 1922. That year a group of businessmen spun off from the chamber of commerce to create the Tucson Sunshine-Climate Club. The Tucson boosters advertised Tucson's attributes in national magazines. Ads focused on the warm winters and ever-present sunshine: "Children of the Sun live here, brown, sturdy, rosey-cheeked—growing into robust, vigorous youths." Tucson was a place "where winter never comes."[55]

Phoenix made its move in 1923, creating the Phoenix-Arizona Club to launch a national ad campaign.[56] The boosters sought to lure tourists by spreading the image of "Delightful Phoenix, the Garden Spot of the Southwest." Phoenix was not only growing as a center of business and commerce but also becoming the "winter playground of the Southwest." Ads ran in national-circulation magazines such as *American Golfer*, *Better Homes and Gardens*, *Time*, and the *Atlantic Monthly*. Once tourists were lured to Phoenix, the next task would be to convince them to stay longer and perhaps even set down roots. Improving the appearance of the city would contribute to the effort to attract new residents. To facilitate this process, the Valley Beautiful Committee sought to improve the city's physical image by launching a campaign in 1926: Let's Do Away With the Desert. The committee asked residents to plant grass and flowers, especially roses, in an effort to rival Pasadena for its "natural" beauty.[57]

By 1926 the Phoenix Club had grown to 550 members promoting Phoenix also as a place where "winter never comes." Over the three years since its formation, the club had spent $125,000 on its ad campaigns. The effort to attract greater numbers of tourists was helped by improvements in the transportation links to Phoenix. Within the state, Phoenix was centrally located, but national trunk lines bypassed the central city. The Santa Fe Railroad took a northern route through Flagstaff, and the Southern Pacific traveled the southern route through Tucson. Phoenix did not acquire service on the main line of the Southern Pacific Railroad until 1926. Prior to this visitors had to transfer to branchline trains from the main lines to the south and the north.[58]

Phoenix also made moves to initiate air service to the city, although the process took longer than might have been expected. Luckingham asserts that Phoenix acquired regular air service in 1927, but this seems very unlikely. An Army Air Corps inspection in November 1927 reported to the mayor and council that sixty thousand dollars in improvements would have to be made to the Phoenix airfield, established in 1924, to achieve a Triple-A Airport designation. Significantly, the airmen had flown from their base in San Antonio and had landed in Tucson, driving to Phoenix to make their inspection. A year later, in 1928, runway improvements had been made, but the terminal and hangar buildings were still under construction. Scenic Airways, a tourist operation based at the Grand Canyon, announced in December 1928 that it would be picking up passengers at the new Phoenix airport, but this hardly constitutes a scheduled travel option to and from Phoenix. In June 1929, Western Air Express announced a new route from Kansas City to Los Angeles that would include a stop in Arizona, but the location was Kingman, not Phoenix. In part the decision to fly the northern route had to do with a common practice in the early years of commercial aviation. Airline tickets generally came with travel vouchers for railroads: if the planes had to land because of weather or mechanical difficulties, passengers could be assured of getting to their destination via the railroad, in this case, the Santa Fe.[59]

By the 1920s the different strategies for attracting tourists had become established. In Tucson, promoters of tourism began marketing the local Hispanic culture: Tucson became The Old Pueblo, while Phoenix boosters created The Valley of the Sun. As examples of the business elites' different strategies, in Tucson the opening of the El Conquistador resort hotel in 1928 included dances by Yaqui performers. Both the name of the hotel, its structure—built in the mission style of the colonial Spanish—and the opening ceremonies linked the tourist effort to traditional cultural themes.[60] On the other hand, in Phoenix the Valley Beautiful Committee's 1926 drive Let's Do Away With

Fig. 5.2. Biltmore Hotel, 1929 (CP SPC 108: 4-51: courtesy Arizona Biltmore Hotel Photograph Collection, Arizona Collection, Arizona State University Libraries). The Arizona Biltmore offered guests elegant accommodations isolated from both the urban bustle of the city eight miles away and the bristly ruggedness of the desert setting nearby. At the resort guests could experience the desert in recreational venues such as horseback riding. Within the hotel grounds, however, the desert would be banished. The manicured lawn, hedge row, palm trees, and shrubs at the entrance to the resort appeared as a bulwark against the looming desert mountains in the background.

the Desert sought to push the natural environment further away. Resort hotels in Phoenix continued to market the climate and desert setting, but residents of the community increasingly encountered an urban environment devoid of natural landscapes. The opening of the Biltmore in 1929 also displayed ambivalence toward the natural setting. The hotel "belonged to the desert," but the opening gala included "a group of professional entertainers furnished by L. E. Behymer of Los Angeles." An orchestra provided dance music, but the sparkling sophistication of the opening was meant to be permanent—"Harry Owens Arizona Biltmore orchestra" would play at the hotel every night, or at least on weekends. Hiking and riding trails would be available for guests during the daytime, but the evenings would be turned over to diamonds, fine dining, and dancing. Even the newspaper's fawning report on the opening contained a casual swipe at the local terrain. Camelback Mountain was "old" and "craggy."[61]

Fig. 5.3. Woman diving into the Biltmore Pool (CP SPC 1-153: courtesy Arizona Biltmore Hotel Photograph Collection, Arizona Collection, Arizona State University Libraries). The elegant figure of the woman diving into the Biltmore pool conveys the grace and beauty of the hotel and its grounds, with the desert mountain peaks providing an incongruous coarse counterpoint to the woman's sleek form. The view of the rooms surrounding the pool shows the modern style of the architecture, which served as another counterpoint to the rugged natural surroundings.

In Tucson the desert vistas became part of the community's identity. Local boosters greeted the creation of the Saguaro National Monument in 1933 with enthusiasm and fanfare.[62] The monument became both a tourist attraction and an asset for the community, preserving open space in its natural form to be enjoyed by picnickers, bicyclists, and ambling bird watchers. The tourist promotions in Tucson were the creation of mostly, but not exclusively, Anglo elites, and these businessmen made at least an implicit decision to live within—and profit from—the natural ecosystem. The desert would not be engineered or willed away. It would be sold to tourists, to be sure, but that meant that at least some portion of the natural setting would have to be preserved. Tucson always seemed to settle for what was given and to be less grasping and aggressive, more willing to live with nature's dictates and the community's heritage.

Phoenix boosters were more ambitious in their drive to create a bustling metropolis. The completion of the Roosevelt Dam in 1911 stands as the hallmark of that drive and determination. At times, however, the drive toward metropolitan status turned comical in its frenetic insecurity. Phoenix and the Salt River Valley did not have a history of their own and so a motto was required. In 1921 the chamber of commerce and the *Arizona Republican* ran a contest for a slogan for the Salt River Valley. The winner was announced on May 22 after receipt of eleven hundred entries (the winner would receive a cash award of twenty-five dollars). C. R. Green won for the suggested slogan Rich, Resolute, Ready, Phoenix, Salt River Valley. Other entries that gained notice, but did not win were

Where sunshine turns your efforts into gold.

Harvest prime, health sublime, where Old Sol works overtime.

Health in our sunshine, wealth in our soil.[63]

The Rich and Resolute slogan did not stick. Through the 1920s, boosters in Phoenix tended to use the Gold Spot motto most frequently. Not until the 1930s did an ad agency come up with an accepted moniker: The Valley of the Sun.[64]

Community identities were set by the close of the 1920s, even as Phoenix searched for an acceptable slogan for itself. The rivalry remained. Resolution of the competition came in the next decade, the 1930s.

Depression Proof

By THE CLOSE of the 1920s, the status of the urban rivalry between Tucson and Phoenix was uncertain. Phoenix leaders claimed clear superiority, and several scholars have taken the boosters' assertions for fact: "As Phoenix goes, so goes Arizona."[1] Closer examination, however, shows that the decade closed with Tucson still in a viable position of competition. Phoenix possessed the larger population and enjoyed an increasing economic advantage over its neighbor to the south, but Tucson businessmen and government leaders felt optimistic about their city's prospects. Rather than the twenties, it was the decade of the thirties that irrevocably widened the economic distance between the two cities. In both locations, Depression conditions curtailed growth and optimism, but Tucson felt the effects of the economic collapse more greatly than did Phoenix. Population statistics show marked differences between the two cities in the declining growth rates of the 1930s (see table 6.1).

As the comparative rates of growth indicate, both cities grew at about the same pace through the 1920s, but their rates of growth varied greatly during

6.1   Population growth in Phoenix and Tucson, 1920–1940

	Population			Rate of growth (%)	
	1920	*1930*	*1940*	*1920–1930*	*1930–1940*
Phoenix	29,053	48,118	65,414	65	35
Tucson	20,292	32,506	36,818	60	13

Population figures derived from U.S. Bureau of the Census, *Census of the United States*, Fourteenth 1920, 1:82, 180; Fifteenth 1930, 1:92: Sixteenth 1940, 1:34.

the next decade. Both cities saw their population increase more slowly, but in Tucson the declining rate of growth approached a position of stasis. The rate of growth slowed in Phoenix by almost 50 percent; in Tucson the decline in the rate of growth was almost 80 percent.

The economic calamity confronted city leaders with severe challenges but also presented civic authorities with new opportunities. The hope in both cities was that the local economies would prove to be "Depression proof." The two cities came through the Depression larger, and in some ways healthier, than before, and so the hope for immunity from the economic collapse was in some ways realized. In terms of the cities' relationship with nature, the Depression served to curtail for a time the sprawl, pollution, and other manifestations of urbanization. At least for another few years, Phoenix and Tucson remained desert cities closely linked to their natural surroundings and circumstances.[2]

Depression-era economics and politics affected the two cities, but not entirely negatively. In many ways the cities fared well during the Great Depression, particularly in the development of the municipal water systems. The desert surroundings of Tucson and Phoenix had always made water a critical issue, first for the main economic prop of agriculture and later for consumer-based domestic uses. Central to agriculture and the local economies, water was also at the heart of politics in the two communities. The significant political debates were often local—arguments over bond issues, for example—but during the Depression national politics took on added importance. The election of Franklin Delano Roosevelt in 1932 and the advent of the New Deals in 1933 and 1935, with their public works programs, benefited both cities greatly. The existence of federal subsidies allowed both cities to expand and improve their municipal water systems far beyond the abilities of the two communities individually. Phoenix previously had enjoyed a beneficial federal program—the

Salt River Project—but the receipt of federal largess in Tucson constituted a new and much-appreciated subsidy.

Stretching back to antiquity, two sources of water traditionally served residents of Tucson: the flowing stream and shallow wells sunk into the floodplain. In the nineteenth century, as the community spread to the east and away from the river, the traditional sources of water became impractical for many of the community's inhabitants. Initially, Tucsonans simply dug wells on their own property, including lots within the town site, finding water within easy reach. Unfortunately, many of the wells provided bitter water tasting of alkali, while others simply ran dry after an initial gush. This ad hoc system of water delivery in Tucson lasted until the Tucson Water Company opened its first mains in 1882.

The initial source of water for the municipal system was the stream flow six miles upstream from the town. To augment the modest flow in the river, workers dug a head cut into the river channel so as to access both the surface and shallow subsurface flow of water. From the head cut, water flowed in a flume constructed of redwood into a forebay—a boxlike structure of timbers —that held three hundred thousand gallons of water. From the forebay, a small steam pump lifted the water into an eleven-inch water main that carried the water four and a half miles to Tucson. Workers constructed the main in place, using square sheets of metal formed and riveted together and coated with tar. The flume and main traversed a pastoral landscape of fields and pastures. Once in town, the main spidered out in a web of smaller mains and laterals. Gravity provided the water pressure in the city system.[3]

Initially the regularized flow of water through the mains provided a clear benefit to the community. In addition to providing the desirable amenity of water that was available at the turn of a tap, the water company worked in conjunction with the city government to provide public conveniences and an improvement in the city's appearance and beauty. The city council announced in 1888 that free water would go to anyone who planted a tree along one of the city's streets. Three years later, the city council installed a drinking fountain on Church Place. "It will be of cast iron and have conveniences for both man and beast."[4]

With increasing convenience came heightened expectations for reliable service. The system was initially up to the task but ultimately proved vulnerable to increased demand and climatological variability. Because the system depended on a single source of water and a single delivery trough, any diminution in flow would result in a serious collapse of water pressure. The most distant taps on the eastern fringe of the town would go dry first as the declining service retreated toward the river. Interruptions could be caused by declining flows at the source or by any break or leak in the redwood trough or sheet-metal main. Droughts remained the most serious threat—dry cycles remained clear and obvious in their effect, even for urban residents. Eventually the municipal water system created a thorough immunity from changing weather cycles, but in the early years the fragile utility did little to change the basic awareness of environmental realities among city residents.

A prolonged drought in the early 1890s made clear the limitations in the city's system. Additional sources of water had to be found, and the process began in earnest in 1893 with the development of wells to augment the city's supply of water. The city dug the wells near the original head cut at Valencia Road, establishing five wells within a radius of fifty feet and at an average depth of twenty feet. Pumps that could deliver more than 1 million gallons a day capped the wells. As the newspaper hopefully reported, "Residents in the eastern end of town will have no cause hereafter for grumbling."[5]

Over the next seven years the company's pumping capacity increased to more than 2 million gallons a day, which allowed the delivery of water to city residents for domestic uses and irrigation water for the cultivation of crops. The water company owned 640 acres of farmland near the head cut and sold water to nearby farmers. The sale of water to both urban and rural customers grossed the Tucson Water Company $18,000 a year in 1900, which provided a healthy profit above the operating costs of $10,560. The system by 1900 delivered water to 625 connections, including sixty-two fire hydrants. More than eight and a half miles of mains linked the connections to the redwood flume. This was the system that the City of Tucson bought for $109,000 in 1900 as part of the Progressive Era reform of municipal utilities.[6]

Questions of adequate supply and sufficient pressure in the system confronted the city-owned water utility, just as those twin problems had dominated the life of the private company. Given the modest flow in the river, virtually nonexistent during dry cycles, the Tucson Water Company continued to add wells to the system, which by 1922 had doubled the supply of water. But increasing the supply only addressed half of the problem. Additional mains and feeder lines had to be constructed to connect the new wells to the system and to expand the utility to new residential areas on the eastern and northern fringes of the city. To expand the system to meet the increasing demand required seven bond issues from 1893 to 1922. By 1922, mains linked more than a dozen wells in two zones in the basin. The eastern zone was eighty feet higher than the zone nearer the river. To provide equal water pressure throughout the system, the city maintained its main booster station to pump the water uphill at Plant No. 1 in its original location at West Eighteenth and Osborne streets. To aid in providing water pressure for northeast residents, the city also constructed a round metal reservoir holding 1.5 million gallons of water on the northwest corner of Campbell Avenue and Second Street.[7]

By 1923 the city's water system had expanded to provide ample water for its twenty-five thousand residents. The reliable supply of groundwater had increased to 14 million gallons a day. That volume could easily provide the 176 gallons of water per person per day that was the average consumption in Tucson. The system could even meet the peak summer demand of 227 gallons per person per day. Peak demand resulted in part from the practice of flood irrigation for lawns and gardens. Tucsonans typically watered their grass and trees by flooding their lawns with a foot or more of water. The ponds were contained in grass-covered berms, with small flood gates within the berms allowing the transfer of the irrigating water from one section of the lawn to another. The University of Arizona campus also used this type of watering system, and the old mechanisms and berms remain on the original parts of campus. The supply of water seemed bountiful in the moist 1920s. Such was the optimism of the day that the head of the water department suggested that the system could provide sufficient water for more than a doubling of the city's population. The future seemed rosy.[8]

But droughts always lurked; if they were not quite ever present, they were common enough to be nominally routine. The growing dependence on groundwater from multiple wells had begun during the dry 1890s. The desert heat was more palpable then; air conditioning was in the distant future. The desert surroundings intruded into the consciousness of the community, making water scarcity a painful fact of life. Conservation efforts came naturally.

Calls to conserve water stemmed from three realities confronting residents of Tucson: the volume of water at the source, the reliability of the delivery system, and peak rates of demand, especially during the summer, that stretched both the volume at the source and the capacity of the delivery system.

The first reference to water conservation came a month before the city announced a plan to dig the first wells near the head cut. The newspaper announced the softly worded request: "It has been suggested that some plan should be adopted by which all irrigation of gardens, lawns and trees in Tucson should be done from six o'clock in the evening to four o'clock in the morning. This plan would be much better for the gardens and lawns and would make the water supply ample during the dry season of the year."[9]

In 1893 the issue was volume. The single source and open flume presented the community with a clear limit to water that soon pushed the privately owned company to develop additional sources to augment the volume in the delivery system. Ten years later the city-owned utility again called for restraint in lawn watering, but by 1903 the state of the infrastructure was as much an issue as the overall volume in the system:

> Notice to Water Consumers:
>
> Owing to the increased consumption of water so far in excess of the present means of supply and the decrease in the underground flow to the now existing wells, it becomes necessary to curb the sprinkling and irrigating of lawns and trees, until the installation of the new pump ordered by the city, and the completion of the new well now under course of construction, to the following hours, viz.—
>
> Sprinkling and irrigating allowed only between the hours of 5 a.m. and 8 a.m. and between 5 p.m. and 8 p.m.
>
> Trusting that the fairminded citizens of Tucson will bear with us in this proposition, Yours respectfully, Philip Contezen, W M Ride, F. J. Villaescusa. Water Committee.[10]

Drops in water pressure and diminishing flows from wells caused Tucsonans to conserve their meager water supply and generated complaints and calls to expand the water system. Concern would heighten during dry spells and then subside during wet cycles. The expansion program during the early 1920s had created a supply system with surplus capacity, and so the conservation ethos waned. By the end of the decade, however, concern began to mount. The expansion of the city in size and population, as well as oncoming drought conditions, caused the city to look for ways to increase its supply of water. In the process, a major transition started south of the city: farmland was converted to urban uses. On June 30, 1929, the city acquired one hundred acres south of town and near the city's well field and delivery system. The farmland included two wells and cost thirty thousand dollars. Water utility workers quickly added the former irrigation water to the city system.[11]

The acquisition of irrigation water for urban uses created the appearance of competition for water resources between the city and farmers. In truth the competition started when the city first began diverting water into the redwood flume. Solomon Warner operated a flour mill near the city, and he blamed the city's system for lowering the level of his mill pond to the point that there was insufficient water to operate the mechanism.[12] Warner's complaint remained isolated, however, as valley farmers increasingly relied on wells and pump technology to irrigate their fields at about the same time the city had begun using wells to augment the city's supply of water. The widespread reliance on wells mitigated against the appearance of competition for some time, as all water users tapped the shallow aquifer. By 1930, however, aquifer levels had begun a noticeable drop and complaints mounted. Farmers criticized the city for its acquisition of farmland solely for the purpose of adding its water to the city's system, claiming the urban uses required more or less constant pump-ing, while irrigation required periodic operation of wells. Agricultural uses ac-tually required much more water than did domestic uses, but the appearance of competition between the city and area farmers created in 1930 a legal chal-lenge to the city's acquisition of farmland the previous year. The obstructionist suit caused the city to delay future land acquisitions. Instead, the city in the 1930s shifted its water strategy to the development of a more efficient delivery system and an increased storage capacity for the city utility.[13]

First came the plan to build a storage reservoir near the well field and pumping plant south of town. Construction of the project started in 1933, in part with the assistance of a ten-thousand-dollar loan from President Herbert Hoover's Reconstruction Finance Corporation (RFC). As the Great Depres-sion deepened in the early 1930s, and with reelection pressures mounting, Hoover had initiated several relief programs in 1932. One of these programs was the RFC, which was designed in part to assist local governments in the construction of public works projects that would boost employment opportu-nities for local residents. Franklin Roosevelt's victory in November 1932 placed Hoover's programs in limbo, and local governments scrambled to adjust to the change in administrations in March 1933. In Tucson's case, construction of the reservoir got a boost in 1934 with a New Deal loan of $250,000, which allowed the project to increase in proposed size from 5 million gallons to 7.5 million gallons. Unfortunately, the Public Works Administration (PWA) funds would only cover 45 percent of the total cost of the project. The city would have to

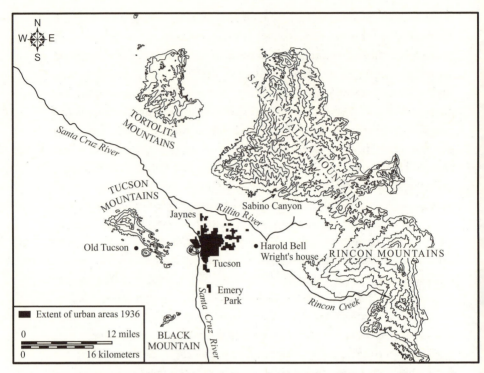

Map 6.1. Tucson 1936. By 1936 the City of Tucson had begun its expansion steadily eastward from its proximity to the Santa Cruz River.

provide the other 55 percent, which would require a bond election that city officials considered problematic, given the community's pinched circumstances. City leaders waited almost four years until improving economic conditions in August 1938 made the prospect of a bond issue more reasonable. Voter turnout was incredibly low on August 1, 1938; only 435 of Tucson's property-owning voters bothered to cast ballots. As the newspaper reported, "Voters evidenced a marked indifference to the whole thing." Fortunately for the water utility, a majority of the 435 approved the $277,000 in bonds.[14]

In addition to increasing storage capacity, the PWA project would also help in developing the delivery system. By 1934 maintaining water pressure had become difficult and expensive. The city had expanded in size several miles to the east, and the increasing distance and elevation from the river required constant pumping to maintain water pressure. New electric pumps had replaced the original steam models, although one old steam pump remained in place at the south side facility for standby and emergency service. The electric pumps were much more efficient than the steam contraptions, but they consumed a lot of electric power. To save the costs of pumping and to create reliable water pressure, the city planned to build two elevated storage tanks. The pumps would fill the tanks, and then gravity would provide the constant water pressure in the system. Each tank would hold 1 million gallons of water. With approval of the bond, construction of the reservoirs began at Elm Street and Randolph Park, then on the eastern edge of the city.[15]

In another move to improve service to residents, the city began in 1938 the process of acquiring private water systems. The effort to purchase farmland for its water had resulted in resistance, but the city was successful in acquiring privately owned suburban systems. The city annexed two neighborhoods in 1938 and 1939: San Clemente and Jefferson Park. In each case the city purchased the developments' private water system and incorporated it into the city utility. Residents generally applauded the move since it resulted in better service at less cost. Over the ensuing decades the city purchased 132 private systems at a cost of $26 million.[16]

Reliable flow and pressure became institutionalized in Tucson by the close of the 1930s. In the process Tucsonans acquired the ability to disregard at least one aspect of their desert surroundings. Blazing summer temperatures remained unignorable, but drought conditions became abstract in their significance. Water flowed through the taps regardless of the outside temperature, and rainfall deficiencies that parched the surface of the desert had little effect on the drip from the hose bib. The water utility's expansion had clear environmental effects, shaping residents' relationship with nature. Most obvious to the community were the costs—financial and political—associated with the expanded city system. Tax revenues had to be raised and augmented from time to time to maintain and occasionally expand the utility. Water remained a topic of political discussion in the community, but the debates and arguments took on a disassociated quality—the issues were mechanical and financial, not hydrological or environmental.

The awareness of New Deal funding and the willingness of federal agencies to subsidize a wide range of public works projects generated additional proposals to benefit the community. The chamber of commerce resurrected the old plan to build a dam in Sabino Canyon. The chamber, with the assistance of the city engineer, financed a survey of the canyon and creek in 1931 and two years later initiated the process of obtaining permission from the Forest Service to build a dam in the canyon. The proposal envisioned a dam 250 feet high that would create a lake two miles long and seventy-six feet deep.[17] The dam would store water for irrigation and flood control, as well as provide a recreation setting for valley residents.[18]

The federal connection was clear from the beginning. The chamber targeted two agencies. First the chamber of commerce received Federal Emergency Relief Administration (FERA) funds to build a road up the canyon to the dam site, which allowed for the finalization of the engineering plans. These included the estimate that the lake would contain nine thousand acre feet of water. The road wound up the canyon several miles, crossing the creek nine times. Each crossing required a one-lane concrete bridge that formed a check dam in the creek averaging about eight feet in height. About one hundred men worked on the road project beginning in October 1934. Ultimately FERA's contribution to the project amounted to the road construction and little else. Citing a lack of progress, FERA canceled its support for the project. Shifting their bureaucratic target, the county supervisors in 1937 applied for $750,000 in Works Progress Administration (WPA, which replaced the PWA in 1935) funds to build the dam and complete the project. The Army Corp of Engineers had previously estimated that the dam project would cost more than $1 million and provide labor for one thousand men for a year. WPA projects generally required local residents to pay about 55 percent of the cost of projects, and so city leaders estimated that Tucson's share of the project's cost would be at least six hundred thousand dollars. Up to this point the chamber of commerce had spent a total of six hundred dollars on promotions of the project. Local political leaders now had two PWA projects awaiting their local contribution; the proposed water system improvements required more than two hundred thousand dollars in bonds, and now the dam proposal would require additional and more costly bonds. Two factors seemed to affect the city's analysis of the dam project's viability. First, a clear rationale pointed to the necessity of the water system improvements; these would take precedence over a primarily recreational project. Second, the city government calculated that the community would never agree to fund both projects during the difficult economic conditions. City leaders still hesitated in 1937 to bring the smaller water system bond issue up for a vote. Given the cautious mood in the city council, the dam project had little chance to proceed. For lack of the local contribution, the dam project quietly died.[19]

The road remained, however. Soon Civilian Conservation Corps crews went to work facing with native stone the small bridges over the creek, and the canyon became an asset to the community that had not been foreseen by the dam proponents. Instead of "parexcellent fishing" and "unexcelled boating" on the lake, Tucsonans came to cherish the lush riparian area within the high walls of the canyon. The road provided a scenic drive with many opportunities for picnicking, swimming, rock climbing, bird watching, and simply enjoying the natural setting. In one specific example, cyclists came to enjoy the challenge of the steep three-mile uphill climb and then the thrill of the daredevil downhill rush. In short, Sabino Canyon, as a destination of clear environmental significance for both residents and tourists, became an integral part of the community after the road, but not the dam, was built in the 1930s.[20]

Phoenix leaders also had to face repair and maintenance needs as well as calls for expansion and improved service during the 1930s. Likewise, Phoenix enjoyed the benefit of federal assistance in some of its water system improvements.

Of immediate concern in Phoenix was the condition of the redwood pipeline from the Verde River. Completed in 1922, by 1929 the wooden system had begun to spectacularly fail. Small leaks underground would result in oozing, muddy quagmires, while large and sudden leaks would send columns of water shooting up in geysers a hundred feet high. City officials proposed a $4.8 million bond program that included construction of a concrete pipeline in 1929, but on two occasions city voters rejected the bond. Before the vote in December a judge had to step in to halt an effort to cancel the election. Opponents had attempted to get an injunction seeking to either cancel the election or at least delay it until the spring, when a new city commission would take office. With the judge's intercession the vote took place as scheduled on December 4, 1929. Voters defeated the bond issue but approved an amendment to the city charter providing that local labor be used on city projects. Full awareness of the extent and depth of the Great Depression would not come for some months, but already concern over unemployment had arisen in the community. City officials blamed the defeat on light turnout: 3,355 votes from 8,700 registered voters. In fact, voter turnouts remained fairly consistent throughout the decade. A hotly contested and contentious vote three years later garnered thirty-four hundred total votes, which brings into question the light-turnout analysis.[21]

Another vote on the 1929 proposal took place in February 1930. The margin of defeat actually increased from 54 percent opposed in December to

57 percent opposed in February. With a second defeat in a little over two months, city leaders slightly revised their analysis from low turnout to a general condition of apathy. An indication of the relative disinterest can be seen in the newspaper coverage of the elections. On the day before the election, a tiny article announced the upcoming vote while the lead story, with banner headlines, covered the negotiations between California and Arizona over Colorado River water. On the day of the election a bigger story proclaimed the "necessity" for the bonds, but once again the nonelection lead story announced in banner headlines the formation of a "bollworm fund" to aid cotton farmers. Only the defeat of the bonds brought the issue to the forefront of the news coverage, but even under the scrutiny of the press, nothing in the report explained with any certainty why the voters had rejected the bonds so thoroughly.[22]

A new city government took office in May. In the meantime, the problems with the redwood pipeline had continued, with additional leaks. The new city commission considered the former proposal and revised it slightly downward to $3.4 million in bonds. In another concession to public concern, the commission announced the creation of an advisory board of leading businessmen "which will be in constant charge of all financial matters in connection with the expenditures of bond funds, will supervise all disbursements and the letting of all contracts, subject to the final approval of the city commission." On June 25, 1930, voters overwhelmingly approved the bonds for a concrete pipeline from the Verde River, as well as the bonds for sewage projects, park development, and other projects. Construction of the new conduit began in late December 1930 and was completed the following year.[23]

The new pipeline generally followed the route of the original redwood pipe, except for a new right-of-way through the Fort McDowell reservation. The city had obtained the new right-of-way in August 1930 as part of an effort to obtain a new well field on the reservation near the Verde River. Successful in the acquisition of the right-of-way, the city failed to acquire the new well field. Changes in federal Indian policy had complicated the task of negotiating with the Bureau of Indian Affairs. Efforts to obtain new wells on the reservation continued through the 1930s without success, although the city was able to augment the supply of water to customers simply by regularizing the flow and eliminating the more or less constant leaks in the old redwood pipe.[24]

With the completion of the pipeline came the harsh reality of paying the bill, specifically, servicing the municipal bonds that the voters had approved.

City leaders had to either raise taxes or increase service fees sufficiently to pay the $1.3 million interest payments over the life of the bonds, and that proved difficult during the period of economic stagnation.[25] Phoenix in general fared pretty well during the Depression, but city leaders needed an expanding economy and tax base to pay off the bonds. With a flat budget and the prospects of declining tax revenues, city leaders had to contemplate cuts in service and personnel as bond payments came due. A solution offered itself in the form of the increased water supply: the city could sell the water and use the proceeds from increased water department revenue to service the bonds. Conveniently, there were hundreds and ultimately thousands of new customers for the city's water just outside the city limits. Two groups had begun requesting the clear and sweet Verde River water: individual homeowners relying on well water and residents in new subdivisions served by private water systems.[26]

Well water in the valley often tasted bitterly of minerals and alkali. In addition, wells became tainted at times with sewage emanating from septic tanks. Many residences relied on septic tanks as sprawling developments outpaced city sewage systems. Environmental problems often arose as systems failed or soil conditions proved to be unsuitable. In many parts of the Southwest, including the Phoenix and Tucson basins, partially compacted caliche characterized much of the substrata in which developers placed septic tanks and leaching fields. The hard subsoil held moisture rather than transmitting it, creating lingering cesspools that offended both smell and sight. In part because of these local soil conditions, Phoenix leaders expanded the city sewers into the fringe neighborhoods in the 1930s. Well users often received city water and sewer service at the same time. Continuing sprawl, however, especially during the boom years during and following World War II, compounded the problem; the so-called septic tank suburbs continued to appear into the 1950s.[27]

Other potential customers for city water were those residents served by private systems in subdivided neighborhoods. The private systems generally relied on well water obtained within the property. The same problems in taste and sanitation plagued the fringe neighborhoods, plus they faced difficulty in maintaining water pressure and reliable service. The Depression presented the private systems with additional difficulties: many of the small systems fell into disrepair as maintenance budgets melted in the face of economic decline. Through the early 1930s both individual well users and neighborhood residents requested water service from the city. Often annexations resulted from the initiative to provide water and sewer connections. By adding taxable property to the city, annexations increased the city's tax base and bonding capacity. The new city residents also paid fees for city services, which further increased the revenue flowing into city coffers.[28]

Federal loans and public works projects during the Depression assisted in the expansion of the Phoenix water system. First to receive service as part of a local and federal initiative were 281 residents relying on wells. These were individual customers outside the city limits who were not part of an organized subdivision with a private water system. The RFC provided the labor used in extending the city's water lines to the new customers, most of whom lived close to the Verde River pipeline. The construction took place during the summer of 1933. City officials estimated that the new customers would contribute seventeen thousand dollars to the city's revenue. As a government official summarized, "Extension of city water service into outside areas . . . not only will increase city revenues and allow the city to dispose of the large available water surplus at a profit, but also will remove a serious menace to public health which exists in contamination of well water."[29]

The city next targeted more than a dozen neighborhoods to the north and east of the city limits. From August to October 1933, city leaders prepared proposals for projects that would extend water and sewer lines to the fringe residents as well as improve storm drains and other infrastructure needs. Federal assistance would cover 30 percent of the cost of the projects, and so another bond issue would be necessary to provide the city's share. City officials and other proponents of the bonds lobbied hard for their passage as opponents mounted their own campaign to defeat the bonds. Both groups staged rallies at the Phoenix Union High School. Two nights before the vote, opponents called for a gathering to discuss their grievances. About three hundred people gathered to hear suspicion that the bond funds would be reallocated or misspent. Opponents also criticized the commission's effort to link changes in the city charter to the bond election. The proposed amendments to the charter would increase the terms of commissioners from one to two years. If passed, two sitting commissioners (who supported the bond and the amendments) would keep their seats for another year, as one opponent surmised, "so that they may spend the money." The night before the election supporters of the bond organized a large rally at the high school following a torchlight parade.

Marchers carried "red fire" torches as well as noisemakers in what organizers called "a march for the unemployed." After the march, a large crowd gathered at the high school to hear supporters trumpet the value of the bond and char- ter amendments.[30]

On December 9, 1933, city voters narrowly approved $1.52 million in bonds to finance the city's share of the projects' cost. They also approved the charter amendments. Proponents celebrated while the opposition fumed and plotted. Passage of the bonds could be judged a clear benefit—the public works projects would create eight thousand man/months of work for unemployed Phoenicians—but it could also be considered mistaken and misguided. The bonds would increase the indebtedness of the city government. Opponents complained that the city already owed a cumulative $8 million in bonds, which it had no way to repay. They also argued that the planned bond repayment scheme was illegal. Bond proponents had assured voters that repayment of the bond would come from an increase in fees paid by new water and sewer cus- tomers. No tax increase would be necessary to retire the bonds. Opponents claimed that this repayment idea violated the state constitution. Lawyers among the opponents stressed that state law required that municipal bonds be guaran- teed with ad valorem taxes, not assurances of future revenue increases through fee payments. Other critics claimed that projects in the bond package were unnecessary and wasteful. The proposal to spend $740,000 for a municipal golf course garnered the ire of one opponent, who complained, "Not one in 100 citizens living south of the railroad tracks would benefit [from it]." On the other hand, supporters of the bond claimed that the golf course would enhance the "city's attractiveness as a winter resort community." Lastly, an opposition minister railed against the "deplorable moral condition" of the city, which he blamed on the "laxity" of government officials. To add insult to the perceived injury, these same government officials were using the New Deal public works apparatus to ensure their political survival. The minister claimed that RFC workers "had been sent out on behalf of the election." The anger of the op- ponents was palpable. Having narrowly lost the election, opposition lawyers shifted their focus to the courts.[31]

The legal challenge to the bond issue worked its way up to the Arizona Supreme Court over the ensuing months. As it turned out, the case turned on the repayment scheme. The court's decision vindicated the opposition lawyers by asserting the need to rely on ad valorem taxes to guarantee municipal bonds, but the court's decision ultimately disappointed the opponents. The bond election stood with the legality of the vote upheld. The court simply required that the city commission drop its reliance on fees to guarantee the bonds.[32]

As the courts considered the legal questions, the PWA hesitated to approve the projects. Ultimately the legal challenge delayed the projects but did not stop them. Late in August 1934, the PWA administrators in Washington announced that they were satisfied with the legal adjustments in the bonds and okayed the projects. The PWA also loaned the city funds to commence the basic engineering and preparatory work. City workers had been laid off during the legal squabble. The PWA money allowed the workmen to be rehired.[33]

With the bonds certified by the courts and the projects approved by the federal government, the city began the process of selling the bonds, awarding the contracts, and commencing the work. Construction started in early December 1934, one year after the bond election. City engineers and contractors estimated that the work on the water and sewer projects would extend into mid-May. At the height of construction, 495 workers gained employment on the water and sewer projects. The city still hoped that the projects would be self-liquidating. Officials estimated that the sewer extensions alone would generate four thousand dollars per year in increased fees starting in 1935.[34]

Before workers completed the expansion, an awareness arose that the project would fail to achieve the city's revenue goals. With additional bonds to be serviced, even more city revenue would be necessary—the city made an initial payment of eight thousand dollars in interest on the bonds in 1934 and would owe another seventeen thousand in interest by 1939—but city officials realized that the new mains would result in no additional revenue for the water department and city. Instead of generating additional revenue by hooking up new customers, the mains would remain capped and unused unless additional structures were built to attach the new city mains to the private systems in the fringe neighborhoods. The private systems were either in a state of disrepair or simply ill equipped to connect to the new delivery system. In February 1935, as workers continued the construction of the water and sewer extensions, city officials announced phase two of the water project: "The second half of the work will involve the installation of lateral mains and connecting lines to serve the hundreds of new residents which have been signed up for city water service." For this second phase the city initially requested an additional one hundred thousand dollars from the PWA.[35]

High hopes rested on the water extension. With the nearing completion of the initial project in March, city officials projected an increase of sixty-five thousand dollars in water department revenue in the first year. If this came to fruition, the 1934 bonds would indeed be self-liquidating. Unfortunately, both the new customers—about twenty-five hundred in all—and the city government would have to wait more than two years for the completion of the water project.[36]

As planned, work crews completed phase one of the water project in April and the sewer extension project in May 1935. Although the city failed to receive an increase in water department revenue, the completion of the sewer extensions had a positive effect on the city's finances. More than five hundred new customers received sanitation service, which benefited public health by reducing the number of cesspools on the city's fringe. The new sewer customers also generated a total of seventy-five hundred dollars per year in fee payments. Water department revenue still suffered, but the additional city revenue from the sewer fees softened the blow somewhat.[37]

Over the next two years successive city governments lobbied the PWA for additional funds while they continued to revise the plans for the water project. Included in the revisions were upgrades for the Verde River pumps and other mechanisms at the head of the pipeline, as well as connections to the private system customers. One of the debates among city engineers concerned the specific means of connecting suburban residents to the city system: should the private systems be repaired and upgraded or simply dismantled in favor of new city construction? In the final analysis, the estimated costs of rehabilitation became exorbitant, and the city decided to simply purchase the systems with the intention to replace them. By August 1936, after months and then years of delay, the mood in city hall was frustrated and impatient. On August 4, the PWA announced its list of funded projects for Arizona, and the city's water extension was missing. Three days later the city announced plans to go forward with the extension on its own so that it could finally benefit from the increase in water connections provided by phase one of the project. Fortunately for city taxpayers, later in August the PWA approved the city's revised plan, and late in 1936 construction began. Workers completed the project in the summer of

1937, and the city at last received the benefit of additional customers for city water. The improvements at the head of the pipeline increased the available supply of water by 3 million gallons a day, from 21 to 24 million gallons a day, which constituted a comfortable surplus beyond the current demand. The city's revenue picture also improved, with water department income increasing by sixty-three thousand dollars from 1936 to 1937. City leaders hoped the water department revenue would continue to increase, by as much as another fifty thousand dollars over the next year. Officials projected water department revenues to reach $593,000 in the 1937–1938 fiscal year.[38]

During the Depression both cities used New Deal programs to develop their municipal water systems. In each case city workers upgraded the supply and delivery systems, producing surplus supplies that came into use during the wartime and postwar booms. Industrial production lagged during the early and mid-1930s, but the advances in urban infrastructure laid the groundwork for the expansion in production that commenced in the late 1930s. In the meantime, Tucson and Phoenix struggled to maintain their economic standing, relying increasingly on tourism to soften the economic blow of the Depression.

One of the allures in the two cities was the desert setting, but the increased attention directed toward the natural surroundings caused some of the first signs of environmental degradation. In perhaps the most commonplace occurrence, automobile traffic became a source of concern in the midst of the economic calamity. It seemed that people always found the nickels and dimes necessary to keep gas in the car. The increased traffic included the type that drove Harold Bell Wright out of his cherished home in the desert. Wright faced a dilemma that has recurred at many campgrounds and other outdoor recreational areas since the 1930s: heavy traffic on dirt roads stirs up clouds of dust and collapses the paths into rutted obstacle courses. The inclination of course is to pave the roads so as to eliminate the dust and preserve the roadbed. But paving simply attracts more travel by an increasingly casual population that previously might have shied away from venturing down a dirt track. Wright had supported a bond issue to pave streets in 1930 so as to cut down dust. The result, however, was increased traffic out to his estate at the end of Speedway Boulevard. The uninvited visitors at times behaved rudely and boorishly, peering through his windows and swimming without permission in his pool. Wright continued to return to Tucson for winters through the early 1930s, but in May 1936 he sold his house and moved to California near Escondido, an early victim of sprawl. In the 1950s Wright's widow sold the remaining Tucson property to a developer who planned to subdivide the estate into seven streets and 110 homes. With the approval of Wright's widow, the builder called the neighborhood Harold Bell Wright Estates.[39]

More traffic was the goal of leaders in both cities. Traffic into the cities and travel within the limits of the community constituted commerce in the minds of officials and business owners, as if travelers shed dollars with every passing mile. Since winter visitors were a visible marker of such commercial possibilities, both cities targeted this source of wealth and prosperity. Phoenix boosters in particular promoted their city as a winter tourist attraction and health mecca during the 1930s, and thousands of people responded. Future Republican presidential candidate Barry Goldwater and other civic leaders encouraged this activity as a method of bringing more revenue into Phoenix and the valley—tourism would be a palliative for the Depression. As Goldwater recalled in 1940,

> The natural thing to which to turn [in 1930 and 1931] was the capitalization of our climate, our natural beauties, and the romance of our desert. These natural resources, which had never before been tapped, were subjected to a national advertising program. This program has been continued during the years, and the benefits derived from it can never be fully estimated. It is very safe to say that Phoenix would not be in the prominent position which she now occupies, near the top of the per capita spending column of the nation if it were not for the thousands of winter visitors and tourists who call Phoenix their home during a few months of the year. . . . It is easy to see, therefore, why business men are so unanimously enthusiastic about the continuance and enlargement of a proper advertising program.[40]

Goldwater was correct in describing the positive economic impact of tourism on the local economy. Curious, however, is his reference to the novelty of the tourist pitch, as if the environmental appeal had been entirely new. Appeals to tourists based on the warm winters and dry, healthful desert air extended back to the early 1900s. The 1930s advertising campaign was not unusual because of its newness, but its size and energy were rather remarkable, given the prevalent caution and retrenchment of the Depression. The city commission routinely appropriated tax revenue—$17,500 in 1937—to assist the chamber of commerce in its "national tourist advertizing."[41]

Fig. 6.1. The Camelback Inn, 1936 (CP MCLMB A796B: courtesy McCulloch Brothers Photographs, Herb and Dorothy McLaughlin Collection, Arizona State University Libraries). The Camelback Inn opened to immediate success in the midst of the Great Depression, perhaps ironically, by catering to the most affluent tourists. The inn differed from the Biltmore not in its level of luxury but in its incorporation of the desert landscape into its interior spaces. Native American art work accompanied the Pueblo style of architecture.

An example of the continuing influence of tourism on the local economy can be found in the opening of the Camelback Inn in 1936. In 1924 the Jokake Inn had opened in Scottsdale, and in 1936 the Camelback Inn joined the Jokake at the base of Camelback Mountain. The Camelback Inn cost two hundred thousand dollars to construct and incorporated Native American and desert themes. Indian artwork adorned the interior spaces, and the guest cottages were named after the indigenous varieties of cactus. The Camelback Inn was the only new resort hotel to open during the Depression and may have been seen as a very chancy proposition. The parent company of the Westward Ho had filed for bankruptcy as Depression conditions deepened, emerging from federal receivership in May 1936. Interestingly, the Camelback Inn specifically catered to the most wealthy tourists. Even in the midst of the Depression the strategy proved very successful. The inn's somewhat remote location (twelve miles from downtown Phoenix) appealed to visitors, since the neighboring

Fig. 6.2. Camelback guests playing shuffleboard (CP MCLMB A796C: courtesy McCulloch Brothers Photographs, Herb and Dorothy McLaughlin Collection, Arizona State University Libraries). Promotional photographs advertised traditional recreational activities such as shuffleboard at the resort. Trail rides in the desert also gained prominent display, always with a venerable wrangler and cowboy serving as guide and mentor to the necktied and coiffured guests. This view of the shuffleboard games includes guests in sunning attire as well as the woman observing on the left who is wearing riding apparel.

Jokake interrupted any feeling of solitude and added to the aura of exclusivity. Manager, and eventual owner, Jack Stewart made sure the dude ranch setting (the hotel maintained a private stable with sixty horses at its peak) included luxurious service and amenities. It was the stated goal of the hotel to attract the most genteel guests. Within two months of the opening, guests filled the inn's seventy-seven rooms to capacity.[42]

In addition to gaining another resort hotel, Scottsdale received another boon with the arrival of Frank Lloyd Wright in 1937. Wright returned to the Phoenix area for the purpose of establishing an architecture school, and his arrival coincided with that of several other artists and creative personalities. In the 1930s Philip Curtis and Lon Megargee came to Scottsdale, continuing a trend established in the second decade of the twentieth century when Oscar Stroebel, Jr., and Jessie Benton Evans established homes in the area, drawn by the "incomparable desert scenery."[43]

By the end of the decade, the influx of tourists became a clear fact of economic life in Phoenix. As Barry Goldwater later noted, "The stimuli from the injection of these tourist dollars into the veins of our economic being have been felt by every person doing business in the area. The farmer has sold more produce. The hotels have filled more rooms. The merchants have sold more goods."[44]

The number of winter visitors to Arizona had steadily increased from 1937 to 1940. About 16,000 tourists in 1937 grew to 23,800 in 1938. Then 1939 set new records and generated great profits at the resort hotels: 35,000 winter visitors contributing about $30 million to the state's economy. The increased tourism accompanied the revived industrial production that occurred with Roosevelt's emphasis on military preparedness in 1938 and 1939. Also, the threat of war and then its reality in 1939 limited tourism opportunities in Europe. As one observer remarked in 1940, "The 'See America First' slogan is becoming more generally adopted."[45]

Tucson shared in the tourism boom, and city leaders crowed over the increasing numbers of winter visitors to the Old Pueblo, but subtle differences started appearing in the two cities' promotions. In both cities, newspapers published promotional editions that trumpeted their communities' desirability as tourist destinations. In Phoenix the *Arizona Republic* printed the Mid Winter Resource Edition every year in mid- to late December; in Tucson, the *Arizona Daily Star* published the annual Rodeo Edition, coinciding with the Fiesta de los Vaqueros in February. Both editions described tourist locales, accompanied by splashy photographs, and catalogued the city, county, and state industries and their economic production. In the tourist pitches, both papers played up the state's wonders of nature, from the Grand Canyon to the White Mountains.

Local references to nature began to diverge by the mid-1930s. Desert settings disappeared from the Phoenix report, except for their commercialized manifestations at the resort hotels. Photographs of manicured lawns and stately homes in the city lured prospective residents. Architecture was vaguely indigenous, with stucco walls and arched entrances capped by tile roofs. But the desert was nowhere to be seen. In Tucson, the same sort of claims for sophistication and modernity appeared, including pictures of impressive homes and thriving cityscapes. But these common booster pitches were accompanied in the Rodeo Edition with articles and photographs proclaiming other community assets. Two examples were the Saguaro National Monument and Sabino Canyon, natural components of the community that were sold to tourists and enjoyed by residents.

The 1940 Rodeo Edition represents both the standard tourist pitch and the references to Tucson as a desert city. First and foremost, the newspaper hoped to profit by selling thousands of copies of the special edition, and city boosters hoped the far-flung distribution of the newspaper would generate wide-ranging tourist interest. In 1940, the *Arizona Daily Star* printed twenty-seven thousand copies of the paper and hoped to sell out, as it had the previous year. All forty-eight states as well as the territories of Alaska and Hawaii received copies. The special edition also found its way to thirteen foreign countries, from China to Southern Rhodesia. Furthering the boosterism of the special edition was a report by the Sunshine Climate Club. Officials of the club proclaimed with pride that 16,273 visitors had been brought into the city through direct contacts with the club, and of those visitors about 10 percent became permanent residents. The report of success was meant in part to justify a further report that the club spent twenty thousand dollars annually for its advertising campaign. Promotions of Tucson appeared in twenty-three national-circulation magazines, including *Time, Life, National Geographic, Town and Country, Harper's Bazaar,* and *Travel.*[46]

Tucson is depicted as a desert city in several places. The paper describes Sabino Canyon as "Tucson's Most Popular Playground," drawing 125,000 visitors annually. No doubt most of these patrons of the canyon were city residents. In another reference to the town's natural setting, the 1940 special edition included the article "Natural Assets in Clouds Forecast Bright Future in Film Making." The story referred to the recent filming of the movie *Westerner* in late 1939 and the soon-to-begin shooting of *Arizona,* for which Columbia pictures had constructed a movie set that came to be known as Old Tucson. Samuel Goldwyn, Inc., produced *Arizona,* and a representative of the company explained why Hollywood producers were heading to Tucson: "We came here to get a new and authentic background. . . . Then there's another reason for making westerns here. That's a matter of light and clouds . . . [and] take those pointed cactus you have here. California doesn't have them. And the mountains are different. They look like the kind of peaks you expect to see in the west. Why, even the horses are different. You don't have horses in California like you have here, either."[47]

Natural aspects of the community appear in this movie producer's catalogue of filming resources. Tucson's surroundings simply looked like the West. Mountains and cacti could not be manufactured on a sound stage with sufficient verisimilitude, especially when the local freedom from smog and haze allowed the movie cameras to capture those mountains, cacti, and clouds in clear resolution. Luckily for the movie producers, sprawl in Tucson was heading east toward the Rincon Mountains (and Harold Bell Wright's house), while clairvoyant planners had placed the movie set on the far west side of town over Gates Pass in the Tucson Mountains. Decades would pass before sprawl in Tucson encroached on Old Tucson's bright sunshine and panoramic desert views.

Two events in the 1930s represent the diverging community identities in Phoenix and Tucson. In Tucson the dam proposal for Sabino Canyon failed to garner enough community support, resulting in a road but no dam and the preservation of the canyon in close to its natural state. In Phoenix, conversely, the community began to enjoy a lush riparian area within its new municipal park. The Phoenix park had replaced the Papago-Saguaro National Monument. In 1930, Phoenix officials and federal administrators had agreed to abolish the monument because of the diminution of the native saguaro cacti caused by pilfering and general urban incursion. The new Papago Park encompassed 1,100 acres of the former monument and would devote 227 of those acres to the new municipal golf course, which had contributed to the controversy over the public works bond issue in 1933. Included in the park, and also emanating from the water bond, was the WPA project to construct a lake—actually eight interconnected lakes—one and a quarter miles long, through the park. The water works would contribute water hazards for the golf course, as well as provide boating opportunities for visitors. In addition, the lakes would be maintained by the state game and fish agency. The ponds would serve as fish hatcheries, providing perch and bass stocks for placement in state streams and lakes administered by the agency. The former natural monument had become a multiuse facility, and prominent among the uses were the water project and the municipal golf course.[48]

Of course Tucson also had golf courses and tried mightily to attract tourists with the appeal of shirt sleeve golf in January. But in Tucson the appeal to tourists included the promise of natural landscapes within the community. Expansive public terrain in Sabino Canyon and the two districts of the Saguaro National Monument graced Tucson. In Phoenix the desert remained present and apparent, but also increasingly walled in and often controlled by private interests in the resorts. On the east side of town the new Papago Park represented the community's truncated relationship with nature. The eleven-hundred-acre park included lakes, a golf course, playing fields for baseball and softball, modest hiking trails, and eventually the city zoo. In 1938 it also came to include Desert Botanical Garden. A small group of Phoenix elites had formed the Arizona Cactus and Native Flora Society, and they convinced the state legislature to lease them 145 acres of parkland for their desert garden. Over the ensuing decades the Desert Botanical Garden developed into a popular attraction, but it remained a small portion of what had once been an expansive natural setting. Phoenix was the Valley of the Sun and a winter playground, where the desert could be willed away.[49]

Part 3

CHOSEN PATHS

1940—1990

The Air-Conditioned Capital
of the World

CLAIMS OF SUPERIORITY in Phoenix continued to waffle between prideful braggadocio and assertions of political and economic reality through the 1940s. Increasingly, Phoenix leaders spoke of their city's position as the center of a burgeoning metropolitan region. In the 1940 census, the metro population in Phoenix reached 121,828. Unfortunately for Phoenix boosters, the census bureau required higher populations to be officially recognized as a "metro district." Either the central city had to have a population of 100,000 or the metropolitan region had to have a population of 150,000.[1] Phoenix fell short in both categories.

But out of this modest disappointment came great optimism, primarily because of improving economic conditions. Phoenix had come through the Depression in better shape than Tucson had, although both communities looked to the future with great expectations. From its larger economic base, Phoenix was poised to expand economically at a greater rate. The gap in size and population between the cities was widening, but in the 1940s the communities shared more commonalities than variances. The towns were still bound by their desert surroundings. The desert confronted community leaders with both attributes that had to be overcome and benefits that could be enjoyed. Whereas mild winters attracted hordes of tourists, blistering hot summers drove away many potential permanent residents. Perhaps the greatest limitation to the cities' growth potential was the summer heat. Key to overcoming this obstacle were advances in air conditioning. Other qualities of the desert provided obvious benefits. In one example relevant to the 1940s, clear skies and wide-open spaces equated to more or less perfect flying conditions, and both cities used their desert conditions as selling points when lobbying for the establishment of military bases and pilot-training facilities during World War II.

In 1940 the onset of World War II for Americans remained almost two years in the future. The distance in time and geography provided for heightened awareness tempered by insular complacency. Given the prevalent isolationism that had developed since the First World War, many Americans considered this new conflict to be none of their business. Increasingly obvious, however was the economic expansion brought on by the expanding war overseas. Additional federal spending resulting from President Franklin Roosevelt's push to expand and modernize the military in the name of prudent preparedness caused a boost in the local economies of Phoenix and Tucson. In both cities military bases and training centers took advantage of Arizona's natural attributes, including its dry climate and clear air.

The federal government first instituted plans in February 1940 to militarize Tucson's municipal airport. Later named Davis-Monthan Air Field, the base included extended runways of sufficient length to handle the largest Army Air Corps bombers. The longest of the three new runways was 7,000 feet long and 150 feet wide. Additional hangars, barracks, and other facilities went up as the field grew to almost two square miles, four times larger than the city's original airport. The City of Tucson had lobbied hard for the base, using the assistance of the chamber of commerce to boost the valley's 306 days of sunshine a year. Local businessman Monte Mansfeld chaired the chamber's aviation committee; he traveled to Washington, DC, twice as a liaison between the city and federal officials. Included in the negotiations was an offer by Tucson to put up $43,600 in funds for the acquisition of land and as a contribution toward the construction costs of the base. The lobbying paid off in September 1940 when the Army Air Corps announced that the Tucson base would house a bomber group and headquarters staff, specifically, First Bombardment Wing headquarters, Forty-first Bombardment Group (medium), Thirty-first Air Base Corps. From about two dozen personnel in early 1940, the base population of headquarters staff, pilots, and ground crews expanded to 3,320 in early 1941. City officials welcomed the military installation and its personnel, but the loss of their municipal airport required the acquisition of a site for the new city airfield. The city council had acquired more than sixteen thousand acres of scrubby desert in the vicinity of the original airfield. Some of the land had contributed to the establishment of Davis-Monthan—the city had presented the land to the air corps as a gift—and then the city used another twenty-five hundred acres for the new municipal airfield about two miles southwest of the Army Air Corps base.[2]

Almost a year later, in January 1941, Phoenix leaders announced the creation of a military aviation training facility west of town. The city paid forty thousand dollars for more than fourteen hundred acres west of Glendale, charging the War Department one dollar a year in rent. The investment calculus was clear, as explained by W. J. R. Sims, aviation booster and city commissioner: "Base development will bring to the Valley an estimated income of $3,500,000 per year, in addition to the $1,500,000 initial cost of establishing the field. . . . This seems good business in anybody's language." The city's efforts first benefited local contractor Del Webb. Webb's company constructed the base, eventually called Luke Field in honor of the World War I flying ace Frank Luke, Jr., from Phoenix. Webb's first government project had come the previous year when his company received a cost-plus contract to expand Fort Huachuca in southern Arizona. The successful completion of that project opened the door to more government contracts, including Luke Field and another military airfield near Mesa. The Mesa Military Airport—later called Williams Field—grew in size to rival Luke Field. Late in the summer of 1941, Luke was graduating its first forty-three pilots just as Williams Field welcomed its first group of trainees.[3]

In addition to the two military training facilities, Phoenix obtained a privately operated pilot instruction base north of Glendale. Known as Thunderbird Field, the base trained novice pilots in basic flying skills. The Southwest

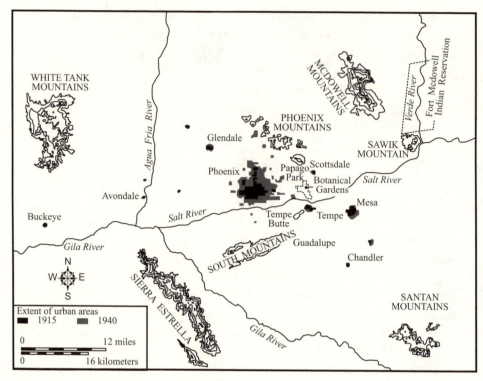

Map 7.1. Phoenix 1940. The Phoenix Basin, showing the expansion of the metropolitan area with development still limited to west of the Phoenix Mountains.

Airways Corporation operated the field and profited by charging the students tuition. The U.S. Army paid the tuition for the prospective military pilots. By the summer of 1941 the facility had 110 U.S. pilots and about 50 pilots from Britain engaged in basic flight training.[4]

The three bases in operation near Phoenix by the summer of 1941 might seem to indicate that Phoenix enjoyed the superior position of leadership in aviation over Tucson. Military organization, however, suggests otherwise. A brigadier general commanded the bomber wing headquartered at Davis-Monthan in Tucson. When the first forty-three pilots graduated at Luke Field in August 1941, Brigadier General Frank D. Lackland traveled to Phoenix from Tucson to award the pilots their wings and commissions as second lieutenants in the Army Air Corps. He also congratulated the commander at Luke Field,

Lieutenant Colonel Ennis C. Whitehead, for a job well done. Within the military hierarchy, at least, Tucson ranked higher.

Tucson received its second military airfield in the spring of 1942. The Army Air Corps established the Marana Air Base northwest of Tucson in April. The base sprawled over 2,080 acres of desert (acquired by the City of Tucson for three dollars per acre, and leased to the Army Air Corps for one dollar per year) beyond the cotton gin town of Marana. Farmers at Marana grew mostly cotton on the acreage near the river channel, relying on wells and pumps to irrigate their crops. The airfield occupied grazing land in the desert several miles from the cultivated area. Construction on the base began in April, but the military attempted to keep the project secret for several months. Local reporters tried to gain access to the site but were thwarted by military guards. Nonetheless, clouds of dust arising from the base gave evidence of feverish work. Later the air corps announced that secrecy had been maintained in case West Coast air units had come under bombing attack in the months after Pearl Harbor. In that eventuality, the units would have been evacuated to the new base at Marana. By the time the air corps activated the base in July, the fear of aerial attack on the West Coast had subsided, and the base at Marana grew through the war to become the U.S. military's largest basic pilot-training facility. During the three years of its operation, from 1942 to September 1945, the base trained more than ten thousand pilots.[5]

Both cities received additional military bases and training facilities during the war. The air corps built Ryan Field west of Tucson and Thunderbird II north of Scottsdale, and the army established—with Del Webb receiving most of the contracts—desert training facilities outside of Phoenix and Tucson. Thousands of soldiers and airmen cycled through the bases and often spent their furloughs and off time in the desert cities. The military men lounged in the cities' parks and swam in the municipal swimming pools. Officers relaxed in the resort hotels' bars. In Tucson, the El Conquistador Hotel came to serve as a surrogate officers' club for personnel from Davis-Monthan Air Field.[6]

Defense industries, also attracted to the region by the climate and open spaces, quickly followed the military bases to the desert. Another factor leading to the establishment of defense plants in Arizona was the federal policy to disperse industry inland away from possible air attacks on the West Coast. Both cities enjoyed the same environmental attributes sought by the defense industries, but Phoenix far surpassed Tucson in attracting new manufacturing plants to the city.[7]

Phoenix first received a defense plant a month before Pearl Harbor. The Goodyear Tire and Rubber Corporation had a long presence in the valley, mainly through its cotton-farming subsidiary, the Southwest Cotton Company. The Goodyear company also manufactured airplane parts. In July 1941 the government agreed to put up five hundred thousand dollars to build an airplane parts factory that would be operated by the Goodyear Aircraft Corporation. The defense plant's neighbor to the south was one of the cotton subsidiary's huge cotton farms. Paul W. Litchfield, the head of the Goodyear Corporation, had been integral to the negotiations for the defense industry location in Phoenix. Litchfield had wintered in the valley for many years and lobbied in Washington for the plant with both a corporate sensibility and an awareness of local conditions. The corporation earlier had established Litchfield Park in the western valley mainly to house cotton workers, and now another town, Goodyear, grew up around the defense plant to house the engineers and technicians. The defense plant opened in November 1941.[8]

The defense industries worked closely with the military services to make sure that the manufactured goods performed to the military's specifications. Contributing to this process of research, development, and manufacturing in Phoenix, the navy established the Litchfield Naval Air Facility in October 1943. Navy personnel at the new base collaborated with Goodyear engineers and tested results to make sure parts and aircraft performed at the desired level. In some cases the Litchfield facility received mere shells of aircraft and fitted them completely with the necessary equipment.[9]

Tucson also received a defense plant during the war. The Consolidated-Vultee Aircraft Corporation established a facility at the new civilian airport southwest of the base at Davis-Monthan. The Consolidated plant included three huge hangars for the modification of B-24 bombers flown to Tucson from their points of manufacture in Detroit, Fort Worth, and San Diego. The Ford Corporation and other manufacturing firms mass-produced B-24s during the war, but in the process of rapid assembly line construction the heavy bombers often left the plant in mediocre condition. Some were outright "clunkers." The Consolidated plant in Tucson modified the bombers to make them more serviceable for their ultimate use. It also outfitted the planes with additional equipment as improvements in avionics, radar, and other technologies came online.[10]

Fig. 7.1. Litchfield Naval Air Facility, 1946 (CP MCL 31989: courtesy Herb and Dorothy McLaughlin Photograph Collection, Arizona State University Libraries). The U.S. military, with enthusiastic assistance of Phoenix leaders, established Luke Field in 1941 and the Litchfield Naval Air Facility in 1943 in the far west valley. The air fields relied on the desert climate and open, pastoral landscapes outside of Phoenix. This 1946 photo shows the Litchfield facility after the war, when it became a storage facility for mothballed aircraft. The pastoral surroundings remained until sprawl in the 1960s began intruding into the bases' remoteness.

Strengthening its superior industrial position, Phoenix gained two additional defense plants during the war. In each case, the federal government subsidized the operation. In March and November 1942, Alcoa and AiResearch, respectively, opened plants to manufacture airplane parts in Phoenix. Alcoa's plant occupied three hundred acres at Thirty-fifth Avenue and Van Buren Street. The AiResearch operation initially moved into buildings near Sky Harbor Airport. These two facilities employed more than five thousand workers during the war and represent the advantage Phoenix achieved over Tucson in its expanding industrial base. Both cities benefited from expanding wartime production, but Phoenix gained a greater advantage and extended its lead over Tucson in size, population, and economic potential.[11]

In part the enthusiasm for prospects in both cities came from a fresh advance against the limiting environmental realities of the cities' desert surroundings. Both cities had acquired sufficient water supplies to support growth,
accomplished with the vital assistance of New Deal initiatives. Now the oppressive summer heat came under assault. Air conditioning would entice burgeoning populations of year-round residents with its promised softening of
the harsh climate. Given our current dependence on the technology of refrigeration, it is difficult to imagine a time when desert living required more accommodation than remediation of the arid surroundings.

A wide range of traditional mechanisms had allowed desert residents to
tolerate the summer heat, albeit without the convenience or efficiency of later
technological solutions. Thick adobe walls pierced infrequently by small windows insulated the interior spaces of Hispanic dwellings from the bright sunshine and soaring temperatures of summer. The transition to wood frame and
brick structures during the early days of Anglo settlement changed the fundamental character of residences and businesses, but also included traditional
means of dealing with hot temperatures. High ceilings, transoms over door-
ways, and double-hung windows provided for ample air circulation. In a style
transplanted from the deep South and Texas, wide verandas surrounded residences, often on all four sides, keeping outside walls and windows constantly
shaded. In a variation for the dry desert, one or more sides of the veranda became sleeping porches after nightfall. Wet bed sheets would be hung from the
outside eaves of the veranda. The dry desert breeze would reach the veranda
after passing through the wet sheets. As the moisture evaporated from the
sheets, the air temperature would drop as much as twenty degrees. This practical application of evaporative cooling survived well into the twentieth century, as I can attest from sleepovers at my grandmother's house in southern
Arizona in the early 1950s.

From these homespun origins, evaporative cooling led to the famous
swamp coolers: ubiquitous boxes placed on roofs or attached to outside windows of homes lacking verandas. First known as excelsior coolers, the mechanisms lowered the temperature by raising the humidity, thus leading to the
swamp cooler designation. The coolers were and remain simple contraptions
containing a water pump that saturates excelsior cooler pads suspended around
the vertical sides of the box: four sides on a roof-mounted cooler, three sides on
a window-mounted cooler. Inside the box, an electric motor and fan pull outside
air through the wet pads and distribute the cooled air through the interior

spaces. To be effective, the evaporative coolers require low ambient humidity—a common circumstance in the Arizona desert, where humidity is often single digit. The price paid for cooler air includes higher electric bills, higher interior humidity and its associated issues of dampness and mold, and less quiet in the household as the electric motor, fan, and water pump drone and hum. By the mid-1930s, these simple, often homemade, appliances, were commonplace in both cities.[12]

Refrigeration units using chemical refrigerants and mechanical compressors became available in the 1930s. Initially expensive and cumbersome, the new air-conditioning units provided clear advantages of convenience and comfort, tempered only by the costs. Included in the trade-offs were the high energy demands of the refrigeration units as well as the later concerns over polluting chemicals and gases.[13] As initial costs dropped with the spread of the technology, and the cost of electricity remained low, air conditioning became commonplace in the two cities in the 1950s. Stores and restaurants switched to refrigeration, along with hotels and motels, factories and businesses, and increasing numbers of homes.

Residents achieved at least the prospect of defeating the summer heat. You could live in an air-conditioned house, drive to and from work in an air-conditioned car, and work, shop, and go to school in climate-controlled buildings. The oppressive heat became for many a mere nuisance rather than a seasonally unavoidable burden in the desert cities. As boosters proudly proclaimed in 1940, "Phoenicians do not move to new localities when they desire a climatic change. They change the climate!"[14] Civic leaders also asserted that the newly cooled interior spaces promoted health and productivity. Absenteeism would diminish as the indigenous siesta mentality disappeared. No longer a time to nap and relax in the shade, afternoons became just another part of the work day. Lethargic and accident-prone workers—Phoenix employers had come to expect "summer mistakes"—would also perk up. Technology seemed to have finally conquered the desert environment, allowing human society to force its own concepts of time and space onto a pliant nature. Encased and insulated, human residents of the cities could at last ignore, if they chose, their desert surroundings. As the *Arizona Republic* asserted in 1940, "Phoenix is truly the air-conditioned capital of the world."[15]

The natural attributes of climate and terrain helped boosters attract business and industry, in addition to military installations, to the two cities. Critical in this effort was the assault on the summer heat. Tourists might be lured to the desert during the mild winters, but manufacturing concerns required year-round residency. An additional dilemma faced boosters in their effort to increase industrial production in the two cities: industry often came with smokestacks, and the prospect of increasing air pollution might kill the goose that laid the golden tourism egg. Cognizant of this threat to their communities' self-image as healthful and natural locales, civic leaders made it a priority to attract clean industries, primarily electronic and other high-tech manufacturers, who would bring smokeless factories to the desert. Fortunate developments in industrial production benefited city boosters in their effort to attract clean factories. No longer tied to specific locations for their natural resources, fuel supplies, or transportation networks, new electronics manufacturers were free to locate wherever they chose. Transportation was still important, but the smaller finished products could be packaged and shipped via trucks or planes. As a result, railroad connections diminished in significance. Likewise, manufacturers of electronics and other products lost their connection to highly capitalized plants in established industrial centers in the East and the Great Lakes region. Free to pull up stakes and locate virtually anywhere executives chose, many postwar industries became footloose.

Workers in these new manufacturing plants tended to be highly skilled. The electronics companies hired engineers by the score and relied on colleges and universities to churn out class after class of these new entry-level workers. Even the assembly staff working on the shop floor had to have a relatively sophisticated technical understanding and training. With higher skills, workers found themselves in a seller's market. Corporations had to compete for quality engineers and technicians. Wages and salaries increased, and corporations felt the need to offer increased benefit packages as well as other amenities. Factories became campuses. Executives came to be concerned with recreational and lifestyle opportunities for workers. In 1953, University of Arizona researchers queried Motorola executives about their decision to locate in Phoenix in 1948. In their response, the executives identified the city's "outstanding climate and its nation-wide reputation as a resort and health center" as an important factor.[16]

Without air conditioning, however, the desert cities could hardly expect their resort image to translate into industrial expansion. The same executives who noted Phoenix's resort identity also referred to "only one drawback." Specifically, the summers of 1951 and 1952 had been "almost intolerable."[17] Daniel Noble, Motorola vice president, explicitly connected the advances in cooling technology to the transformation of the desert into a reasonable year-round work environment. He also favorably compared the desert's summer heat to the north's winter cold:

> The agreement is quite general among the [Motorola] families that they will take the four months of summer weather in preference to the winters in the north and in the east. And they point out that a hundred-mile drive north from Phoenix will take them into the cool, wooded mountain areas of pine trees and streams. Where, they ask, in the north or in the east, can they drive out of the snow and ice and the cold in a hundred miles? And then there are the coolers to condition the house; it is a matter of adjusting the mental attitude (with the same straightforward approach one takes in the north and east when providing for heat on a wintry day) to accept heat in Phoenix as something to be dealt with, and to provide for refrigeration cooling during the comparably small number of hot, humid days. . . . Motorola management feels that refrigeration cooling in the plant and in the home is the complete solution to the Phoenix summer heat problem. . . . The occasional superheated periods are as easy to deal with as the short runs of subzero weather in the north. Refrigeration cooling in the home has transformed Phoenix into a year-round city of delightful living.[18]

Of course other important factors contributed to the decision by executives to move their corporate operations to Arizona. The first three defense plants had been subsidized by the federal government. In the postwar years, state leaders continued the effort to attract industry by softening the tax burden on manufacturing industries. For example, in 1955 the state legislature modified the state sales tax, repealing the 2 percent tax on manufactured products sold to the federal government. As a result new corporations such as Sperry-Rand moved to Phoenix, and existing defense industries in both cities expanded their local plants.[19]

Historians such as Bradford Luckingham and Thomas Sheridan see the tax reform bill as a clear indication of the Phoenix advantage over Tucson, referring to the opposition to the bill in the state legislature that arose among representatives from Tucson and Pinal County. Luckingham says Tucson harbored "considerable opposition from established interests" who resisted the effort to recruit defense industries. This is somewhat misleading. The question motivating debate about the tax reform bill concerned the displacement of the tax burden from defense industries and the transference of the tax burden to existing industries, particularly mining. Huge copper-mining operations were located in Pima and Pinal counties. The fear was that the tax benefit for the defense industries would create an additional tax liability for the mines. Phoenix business and political leaders pushed their tax reform agenda with single-minded determination, while Tucson officials advocated a more diversified approach that would continue to support traditional industrial activities.[20]

Motorola was one of the biggest, but many more corporations moved to the desert cities during the postwar boom. Phoenix acquired hundreds of factories during the 1950s. In the midst of this expansion, manufacturing surpassed agriculture as the leading source of income in Phoenix; from less than $5 million in 1940, manufacturing income increased to more than $435 million in 1963. Agriculture slipped to second, and tourism occupied third place as a source of income. During the boom, manufacturing employment tripled in Phoenix, as corporations such as Motorola, General Electric, and Sperry-Rand moved to the Valley of the Sun. By 1960, Motorola alone operated three plants in Phoenix and employed more than three thousand workers. The company had the largest payroll in the city.[21]

Tucson shared in the expansion of industry during the postwar boom, but to a lesser extent than Phoenix. In 1951 Howard Hughes established the state's largest defense plant in Tucson, just south of the municipal airport and Davis-Monthan Air Base. Hughes executives cited the natural attributes of the desert city—open spaces, clear dry air, recreational benefits—as reasons for locating in Tucson. By 1959, Hughes Aircraft employed more than five thousand workers, making the Hughes operation the largest employer in the state. Unfortunately for Tucson, the Hughes plant was Tucson's only large defense manufacturer. Of the state's top five manufacturing operations, Tucson had the first, but Phoenix had the next four: Motorola and AiResearch each employed more than three thousand workers, Reynolds Metals employed more than two thousand, and Goodyear Aircraft employed seventeen hundred at its Litchfield Park plant. By 1960, Phoenix had more than five hundred factories employing almost thirty-one thousand workers, which accounted for 63 percent of Arizona's total manufacturing employment. Tucson had 130 factories employing eighty-seven hundred workers. Tucson's share of the state's manufacturing employment stood at 18 percent.[22]

Environmental factors such as climate and geographic location played critical roles in supporting urban growth in both cities. With growth came

Fig. 7.2. Motorola in Phoenix (Arizona Historical Society/Tucson, AHS Photo Number 55661). Motorola established its first manufacturing plant in Phoenix in 1948 and continued to expand its Phoenix operations through the 1960s. The electronics firm typified the type of industrial manufacturing that Phoenix boosters most desired. Free from belching smoke stacks and employing hundreds of highly paid engineers, the Motorola plant represented the economic base to Phoenix's advance to metropolitan status.

consequences, however. The urban expansion of the cities greatly affected the surrounding environment. Tucson's smaller growth rate exerted less pressure on the city's natural surroundings, while the exponential expansion of Phoenix placed tremendous pressure on the natural props for the metropolitan structures. Once again, the status of municipal water supplies sheds light on the evolving relationship with nature in the desert cities.

Tucson's water system steadily expanded in the years following the war. Depression-era improvements had carried the city through the war, but increases in population and size accomplished by postwar annexations required additional supplies and infrastructure expansion. Postwar sprawl in Tucson, as in Phoenix, was largely a private endeavor. Developers simply acquired parcels of land and placed subdivisions down with varying degrees of care and skill. In

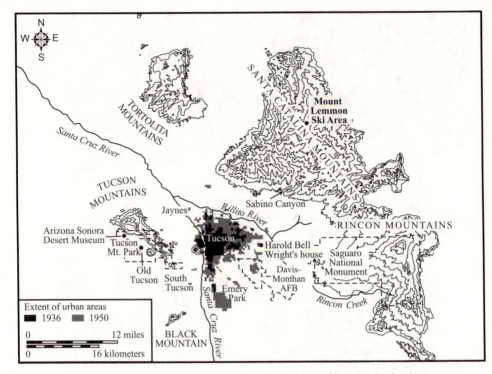

Map 7.2. Tucson 1950. Sprawl in Tucson filled the basin, and low-density development covered the foothills of the Santa Catalina and Tucson Mountains. Already, large preserves of natural landscapes existed in the Saguaro National Monument and Tucson Mountain Park.

many cases, the suburban neighborhoods appeared outside the city limits and therefore were free of city zoning regulations. County controls were modest, to say the least. Also, the neighborhoods were beyond the reach of existing water and sewer service. Developers in Tucson often found it most economical simply to dig a well capped with a pump within the confines of the subdivision. The builder then created a private distribution system to serve the development's homeowners. In many annexations the city acquired private water systems along with the homeowners. When these were suitably constructed and maintained, the municipal utility simply incorporated the new subdivisions into the city system. In other cases, however, the city acquired private systems in poor condition. In steps that ranged from painless to contentious, cooperative to litigious, the city system grew through the 1950s by hooking up individual residents and entire neighborhoods. In 1945, the city system relied on groundwater supplied by nineteen wells. Thirty-three wells, including many formerly private wells, served city residents in 1950. By the end of the 1950s, the city had acquired forty-three private water systems.[23]

The expansion of Tucson's water utility through the 1950s required two major bond issues, which passed in 1951 and 1953 without major contention. In each case the bonds provided for expanding the city system as well as building new reservoirs and acquiring new wells. Water rates also went up slightly. The construction of mains, laterals, and reservoirs took place within a continuum of experience; in this sense, the bond issues contained little that was revolutionary or controversial. One aspect of the system improvements did, however, constitute a new development. Tucson in 1952 returned to the process of acquiring agricultural land for the purpose of transferring irrigation water to domestic purposes. The first of the decade's bond issues included funds earmarked for the acquisition of farmland in nearby Avra Valley. The city continued to purchase farmland to acquire new wells for the city until 1957. Then, just as might be expected after the city's first such effort in 1929, a legal confrontation developed between the city and a corporate farm. The Midvale Farms Company protested the city's actions before the state land commissioner. Claiming a prior appropriation of the groundwater in the Santa Cruz River floodplain, the company argued that the city's plan to dig new wells in the area would deprive them of their resource. The land commissioner agreed, and the city in December agreed to the farm company's right to six thousand acre feet of water per year from the floodplain aquifer.

Competition over groundwater in Tucson contributed to the further development of a conservation ethos. Given the reliance on groundwater alone, supplies always seemed to teeter on the verge of inadequacy. Management of the scarce resource became the hallmark of Tucson's water policy. Tucson would continue to grow in the coming years, and groundwater withdrawals increased accordingly. As the water table dropped and city wells either deepened or went dry, conservation became a reasonable component of the city's water regimen. That policy developed more fully later, but Tucson's contemporary water ethos has its roots in the overdrafts of groundwater and declining water tables that accelerated during the postwar boom.

Likewise in Phoenix, the remarkable growth of the city placed additional pressure on the water utility to keep pace with the boom. The Phoenix water system continued to rely on the Verde River pipeline—improved with the assistance of New Deal subsidies—supplemented with wells in the city during peak-demand periods. Well water in Phoenix continued to disappoint city residents with its alkaline taste. As always the solution to the water quality problem in Phoenix was to increase the supply of sweet-tasting Verde River water. With the exponential growth, however, city managers struggled to keep up with demand. Crisis management took root, with emergency measures and last-minute improvements causing the city water system to lurch uncertainly into the 1950s.[24]

City leaders in Phoenix could hardly be blamed for failing to prepare for the postwar growth rates. One newspaper report summed up the dilemma: "Although many of the city's wartime industries are closed down, the water consumption figure has increased more rapidly since the close of the war than ever before." Specifically, water consumption in Phoenix had increased by 5 million gallons in one year, from 1945 to 1946. By April 1946, peak demand for water in the city had reached 59 million gallons a day. Unfortunately, the maximum flow of water through the Verde River pipeline remained at 45 million gallons a day. The shortfall could be made up by well water, but that resulted in the mixing of foul-tasting well water with the clear Verde water. The city's three reservoirs, capable of storing 35 million gallons, also provided coverage during shortfalls, but the limited capacity of the reservoirs compared to the peak demand made the overall water situation tenuous at best. Other factors also contributed to the crisis mentality. Realtors predicted that thirty-six hundred new homes would be constructed in Phoenix during 1946. The water department projected an average of two hundred or more new water connections every month.[25]

As the heat of the desert spring began to mount in 1946, consumers noticed precipitous drops in water pressure during peak afternoon periods. Water in taps would turn to a trickle. If the fire department opened one fire hydrant and attempted to open the next hydrant in line, the second hydrant would suck air and diminish the flow from the first hydrant. The desired water pressure was a consistent fifty pounds per square inch; shortfalls during peak-demand periods would cause decreases to twenty-two pounds per square inch. Of necessity the city began preparing plans and bond issues to increase water supplies and fund system improvements.[26]

The city first contracted with an engineering firm from Kansas to study the water system and offer recommendations for increased supply and system improvements. To pave the way for acceptance of the project, city leaders re-minded residents that war needs necessarily had superseded water department projects since 1941. System shortfalls now could be addressed, whereas only nine months earlier no such project could even be contemplated. The Kansas engineers presented their report on May 27, 1946. Recommendations included a new well field on the Verde River, a new reservoir in Phoenix, and various other system improvements. The report suggested that the city embark on a twenty-year development program with an estimated cost of 10 million dollars. Balking at the price tag, the Phoenix mayor appointed an advisory committee composed of two bankers and three engineers to study the Kansas report. Eventually the committee recommended a downsized program with a cost about half that of the initial recommendations.[27]

In the meantime, water shortfalls and pressure drops remained a constant problem. To temporarily increase the supply of water, the city in June con-tracted with the Salt River Project (SRP) to use an SRP well within the city limits during emergency periods. The initial arrangement lasted six months, but the city and the SRP renewed the agreement repeatedly. Phoenix mayor Ray Busey and his staff continued work on the water plan and bonds as they searched for stopgap measures. In August SRP officials made a suggestion dur-ing their meetings with city leaders that could result in a permanent solution to the city's water issues. The SRP proposed that the city spend eight hundred thousand dollars to build headgates on the spillway of Horseshoe Dam on the Verde River. The headgates would provide for additional water storage behind the proposed taller dam. In return for its financial contribution to the project, the city would be allowed to use an additional twenty-five thousand acre feet of Verde River water, enough to meet its increasing needs.[28]

Complicated negotiations ensued. The dam had been built by Phelps-Dodge Corporation to provide water necessary for its Morenci copper mine. Since the dam's storage of water would affect downstream users, Phelps-Dodge had worked out agreements with the SRP and other downstream entities. The City of Phoenix also claimed a share of the water, and so the Horseshoe Dam had been constructed within a legal web of water appropriations regulating every drop stored behind the dam. Now the city and the SRP were proposing to store more water behind the dam. With so many interested parties—including virtually any water user downstream from the dam—the city-SRP plan faced many obstacles.[29] City voters approved a bond including funds for the headgates on November 19, 1946. It then took more than two years for the city to obtain all the necessary permissions and legal clearances to move forward with the dam project. Culmination of the approval process finally came in January 1949 when the state land commissioner okayed the headgate project. Construction began soon thereafter, and in June 1950 workers completed the spillway additions. With the increased height of the dam and headgates, Horseshoe Dam could now store more than 140,000 acre feet of water. Unfortunately for the City of Phoenix, a severe drought accompanied the completion of the project. When the new structures became available to store water, the surface of the lake rested far below the spillway. Eight years of drought had left only thirteen hundred acre feet—less than 10 percent of capacity—in storage behind the dam.[30]

On paper, at least, the city had sufficient water to meet the ever-increasing demand. The 1946 bond projects also included infrastructure upgrades that allowed the water utility to deliver water to consumers with consistent pressure and reliability—as long as supply kept pace. The city was mechanically capable of drawing as much Verde River water as it needed, but legal restrictions regulated the city's draw. The SRP had the task of monitoring the city's draft, since all of the Verde River's flow legally had been allotted among the downstream users. By the summer of 1951, the city's draw of water had reached a critical stage. On July 4, 1951, local newspapers informed residents that Phoenix had used sixteen thousand acre feet of water in the first six months of the year, leaving it only four thousand acre feet from the Verde river for the rest of the year. As city leaders began warning residents that water rationing might be necessary, officials looked to the SRP for assistance. The agricultural interests in the SRP were feeling just as pinched by the drought as the city was, and no easy solution presented itself. Bill Pickrell, president of the SRP Water Users Association, warned the city early in July that at its current rate of withdrawal, the city could only take water from the Verde River for ten more days.[31]

Phoenix had arrived at a critical moment in its relationship with the desert, but at this crossroads in its water policy only a few believed that the time had come at last for a conservation ethic in the state's largest city. The water ethos in the city is exemplified by events in the spring of 1946, when a crisis in rising demand threatened to derail the city's expansion. As city manager Odd Halseth reported, part of the rising demand resulted from waste:

City fathers still are harassed by citizens who use water to excess in their coolers. They still are bothered by those who turn on the hose at night and leave it until morning—despite publicity about the water shortage.

Steps to correct those conditions are difficult to take—and there's always someone else who crops up with a midnight-running hose.

The answer lies in more reservoirs, more pipelines, more supply, extending the grid system inside the city—and that can be done only with a bond issue.[32]

Halseth's solution—more, more, more—expresses the Phoenix water ethos. Conservation was sometimes discussed or suggested, but the acquisition of greater supplies of water always seemed eminently possible in Phoenix. In 1951 it remained just as possible as it had been in 1946 and earlier. The SRP controlled much more water than the city could ever use, if only an agreement could be reached to share the bounty produced by the federal reclamation project. Negotiations between the city and the SRP started on July 5, 1951, and continued over the next five months. The discussions started during calls for conservation and heightened concern for wasteful practices. But ultimately the crisis of July was averted by the most natural of circumstances. The summer monsoon arrived in mid-July and continued to thunder and roar until all the rivers flowed and all the reservoirs filled. Once again, Phoenix had dodged the conservation bullet.[33]

Negotiations between the city and SRP culminated in early 1952 with an agreement that allowed the city to acquire ample water supplies. As Phoenix spread across the valley—in a process dating back decades—subdivisions often replaced farmers' fields. Since the SRP included most of the Salt River Valley, many of these new suburban residents occupied both City of Phoenix and SRP land. A legal obligation came with owning SRP land, namely, the payment of fees that went toward the repayment of the federal reclamation project. The fees were the recompense required by the original reclamation legislation: in return for the irrigation water landowners would pay for the project that provided the water. Since this involved liens and assessments, we may assume that the suburban homeowners would have learned of these obligations at the closing of their mortgages, if not sooner. But since the assessments on subdivided lots were small, and the SRP lacked the ability prior to computers to calculate the bills, send the statements, and collect the payments for tens of thousands of new minuscule accounts, many homeowners never received a bill or simply failed to pay their assessment obligation to SRP. Furthermore, homeowners never received irrigation water. The city water utility served the homeowners occupying SRP land. The unused irrigation water reverted to use by SRP farmers.[34]

The city and the SRP reached agreement early in 1952. The city agreed to pay the reclamation-related assessments and fees for all the SRP land subdivided within the city. The settling up came to two hundred thousand dollars, and the city agreed to continue paying the annual fees thereafter. In return the city received the former irrigation water that previously had reverted to the SRP farmers. Since homes and families, even pursuing the most egregiously wasteful practices, used much less water than did agriculture, the city obtained a bountiful supply of excess water that would increase with every new subdivision and annexation that included SRP land. At last the future of water supplies in Phoenix seemed secure. Only the issue of water quality remained.[35]

The bountiful quantity of water required treatment prior to delivery to households, and this placed a mild burden on the city water utility. With the agreement between the city and the SRP in 1952, the city began the process of acquiring the land necessary for the construction of the Squaw Peak Water Treatment Plant. The plant allowed Phoenix to take water directly from the Arizona Canal for delivery into the city system. Construction on the plant began in November 1952, and the SRP water started flowing into the city system early in 1953.[36]

The Squaw Peak plant was the first of many water treatment facilities built by the city during the sprawling boom times. Although a financial burden accrued to the city in the construction of multiple treatment plants, the city benefited from the experience gained in the treatment of mineral-rich water before it reached homeowners. In contrast, Tucson's groundwater required little if any treatment prior to delivery to customers. When mineral-rich Central Arizona Project (CAP) water arrived in Phoenix and Tucson in the 1990s, the outcomes were very different. The decades of experience with water treatment by the Phoenix water department turned out to be very useful when the treatment of CAP water became an issue. Phoenix adapted to CAP water with little fanfare or difficulty. In Tucson CAP water arrived amid controversy and litigation. The negative outcomes in Tucson resulted, in part, from the lack of experience among Tucson water system engineers and managers. Phoenix water managers may have complained from time to time in the 1950s and 1960s about the cost of building and maintaining the treatment plants. The benefit from their experience compounded over time and matured to significant use-fulness decades in the future.

Phoenix failed to achieve its goal to be declared a metropolitan area in the 1940 census, but with a growth rate of 63.3 percent through the 1940s, the city's population reached 106,818 in 1950. Ironically, the census bureau lowered its thresholds of population required for recognition as a metropolitan area to fifty thousand in 1950.[37] If that had been the criterion in 1940, Phoenix would have reached the coveted label ten years earlier. In 1950, Phoenix at last achieved official recognition of its metropolitan status. The census policy proved a boon for Phoenix boosters, long pursuing the goal of regional superiority. Tucson had not achieved the required threshold of population, and so, even though the city possessed a significant fringe population outside its city limits, the census counted those fringe residents as county, not city, inhabitants. Phoenix boosters were quick to advertise their advantage, seeking to parlay their metropolitan identity into even greater levels of growth and prosperity during the postwar boom.

The 1960 census reported remarkable growth during the decade, which gave statistical verification of the boom and sprawl conditions that had confronted city leaders during the 1950s. Both Tucson and Phoenix experienced growth rates surpassing 300 percent. The anomalous spurt in population size and geographic expansion pushed Phoenix further into the realm of metropolitan status, while Tucson's phenomenal growth at last marked the city's maturation to big-city existence. Although many Tucsonans clung to the concept of their city as a small town, the sprawl and congestion caused by increasing population levels confronted Tucson residents with an urban reality that challenged cherished images of their community.

Leaving Tucson? Take a Friend

Tucson's growth rate of 368.4 percent during the 1950s actually surpassed Phoenix's growth rate by more than 57 percent. Nonetheless, the population of Phoenix was more than double that of Tucson in 1960, maintaining a level of superiority first established in 1950. Phoenix had marched self-confidently toward regional supremacy and continued its pursuit of ever-greater metropolitan status through the ensuing decades. To some this drive for expansion conformed to time-honored and commonsense policies, while to others the drive for greater size and population came to represent a sort of Malthusian tragedy. The debate created the first crack in the progrowth consensus in Phoenix. A crosstown freeway proposal unexpectedly failed, and developers found their access to building sites on Camelback Mountain cut off when the city acquired and preserved the scenic location for public use. Despite these nascent obstacles to further development the Phoenix metro region continued to advance over the desert. Sprawl continued apace, and water usage remained a matter of conspicuous consumption.

In Tucson, some leaders bemoaned their city's second-class status in the state and pushed for greater efforts to expand the population and local economic base. Others in Tucson focused on the city's Old Pueblo identity, seeking to preserve the traditional and historic uniqueness of the town, which rampant growth seemed to threaten. Bumper stickers appeared in the 1960s inquiring and suggesting, "Leaving Tucson? Take a friend." Unfortunately for the preservationists, few residents heeded the call. Sprawl continued to advance over the basin floor and beyond. As in Phoenix, voters in Tucson refused to support the construction of a crosstown freeway. Unlike in Phoenix however, the defeat in Tucson surprised few. Residents of the Old Pueblo sought to preserve elements of small-town culture despite the persistent sprawl of the city. In one example of the effort to promote small-town neighborliness, the Tucson Meet Yourself program flourished for a few years in the 1980s. Once a month downtown streets became pedestrian walkways lined with street vendors, musicians, and food stalls. Young and old, families with babies in strollers—every class and race and ethnic group seemed to turn out for the good times. Eventually the event succumbed to common urban circumstances of aggressive panhandling, bold and public alcohol and drug use, and generally declining downtown conditions. Tucson's contradictory self-image became entrenched: small and intimate as the Old Pueblo while at the same time a sprawling, post-modern desert metropolis.

Census statistics give a numerical indication of the remarkable population growth during the postwar boom in the two cities. Phoenix maintained its size advantage, more than doubling Tucson's population, over the four decades from 1950 to 1980. Nonetheless, Tucson's expansion to more than two hundred thousand people in 1960 moved the community clearly into metropolitan status. Both cities continued to grow after the boom years ended, although growth returned to more typical rates for the two communities.

The physical size of the cities increased along with the population. Both cities maintained an attachment to low-density, sprawling expansion. Rarely with any planning or governmental oversight, new subdivisions multiplied across the desert floor. Claims for healthful lifestyles and natural domestic settings accompanied the booming expansion, even as air pollution and visual clutter increased. Finally traffic congestion arose in both cities as reliance on individual automobiles for commuting and personal travel across the urbanized area brought both cities near gridlock. Both communities faced the dilemma of

8.1 Population growth in Phoenix and Tucson, 1950–1980							
	Population			*Rate of growth (%)*			
1950	*1960*	*1970*	*1980*	*1940–1950*	*1950–1960*	*1960–1970*	*1970–1980*
Phoenix 106,818	439,170	584,303	789,704	63.3	311.1	33	35.2
Tucson 45,454	212,892	262,433	330,537	23.4	368.4	23.3	26

Population figures derived from U.S. Bureau of the Census, *Census of the United States*, 1950, 1:3–7; 1960, 1A:4–7; 1970, 1A, Sec. 1:4–10; 1980, 1, part 4A:4–12.

trying to balance continued growth while maintaining a beneficial relationship with their fragile desert environments.

During the postwar boom Phoenix sprawled mainly west. Developers followed the lead of master builder William Levitt by establishing scores of low-density suburban neighborhoods in the Valley of the Sun. The chief architect of this pattern of development in Phoenix was John F. Long. Thousands of job-seeking immigrants, many of them World War II veterans who had traveled through the Southwest during their military service, flooded into the valley seeking to join in the postwar Sunbelt boom. Long in part met the demand for low-cost housing by establishing the village of Maryvale (named after his wife) on 37.8 square miles in the western valley in the mid-1950s. Long continued to develop the area through the 1960s. The population by 1970 was 66,136, almost universally housed in detached, single-family homes. Typical houses in the village had three bedrooms and were placed on small lots. Houses built in 1960 were selling for a modest sixteen thousand dollars in 1969.[1]

Long was just one of the developers who benefited from the conversion of agricultural land to domestic purposes. As the urban area spread progressively west, property values increased in the neighboring agricultural plots. Eventually the value of the farmers' property would surpass the profit potential of cultivated crops. At that point farmers would sell their land to developers and move their agricultural pursuits farther out into the desert. In some cases land values increased one-hundred-fold. By 1977 builders were converting more than fifteen square miles a year of agricultural land into low-density, single-family homes. In one example in Deer Valley, a citrus grower turned 454 acres of groves into a multifaceted development: 90.6-acre shopping mall, 199-acre commercial district, and 164.3-acre residential development.[2]

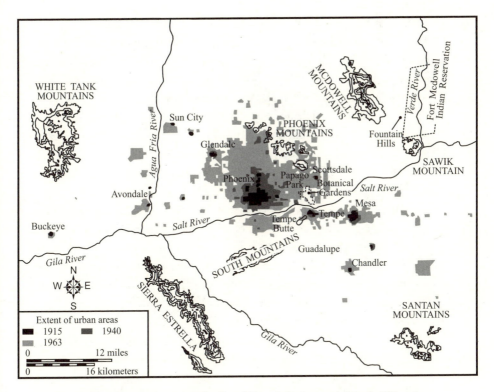

Map 8.1. Phoenix 1963. By the 1960s, the City of Phoenix had expanded to abut its metropolitan neighbors. Annexation wars accompanied the expansion as bordering communities
sought to control suburban development on the few remaining open spaces within the metropolitan area.

Suburban lifestyles took on fabled qualities, and Phoenix boosters prided
themselves on the community's seemingly ubiquitous swimming pools and
tennis courts, although in truth these accoutrements were the privilege of
the wealthy. The owners of relatively low-cost housing settled for a patch of
grass in the yard and a swing set for the kids in the back. To some the Phoenix
brand of suburban culture became ultrasuburban. As an eastern reporter noted,
"There's a land conscious mentality in Phoenix. People want their yards." Immigrants were also fleeing urban problems associated with more densely settled eastern and midwestern cities. As one observer noted, "People who come
to Phoenix don't want to move into an inner city. They've come to get away
from that." Nearby mountains provided ample opportunities for boating and

fishing, hiking and hunting, and skiing in the winter. The outdoor playground image abounded in booster publications produced by longtime residents but also flourished in the minds of recent arrivals. As prominent local business leader Karl Eller stated in 1974, "I like the Phoenix way of life—the open air, open community type of living." Another businessman gave his own spin on the ultrasuburban lifestyle in 1975: "Employees work from seven till three and can be home in twenty minutes, swimming, playing tennis or golf, relaxing with their families." As Bradford Luckingham recalled, "Often a new housing development in the Phoenix area would be completely sold before there were any houses, streets, sewers, or utility lines on the land."[3]

Both push and pull factors contributed to the tremendous growth in the city. Declining job prospects in the old Rust Belt compared with the expanding job market in Phoenix—the unemployment rate was only 5 percent in 1980—caused much of the immigration. The desirability of desert lifestyles also pulled many new residents into the city. A study in 1980 sought to identify the causes of immigration into Phoenix and found that 22 percent of new arrivals came seeking to enjoy the desert climate. A slightly higher percentage, 29 percent, gave better job prospects as their reason for immigrating to Phoenix. Other new residents cited health concerns, nearby relatives, and a "change of lifestyle" as the reason for their move.[4]

The expanding economy in Phoenix benefited from both the Rust Belt decline and the increasing costs of conducting business in Southern California. Inflated property costs and the increasing congestion in Los Angeles created an industrial and manufacturing migration into Arizona. Many businesses and their employees rejoiced at the lower costs of living and relatively smog-free environment in Phoenix. As one executive remarked in 1978, "I talked recently to some friends in companies on the West Coast and they are thoroughly disgusted with the high cost of land and housing and other problems of being there, such as smog, dense traffic and the fact that they have to live so far from work. They all said they would like to move to Arizona."[5] Although indications of deteriorating conditions—smog and traffic congestion, for example—were evident in Phoenix by 1970, circumstances in the desert city remained preferable to the outlandish conditions in Los Angeles. As the phenomenon increased in the 1980s, observers remarked that Phoenix benefited from this California Slopover.

Rather than following a rationally formulated plan, the remarkable growth in Phoenix conformed to the dictates of entrepreneurial imperatives: developers chose building sites that would maximize their profits. At the most basic level, the cost of land determined a subdivision's viability and profitability. What resulted was a hodgepodge of leapfrogging development. The suburbanized landscape stretched across the desert valley, subdivisions interspersed with farmers' fields. Maricopa County remained a prominent producer of agricultural products. In 1980 it still ranked as the fifth-largest agricultural county in the nation, although increasingly agriculture retreated in the face of urbanization. Neighborhoods grew and spread, but the residue of farming remained visible within the sprawling city. Calls for infill arose in the 1970s, and even the mayor at the time, Margaret Hance, trumpeted the call. With the prevalent probusiness mood in the city, however, nothing came of the effort and the dictates of the free market continued to drive sprawl in Phoenix.[6]

Annexations provided a political framework for the expansion of the city that mitigated against the purely economic, profit-seeking, and basically incoherent pattern of sprawl in Phoenix. The City of Phoenix pursued an aggressive annexation program consistently through the postwar boom and into the 1980s. During the peak period of expansion from 1950 to 1965, the City of Phoenix instituted forty-three annexations, which added 227.8 square miles and 299,173 people to the city.[7] In 1970, Phoenix ranked as the twentieth-largest city in the country, with a population of 584,303. By 1980 the city had grown in population to almost 790,000—ranked ninth in the country—and reached a physical size of almost 330 square miles.[8]

Annexations at times generated resistance, and the annexation wars during the 1960s were particularly acrimonious.[9] The combatants were Phoenix on one side and Scottsdale and Tempe on the other. The first controversy began in March 1960 when the Tempe City Council launched a preemptive strike to avoid being surrounded and cut off by the expansion of Phoenix. As the former mayor of Tempe recalled, "A year or two after Phoenix annexed out to Forty Eighth Street (thereupon becoming contiguous to Tempe at its northwest boundary) rumors began that Phoenix was getting ready to move toward the southeast. This would have cut Tempe off almost completely. Tempe saw red. It became an emotional thing to some extent. Some councilmen saw Phoenix as a monster, out to grab cities."[10]

To forestall the next Phoenix move to the southeast, Tempe took an unusual action. On March 17, 1960, the Tempe City Council annexed a strip of land three feet wide between the Phoenix and Tempe city limits. The strip extended thirty-seven miles along the western border of Tempe and the southeastern border of Phoenix. The three-foot annexation generated protest from Phoenix and from Chandler, Tempe's neighbor to the south. Chandler leaders considered the Tempe move to be potentially threatening to their own expansion. Opponents of the Tempe action sought relief in the courts, and on June 1, 1961, a judge overturned the annexation. Having lost in the courts, Tempe leaders acquiesced to the expansion of Phoenix. No further legal challenges or counterannexation ploys materialized in Tempe, although hurt feelings remained and tempers smoldered in Tempe for years to come.[11]

Another argument over the expansion of Phoenix appeared in early 1961 as the controversy between Phoenix and Tempe worked its way through the courts. Scottsdale had incorporated in 1951 and had grown in population and size through the decade. By 1960 the town was seeking expansion to the west just as Phoenix leaders began to eye expansion to the east. Most of the Phoenix sprawl was going in the opposite direction toward the west, but in the southeastern move toward Tempe and in this small eastward push toward Scottsdale, the city was moving in virtually all directions simultaneously. Controversy arose in 1961 when both Phoenix and Scottsdale sought to annex the same piece of property near Fortieth Street. First Scottsdale annexed the area on January 25, 1961, having gathered the signatures of 53 percent of the residents of the area. The City of Phoenix immediately protested the annexation, pushing its claims in the courts. On behalf of the city, the Arizona attorney general filed a motion in the superior court challenging the legality of Scottsdale's annexation, and on June 5, 1961, the court ruled in favor of Phoenix. Immediately after the ruling, Phoenix annexed the area. As Scottsdale's mayor, M. E. Kimsey later explained, "We had fifty three per cent signers but lost [in the court] on a technicality. . . . In the meantime Phoenix jumped in and claimed fifty per cent signers and annexed right away. How they could get fifty per cent when we already had fifty three per cent is hard to figure."[12]

Hackles had been raised, and the bitterness caused a newspaper editorialist on October 5, 1961, to urge reconciliation: "We live too close together to be always quarreling." Relative peace reigned for a few months, but then another battle over annexation arose between Phoenix and Scottsdale. In 1962, a

Phoenix newspaper gave a succinct account, with the boldfaced headline, "Move Set to Block Scottsdale":

> The annexation war between Scottsdale and Phoenix was renewed yesterday when two annexations were rushed through by the Phoenix City Council in a surprise special meeting. . . . The (nine and three-fourths square mile) area now contains only 30 persons but is in the path of suburban development. Both Phoenix and Scottsdale want to expand this area. . . . [Phoenix] Mayor Sam Mardian said the proposed City of Scottsdale's annexation, scheduled to receive final Scottsdale City Council action Monday triggered the counterannexation by Phoenix. . . . "There is no question in our mind that this area is in the normal path of growth of the City of Phoenix," Mardian said.

This time Scottsdale sought relief in the courts, successfully obtaining a restraining order halting the annexations by Phoenix. Over the next two years the two cities negotiated "spheres of annexation influence," and finally reached agreement in January 1964. Included in the agreement was the promise by Phoenix to rescind its emergency counterannexation, and in April 1964 the city council voted to deannex the contested area.[13]

Phoenix had prevailed against Tempe and reached a stalemate agreement with Scottsdale. Throughout the valley, however, Phoenix continued to grow and sprawl, with little subsequent opposition or resistance. Eventually the Phoenix city limits came to encompass most of the Salt River basin, with the neighboring satellite towns in the valley surrounded and frozen in their geographic shape.

Of course, the municipal water system in Phoenix had to keep pace with the annexations and increases in population. With the 1952 agreement with the Salt River Project, the City of Phoenix had acquired a bountiful surplus of water. The agreement allowed the city to use the water provided for each acre of land within the SRP area as subdivisions within the city limits replaced farmers' fields. The transition from cultivation to domestic uses netted the city a huge surplus of water that could be used to support additional growth. With the supply problem solved, all that remained for the city was to increase the capacity of the city's water treatment plants to allow processing of increasing amounts of SRP water for domestic purposes.

The population growth on the west side required the construction of a new water treatment plant. In late 1961 the city acquired the land for the Deer

Valley Water Treatment Plant. The design and construction phases of the project took almost three years. In September 1964 the plant began processing 80 million gallons of SRP water per day for the use of homeowners in the vicinity of the plant site at Thirty-first Avenue and the Arizona Canal. The City of Phoenix also engaged in improvements of existing treatment plants. The Squaw Peak facility received a facelift that increased its capacity by 20 million gallons a day. In addition, the city built reservoirs to store treated water at the Squaw Peak, Shaw Butte, and Deer Valley water plants.[14]

The regularized water supply allowed Phoenix leaders to avoid instituting conservation measures and contributed to the feeling in Phoenix that desert conditions provided clear benefits with no downsides or liabilities. Conservation of water resources became a topic of discussion in the late 1970s, and some city leaders and community activists encouraged the city's population to recognize their own naturally parched circumstances. In Phoenix, however, water conservation failed to materialize. Encouraging pronouncements issued from city hall urging city residents to install water-saving devices in their homes as well as publicizing the benefits of desert landscaping over grass lawns. In addition, public and private institutions investigated the use of waste water for irrigating purposes, as well as the use of efficient drip-irrigation systems for landscaping. The bountiful supply made it difficult in Phoenix to generate support for such measures. Conservation was a tough sell. Eventually the environmental realities of desert life would impinge on the community ethos in Phoenix, but the 1970s and 1980s saw only halfhearted and timid movements toward water conservation.

This stands in stark contrast to the clear recognition of scarcity in water supplies in Tucson and the state. In 1980 the state legislature passed the Arizona Groundwater Management Act. Concern had mounted that growing urban areas were reaching a point of competition with agricultural areas. In 1980 cities and industry used 8 percent of the water consumed in Arizona, mines used less than 3 percent, and agriculture gulped up 89 percent.[15] The depletion of groundwater had become alarming, and the federal government recognized the problem. Part of the impetus for the groundwater act came from Secretary of the Interior Cecil Andrus. The secretary announced that funding for the Central Arizona Project would be canceled unless the state created a plan for the restoration and regulation of groundwater supplies. The state legislature created the required plan in 1980, but the legislation papered over the lack of consensus in the state over distribution of water resources. Farmers claimed that the act would destroy agriculture in the valley and endanger the entire nation's food supply. They even suggested that tourism would suffer in Phoenix when "fragrant citrus groves and green fields are replaced by high-rise buildings and parking lots."[16]

Further complicating the water politics in the state was the lack of uniformity in water use by urban areas. The cultural distance between Tucson and Phoenix has much to do with the cities' varying consciousness about water. By the mid-1980s, Tucson had established a long record of water conservation policies, while Phoenix persisted in ignoring the ultimate scarcity of water in the desert. Phoenix's failure to enact a city water conservation policy was clearly understood at the time. Karen Smith explicitly criticizes the city's lack of water conservation: "Unlike Tucson, which seems to have managed its much scarcer water supply better, the Phoenix City Council has yet to approve a water conservation policy for the city. As of 1982, Phoenix had a population of one-and-a-half-million people. A city of such numbers cannot long rely on Lin Orme's [the former director of the SRP] prophecy that it will always rain when it is needed." Only in the twenty-first century would Phoenix have to face potential shortfalls in water supply. In the meantime, growth continued unabated, and the Phoenix leadership persistently relied on the surplus of water provided by the SRP to support continued sprawl.[17]

The bipolar relationship with the desert continued in Phoenix. On the one hand, resort owners and the tourist industry marketed desert landscapes and the dry warm climate as positive community attributes. On the other hand, city dwellers and business leaders diligently sought to push the desert to the distant margins of the community's identity. The tourist industry grew through the 1960s and 1970s, surpassing agriculture as the valley's second-largest industry. By one estimate in 1978, tourists contributed $1.6 billion a year to the local economy. New resorts such as La Posada and Mountain Shadows opened, and existing resorts received upgrades and new infusions of corporate interest. In one example, the Marriott Corporation acquired the Camelback Inn in 1967.[18]

Shopping malls proliferated in the valley coincidentally with the expansion of the tourist resorts, but the commercial centers represent the community's effort to marginalize the desert. Shoppers would drive into the massive parking lots in their air-conditioned cars and hustle across the bubbling asphalt to the chilled interior spaces of the new malls. Only in that brief sprint in and out of the stores would the shopper experience the desert climate. Inside the malls waterfalls gurgled and ice skaters twirled. Metrocenter was the biggest of the malls, opening in 1973 on the northwest side of Phoenix. The mall occupied 312 acres, which included the parking lots that could accommodate seventy-six hundred cars. Inside the mall shoppers could find five anchor department stores, countless shops, multiple restaurants, movie theaters, and an ice-skating rink. When it opened, developers claimed it to be one of the biggest shopping malls in the world. Fourteen million shoppers entered the mall in 1979 alone.[19]

Getting to the mall required driving, and the decentralization of shopping centers around the valley contributed to the increase in traffic that came to threaten and eventually overwhelm the once-pristine desert environment. The debates over freeway construction started the resistance to growth in Phoenix, as opponents coalesced around the image of Phoenix as the new Los Angeles. Initially a political consensus supported freeway construction, with only the financial costs serving as a source of hesitation. By the 1970s, additional resistance based on a critique of the freeways themselves mounted to temporarily stymie freeway construction in Phoenix.

Phoenix had lagged behind other cities of similar size in freeway construction during the 1950s and 1960s. Automobile traffic in the meantime had increased exponentially as low-density sprawl dispersed the population thinly over the valley. Whereas the model of decentralization, Los Angeles, possessed a density of 6,976 persons per square mile in 1970, Phoenix residents experienced a settlement pattern less than half as dense, only 3,103 persons per square mile. With such a scattered population, city engineers considered expansion of the freeway system critical. Engineers and traffic specialists had planned the Phoenix highway system in the mid-1950s, but the modest planned expansion had been swamped by the unforeseen growth of the 1960s. In 1960 the city only had seven miles of freeways, with plans to add fifteen miles of freeways over the next few years. Unfortunately, the slow growth in freeway miles left streets congested and freeways jammed. Engineers complained that cities of the size of Phoenix expected highways to carry 40 to 45 percent of automobile traffic. In Phoenix freeways carried less than 8 percent of traffic, which forced surface streets to accommodate much more traffic than they were designed to carry. In normal circumstances, a surface street might be expected to carry ten to twenty thousand cars per day. Because of the huge increase in

Fig. 8.1. Park Central Shopping Center, 1957 (CP MCL 61990: courtesy Herb and Dorothy McLaughlin Photograph Collection, Arizona State University Libraries). The low-density life-style of suburban development in the City of Phoenix included the decentralization of commerce and shopping. Goldwater's Department Store had been a fixture downtown since the nineteenth century. Recognizing the shifting residential patterns during the post–World War II boom, Goldwater's relocated to the Park Central Shopping Center in 1957. The success of Park Central spurred further development of malls. The largest in 1973 was Metrocenter, occupying 312 acres on the northwest fringe of the metropolitan area.

traffic in Phoenix, some streets handled thirty thousand cars per day. The traffic situation in Phoenix compared poorly with other cities of similar size. For example, San Diego, with a population of about six hundred thousand (when the Phoenix population was five hundred thousand), possessed seventy-four miles of freeway. Phoenix had twenty-two miles of highway. Clearly, for Phoenix to maintain its drive for regional supremacy, the coming decade would have to include a massive improvement of the transportation infrastructure.[20]

Ironically, the movement for additional freeway construction met resistance from within the progrowth business community. Prominent in the booster establishment was Eugene Pulliam, publisher of the two main Phoenix newspapers. In the early 1970s, Pulliam led the opposition to a new freeway project that would have traversed the central city in an elevated Inner Loop that rose in places to eight stories in height. Pulliam's newspapers editorialized against the freeway project, criticizing the Inner Loop project specifically and freeways in general. Pulliam considered Los Angeles to be a poor example for Phoenix to emulate, at least as far as its transportation system was concerned. Besides increasing congestion and gridlock, an expanded freeway system would add to the air pollution already affecting the clarity of the desert air. More specifically, he considered the proposed Inner Loop project to be wrong on two counts. First it would needlessly divide the city, with the inevitable effect of creating declining conditions in those areas bisected by the freeway. Specifically, he thought the south side of Phoenix, after being divided by the freeway, would become "a dumping ground." Second, he considered the elevated portion of the project to be a potential eyesore visible from the heart of downtown.[21]

City leaders had hoped to develop a strong consensus behind the freeway project, noting particularly that state and federal contributions would make up the lion's share of the funding. Unfortunately for the proponents of the project, Pulliam's papers unleashed an incredibly slanted and vituperative campaign to defeat the freeway proposal. Editorial cartoons ran on the front page; one depicted a bulldozer crushing houses, with the demolition crew identified as the Phoenix Chamber of Commerce, the Phoenix Real Estate Board, land speculators, and the Phoenix City Council. The vote came on May 8, 1973, and a clear majority—58 percent—opposed the Inner Loop. The setback for city traffic planners held up construction of the project for two years. In the meantime, engineers tweaked the proposal, in part by removing the elevated portion of the freeway. In the next vote, on November 5, 1975, the Pulliam press again opposed the freeway, but a majority approved the plan, and Interstate 10 through central Phoenix began a long-awaited process of expansion and improvement.[22]

By 1980 the Phoenix freeway system had grown to thirty-two miles, but in the meantime sprawl had continued apace and the additional miles of freeway remained congested and locked in stasis during the commuters' rush hours.[23] Thwarting traffic engineers' planned expansions of the system, more and more residents moved to the valley into increasingly distant subdivisions. It seemed that no matter how many lanes were added or new routes created, drivers relying on the controlled-access routes overwhelmed their capacity. In many residents' eyes, the Phoenix highway system remained woefully inadequate, and yet to others, conditions in the valley remained preferable to those in other areas of the country, particularly Southern California.

A more purely environmental debate arose in Phoenix over preservation of Camelback Mountain at about the same time controversy arose over freeway construction. During the 1960s, developers began the slow process of constructing large expensive homes on the lower slopes of Camelback Mountain. Building sites had to be carved out of the side of the hill to provide enough flat area for the homes, with driveway access requiring additional cuts into the face of the mountain. The new homes were clearly visible throughout the valley, especially at night, as residential lights shone and automobile headlights crept up the hillside. Alarmed residents considered the prospect of houses peppering the entire height of the mountain.

In the late 1960s, city leaders purchased the hump of the mountain above eighteen hundred feet, limiting the progress of development up the slope, and placed a moratorium on building within the rest of the Phoenix Mountains. Subsequently, environmentalists and other activists, along with city planners, developed a plan to create a public land preserve throughout the moratorium area. A viable political coalition developed supporting the Phoenix Mountain Preserve, led by Mayor John Driggs. In 1973 his administration backed a $23.5 million bond that voters passed, providing the city with the funds necessary to begin acquisition of the undeveloped area. Driggs later referred to the effort to preserve Camelback Mountain as "the greatest accomplishment in my administration." Remarkably, consensus behind the public land initiative in Phoenix survived multiple changes in administration. Mayor Margaret Hance supported the mountain preserve through her terms in office from 1976 to 1983. In 1978 she supported the expansion of the preserve by nine thousand acres at a proposed cost of $12.3 million. Subsequent administrations echoed the agreement. The consensus was necessary because of repeated efforts by developers to overturn the preservation effort and open the mountains once again to private ownership. As a supporter remarked in 1978, "Still, the picture is far from rosy. Land developers remain poised at the slightest hint that some mountain pieces may be up for sale." Efforts to acquire more acreage in the preserve continued through the decade, including the successful efforts by city leaders to acquire federal funds to assist in the land acquisition. Rising property values made the acquisition of land for the preserve more and more difficult, but the community consensus behind the Phoenix Mountain Pre-serve remained steadfast. As another supporter observed in 1980, "The natu-ral beauty of our mountain horizon, our close-in-mountain slopes and natural areas—this is the very substance of the natural environment that has been so instrumental in the population and economic growth of this region. The grand scale and rugged character of these mountains have set our lifestyle, broad-ened our perspective, given us space to breathe, and freshened our outlook. These mountains are the plus that still over-weighs the growing minuses in our environmental account."[24]

By 1980 the "growing minuses" were all too obvious: increasing air pol-lution, persistent traffic congestion, and more and more of the desert valley bulldozed into the latest version of suburban development. But at last, Phoenix had moved to preserve a natural element of the community. In 1930, the com-munity had acquiesced to the dismemberment of the natural preserve in the Papago-Saguaro National Monument. In the 1970s, community concern over a natural setting finally reached political fruition. It had been a long time com-ing and remained somewhat surprising given the continuing probusiness and progrowth ethos in the community.

Tucson also grew in population and physical size through the decades fol-lowing the postwar boom. As in Phoenix, civic leaders made major efforts to attract industries and expand the economic base of the city. Despite these simi-larities, a fundamental difference developed between the two cities. In Phoenix, opposition to annexations had ended by 1970, allowing the city to expand to its geographic limit with speed and abandon. At the same time in Tucson a slow-growth movement appeared, with elected officials advocating infill and a limit to the expansion of the city. One facet of the slow-growth movement was the effort to revise water utility practices, including raising water rates and charging residents service fees that were related to delivery costs. The politi-cal resistance to growth lasted only a few years and ended with the electoral defeat of most of the slow-growth proponents. Although short lived, the re-sistance to rampant growth in Tucson rippled throughout the community and represented the manifestation of the small-town, Old Pueblo image of the city. Even as Tucson grew to metropolitan status, the desire for uniqueness and the political voice of the smaller-is-better proponents appeared consistently and with occasional voter approval. Developers and businessmen advocated ex-pansion of the economic base in Tucson, just as in Phoenix. In Tucson, however, the booster mentality continually encountered the nay-saying resisters to growth. The resistance to growth in Tucson never succeeded in building a wall around the city, but the slow-growth critique appeared in Tucson with much greater regularity than in Phoenix, exerting an unmistakable effect on the city of Tucson in the 1970s and beyond.

As in Phoenix, business leaders and political officials sought to promote Tucson as a big city suitable for economic advancement. The effort to attract high-tech and electronics firms took on a bureaucratic quality in the mid-1960s, when Democratic mayor Jim Corbett established the Development Authority for Tucson's Economy. The agency used tax dollars to promote Tucson locations for industry and relied on the continued presence of Hughes Aircraft to serve as the model and precedent for recruitment. By 1974, the development agency had attracted fifty-two companies to locate in Tucson, including Burr-Brown Industrial Research Company. A change in city administrations revamped the promotion effort and in the process replaced the development authority with the Tucson Economic Development Corporation. Regardless of the name of the agency, recruitment continued. In 1978, IBM announced plans to establish a research and manufacturing plant in Tucson, and in 1979 National Semiconducter joined the other electronics firms in the Tucson Basin.[25]

The employees of these companies contributed to the flood of immigrants entering the valley and the suburban sprawl eating up more and more of the desert. Tucson developers profited from the expansion of the urban population, but in Tucson the suburban phenomenon became almost anti-urban. As one brochure proclaimed, Tucson residents of the suburbs enjoyed an "uncitified closeness to nature."[26] The same sort of residential accoutrements adorned Tucson homes as those in Phoenix—for example, swimming pools and tennis courts—but in Tucson Old West traditions lingered in the developers' promotions. Not as ultrasuburban as those in Phoenix, Tucson subdivisions reflected desert settings and western traditions. The Tucson version of frontier lifestyle also dominated the recruitment efforts of industrial corporations. Hughes Aircraft, for example, used Tucson's western image as part of its employee come-on: "Arizona was settled by men who dared to be different, who rejected being part of a stereotyped pattern, and carved out a new life in their own frontier. . . . If you are interested in not only a new way of personal life but a different concept of professional life, we would like to talk about specific opportunities for you at Hughes-Tucson."[27]

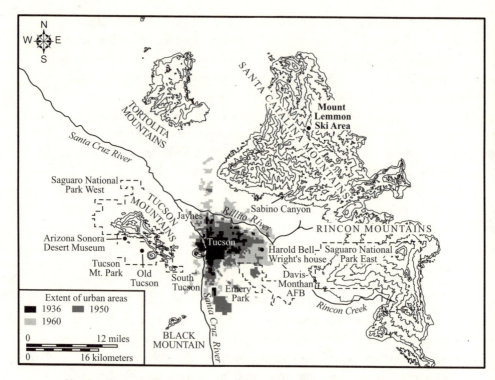

Map 8.2. Tucson 1960. Continuing sprawl in the Tucson Basin began to creep beyond the mountain boundaries. Low-density suburban development had reached the Saguaro National Park on the east, but additional preserves to the west maintained the image of Tucson as a community sensitive to its desert surroundings.

The type of suburban home envisioned by Hughes, and the type promoted by many Tucson developers, was the epitome of low-density housing, the so-called ranchette. A chamber of commerce pamphlet explained the concept: "In the foothills, within 20 easy minutes from downtown, there are many suburban ranch home sites, commonly 4 acres or more in size. There is ample room for swimming pools, putting greens, shuffleboard and badminton courts, playground equipment and stables. Ranch living has become almost standard with Tucson executives who still are within easy driving distance of all the city's commercial and industrial areas."[28] The same sorts of promotions could be aimed at potential residents and winter visitors. Ranch lifestyles, properly sanitized for the genteel audience, appealed to suburban sensibilities: "Facilities for enjoyment of active sports are offered everywhere. The favorite pastime is riding out into the desert on old Indian trails or up into the foothills for a picnic by moonlight, western style . . . vistas are spacious and the western atmosphere is genuine."[29] Arizona's noted pictorial magazine *Arizona Highways* devoted an issue to Tucson three times from 1956 to 1965, and in each case it emphasized the desert environment and western lifestyle. With a nationwide circulation, the magazine's promotion contributed to the city's image as the Old Pueblo, desert city, and winter playground, all rolled into one. Running through all of the community images was the cowboy motif: "Off for a ride in the desert! Nothing can offer sharper contrast to big city living than the care-free individualistic life of the western range, especially when the trees aren't trees, but saguaros!"[30]

Of course most of Tucson's residents lived and worked in much less grandiose circumstances than the chamber of commerce publications advertised. Nonetheless, the foothills lifestyle was real in Tucson and served as a major prop for the city's image as a community firmly in touch with its natural surroundings. The ranch homes in the foothills of the Catalina Mountains stood out as Tucson's most desirable suburban setting. The creation of the foothills lifestyle primarily was the work of one man, a developer with exceptional foresight, a keen eye for the natural contours of the desert terrain, and a healthy distrust of politically mandated zoning codes, John Murphey.

Murphey was a developer, so it would be erroneous to consider him a proponent of slow growth or a preservationist in the model of John Muir, the founder of the Sierra Club. On the other hand, Murphey placed limits on his own quest for wealth by maintaining a sense of balance and propriety. In the 1930s he had purchased seventeen hundred acres in the Catalina foothills and begun slowly selling off parcels for home sites while gradually acquiring additional acreage for development. As a Tucson planner later recounted, "Murphey was a visionary guy and he had a built-in sensitivity to the land. He would walk or ride the whole area before he laid it out, and he took care to site houses on the land in the best way. Without him, God knows what would have happened to the foothills."[31] Murphey's Catalina Foothills Estates came to represent the low-density ranch home model that epitomized Tucson suburban life. To maintain the desirability of the area, Murphey created strict deed covenants and property restrictions applicable to homeowners, relying in part on the advice of noted architect Josias Joesler. Regulations determined the placement of roads and driveways and the issue of vegetation removal. Covenants regulated even the color of roofing material and the placement of garbage containers. The following excerpt from a promotional brochure indicates the developer's vision for the foothills: "It is desired that roads built shall follow and cling to these washes or other depressions of natural drainage as closely as possible." And, "The hills are covered with cacti . . . and have restrictions against their removal except for construction purposes. Catalina Foothills Estates owns over 5,000 acres in the district and has determined to keep it clear of all objection-able commercial enterprises."[32]

Murphey distrusted zoning regulations and relied on his personal real estate dealings to maintain the quality of life in the foothills. He died in 1977, and in his absence the tight control over development of the area slipped and soon deteriorated into the oblivion of commercialism. County zoning ordi-nances allowed much more leeway for development in the area than Murphey had accepted. Soon condominiums and commercial areas sprang up, as well as resorts complete with golf courses and multiple swimming pools. Critics of the new form of foothills development included longtime ranch home resi-dents and social critics, uniting to complain about the county's lack of regula-tion, which had created "a sort of aesthetic holocaust." Some considered the new form of land use to have "'Californicated the foothills' by imposing elegance where wilderness once reigned." By the late 1980s, the foothills area reached a much denser population of forty thousand, and a new round of criticism arose when residents learned that new zoning rules would allow a population increase in the area to eighty thousand.[33]

A vestige of Murphey's development ethos remains in the original por-tion of the Catalina Foothills Estates. The stretch of Campbell Avenue north from River Road still follows the contours of the land in a twisting, single lane that requires modest if not downright slow speed. If the final demolishment of Murphey's vision ever comes, it will proceed from an announcement by the city that Campbell Avenue between River Road and Skyline Boulevard will be widened and straightened to accommodate increased traffic flow. On the other hand, as long as a bit of the old foothills lifestyle remains, Tucsonans residing in those foothills ranchettes will be able to cling to their self-image as an envi-ronmentally aware community.

Most residents of Tucson lived in much less affluent surroundings than the homeowners in the foothills. Nonetheless, all Tucsonans could relate to their desert environment through popular and commonly patronized venues.

Included in these natural areas were the two districts of the Saguaro National Monument and the Sabino Canyon riparian area. Another prominent and popular destination for both tourists and local residents was, and remains, the Arizona-Sonora Desert Museum. A combination zoo and botanical garden, the museum provides escapes from the hubbub of urban life into a natural haven that holds the desert environment in clear reverence. The institution has always possessed an outreach component, educating visitors about the fragility and hardiness of the native environment. The message is clear on all fronts. The desert deserves our attention and respect and, if approached with sensitivity and awareness, rewards our senses with remarkable displays of beauty and grace.

An early supporter of the desert museum was naturalist and social critic Joseph Wood Krutch. The author of *The Modern Temper* had retired to Tucson in 1952 and quickly began working with the museum founders and staff. He became prominent in the museum's outreach program; he even named the museum's educational van the Desert Ark. Krutch's academic and intellectual credentials, as well as his sensitivity and eloquence, made him the leading spokesman in Tucson advocating the preservation of the desert environment.[34]

Krutch began visiting Tucson in the winters in the 1930s and settled permanently when he retired from his faculty position at Columbia University in 1952. His arrival as a permanent resident came just as sprawl took off in gigantic leaps—his preservationist critique emanated from both philosophical and practical concerns. He built his home on five acres of desert east of the city limits, in a physical setting similar to that of Harold Bell Wright's estate at Speedway and Wilmot. Wright had fled from the early manifestations of sprawl. Krutch was reacting to the consequences of rampant growth. In 1955 and 1956, the City of Tucson enacted several annexations that threw the city limits in great leaps across the desert valley. Practically from the moment he moved into his home amidst the pristine desert, Krutch found himself annexed. He first spoke out against urban growth in October 1956 in a talk presented to Tucson's Rotary club: "Whenever I see one of those posters which reads 'Help Tucson Grow,' I say to myself, 'God forbid.' I suggest that the Rotary Club adopt a new motto: 'Keep Tucson Small.'"[35]

The urbanization of Tucson threatened to destroy the natural quality of life in the Old Pueblo that Krutch had initially found so inviting and desirable. Krutch exemplifies another in the long line of health-seeking elites who found

Tucson to be the perfect place to satisfy their personal needs. Sprawl was destroying that perfect place. Krutch understood that in opposing growth he could be accused of opposing progress; he was cognizant of the economic realities of urban life and recognized his own privileged, financially independent position.[36] In 1962, Krutch expressed his "partial solution" for the dilemma facing Tucsonans seeking to maintain both a naturally healthful community and a vibrant and economically expanding city: "Does all this mean that the desert, with all it has meant to many of us and might mean to generations still to come, is doomed to disappear in the not too distant future—unless indeed a fundamental change of heart should take place in the majority of the citizens who direct our destinies? Perhaps. Perhaps, on the other hand, there is a partial solution—namely the reservation of some sections of it as public land explicitly reserved in Parks, Monuments, and Wilderness Areas. It is far more rewarding to be able to live in the desert than merely to visit it. But that is at least better than nothing."[37]

The desert museum constitutes an element of Krutch's partial solution, along with the other natural areas in and around Tucson. Whether the partial solution represents sufficient preservation depends on the observer's point of view. The most ambitious developer likely would consider any preservation to be wrongheaded, just as the ardent preservationist would consider any further sprawl to be an egregious affront against nature. Politically, the significance of Krutch's partial solution came from its ability to suggest reasonable, consensus-building electoral possibilities. I am not asserting a clear cause-and-effect relationship, but it is clear that in Tucson intellectual and philosophical pronouncements in the 1960s were followed by a viable and temporarily powerful slow-growth movement in the 1970s.

Electoral victories in 1972 and 1974 placed reform Democrats in positions on the Pima County Board of Supervisors and the Tucson City Council. The new Democrats advocated planned growth and infill, seeking to promote denser development within the city limits so as to limit the expansion of the city into pristine desert landscapes. Loosely referred to as slow-growth proponents, these supervisors and council members faced opposition from those who supported rapid and restriction-free development. Mostly, but not exclusively, Republicans, the proponents of development and sprawl complained that slow growth would weaken the city's economy and hinder the advance toward citywide prosperity.[38]

The focus of the political dispute became city water policy. The four re-form-minded city council members targeted revisions of city water policy as a rational way to promote more responsible development. Another goal was to bring the city's water policy into a more ecologically sound position of sus-tainability—in other words, to force Tucsonans to acknowledge their desert surroundings.

The impetus for the water policy revision came from within the city's water utility itself. By the early 1970s, the water department was in need of imme-diate rate increases and capital improvement projects. The last major rate re-vision had come in the early 1950s. Since then, the massive sprawl of the city had required the water utility to embark on a huge infrastructure expansion program. One particular difficulty was that the development of the foothills required the city to pump water ever farther uphill, increasing costs for the water department without any ability to recoup the additional expense. In 1976 the water utility recommended a revision of water policy to the city council as well as a $150 million capital building program. On average water rates would go up 42 percent, but the new rate schedule included significant changes. First, customers would be charged higher rates the more water they used, which re-versed the former policy of declining rates for greater volume consumed. Also, the new rates included additional charges for those customers in the highest lift zones. The rate change for individual customers would range from a de-crease of 20 percent to a maximum increase of 185 percent (customers using a great deal of water in the highest lift zone).[39]

The new water policy drew immediate opposition. Front-page headlines announced the new policy and reported on the debates on the city council be-tween the four reform Democrats and the Republican mayor. Despite the protest, the slow-growth majority pushed through the new water policy, as one observer remarked, "with a touch of righteousness and a lot of naivete."[40]

The new policy went into effect in July 1976, and when the first bills went out to consumers later that month, a firestorm of anger and protest erupted. Many water bills doubled, and it seemed as if all citizens saw their water costs increase more than they had expected. Some accused the New Democrats of being disingenuous in explaining the effect of the new policy on consumers' bills. In response to the protest and concern, the city council in August re-scinded the unpopular lift charges and instituted a lifeline rate that would pro-vide basic levels of service at a very modest, subsidized rate. The council's retreat proved to be inadequate to address the anger in the community. It is questionable whether any response by the council could have satisfied the protesters. In September the opponents of the new water policy submitted petitions to the city clerk forcing a recall election. The recall petitions had twice the necessary number of signatures. The next month, in October, opponents announced a slate of roll-back candidates. The opposition candidates promised voters that, if elected, they would roll back the water rates to their pre-reform status.[41]

On January 8, 1977, three New Democrat council members were soundly defeated at the polls (the fourth member of the slow-growth majority on the council had previously resigned and moved out of state). After the election, one of the defeated council members, Doug Kennedy, offered a brief assessment: "The voters had been swayed by the emotional issue of their water bills, and not by the facts surrounding the water rate increases." He was correct in that the water department's crisis remained, regardless of who sat on the city council. The roll-back council members had to face the same water utility circumstances but now from a political position that made significantly raising rates problematic, if not politically impossible. They also had to confront the water department's demand for a $150 million expansion.[42]

The resolution of the water crisis finally came down to something akin to a Joseph Wood Krutch partial solution. Conservation would solve the problem or at least provide a measure of relief that would temporarily allow the community to continue expanding and sprawling. It was called the Beat the Peak program and began with a fifty-thousand-dollar public relations campaign that started in the summer of 1977, only a few months after the recall election. The goal of the water conservation program was to get Tucsonans to voluntarily reduce their average daily water consumption by 25 percent. If that could be accomplished, then the water company's expansion project could be reduced by $50 million. The hope was that each dollar of advertising for Beat the Peak would result in one thousand dollars in savings for future capital expenditures.[43]

And it seemed to work. From an average daily consumption of 190 gallons per person per day from 1969 to 1976, water consumption in Tucson dropped to 163 gallons per person from 1976 to 1996. The water conservation resulted from a wide range of advertising appeals. First, the program's mascot, Pete the Beak, told Tucsonans that they should not water their lawns or fill up

Doc Pete checks the aquifer.
Coloring Page

Where'd the water go?

Fig. 8.2. "Doc Pete checks the aquifer," *The Adventures of Doc Pete* (courtesy Tucson Water). In 1977 the Tucson Water Company began its noted water conservation program and introduced the cartoon mascot Pete the Beak. In 2001 the water utility began producing activity books for children, seeking to inculcate a water conservation ethic among Tucson's youngest residents. The online activity books include puzzles, games, and coloring pages. In this example from 2002, Doc Pete asks, "Where'd the water go?"

their swimming pools on Wednesdays; also, on other days they should only water their lawns during early-morning or late-evening hours. The community also heard about the advantages of desert landscaping and water-saving methods and practices for inside the home. Tucson became a leader in the national movement toward low-flow toilets and shower heads. Teachers lectured schoolchildren not to leave the water running in the sink when they brushed their teeth. Wait staff in restaurants adopted a scowl when asked for a glass of water with a meal. In the 1980s, Tucson became the poster child for water conservation, a status recognized by city leaders around the West, as well as scholars of cities nationwide. Tucson was the desert city that best represented a reasonable accommodation with its natural surroundings.

In the 1970s in Phoenix, Mayor Margaret Hance gave rhetorical support for infill, but no slow-growth movement materialized to obtain a voting majority on the city council. In Tucson the slow-growth movement rose to prominence and then crashed in the recall of 1977, but out of the defeat arose a remarkable water conservation program. Also, the slow-growth proponents in Tucson, although losing their majority status, maintained a voice in the public forum. County supervisor Dave Yetman maintained his position through the 1980s and consistently gave voice to the same sorts of concerns that motivated the slow-growth advocates in the 1970s. In Phoenix such voices remained marginal to the public discourse. The temporary defeat of the freeway had been possible only because of the participation of Pulliam and his newspapers. Likewise, the preservation of the Phoenix Mountains required the support of mainstream political leaders and remained anomalous to the broader community ethos.

In both cities sprawl and expansion continued to the extent of their physical limits. Ultimately, the slow-growth movement in Tucson failed to stop or even slow down sprawl. Likewise, the effort to bring water rates and water consumption policies in Tucson into some sort of rational system also failed. The conservation program was only a partial solution for the problem of water consumption in a desert environment. Water in Tucson was still cheap, it was available at a turn of the tap, and it presented no restriction to the city's growth through the 1980s.

Annexations continued to organize what was otherwise the chaotic practice of development that followed the dictates of maximized profits. In both places, the expansion and annexations extended to their natural limitations. Although Phoenix dominates the basin, it is hemmed in by the surrounding satellite communities and the Fort McDowell Indian Reservation. In Tucson, mountains and public lands in the form of national forest and the Saguaro National Monument—soon to acquire national park designation—limited the city's expansion to the north and east. Likewise, the Tohono O'Odum Reservation limited expansion in the southwest. That left the southeast and northwest, and those were the directions in which Tucson continued to expand.

Both cities are huge, metropolitan, sprawling expanses of glass, steel, bricks, and mortar rising from the desert floor. They consume huge quantities of water, electric power, and fossil fuels and generate equally huge quantities of garbage and waste. On the other hand, residents of both cities think of themselves and their communities as environmentally aware and ecologically responsible. Proponents of both cities think of their communities as the best place to live—if not quite perfect, then at least better than the places that they recently left. Thousands of new residents arrive every year, and they like what they see. At the same time, residents of some tenure look at developments in both cities and shake their heads. Some see decline; others look upon the same scene with optimism. Both cities harbor multiple visions of their multifaceted communities.

Epilogue

FOUNTAINS IN THE DESERT

URBAN SCHOLARS USE two different models for coming to understand the culture and lifestyle of residents of cities. Some consider that a connection to a place runs no deeper than a person's neighborhood, block, or street. This small-district approach focuses on the qualities of day-to-day life. Significant are the social aspects of life, including the various aspects of home life and workplace, leisure-time activities, ethnic identities, and religious affiliations. Often the organizing force for the neighborhood in big cities is the community church, park, or playground, or perhaps a factory that employs area residents. Issues that affect the quality of life are basic and commonplace concerns such as sanitation, security, and opportunities for education and employment. In this approach to city life, the large metropolitan labels fade to irrelevance. Individuals are not residents of Chicago or New York City. Rather, they live in sections or districts within the large city that carry more meaning. They live on the South Side or the North Shore, in the Village or The Bronx. People live in communities that are much smaller and more intimate than the metropolis.

The other way to approach a city and its inhabitants is to focus on the larger identity. Proponents of this approach acknowledge that individuals require specific abodes and means of subsistence within the urban milieu, but suggest that the relevance of urban life is directly related to the functionality and cultural vibrancy of the metropolis itself. This way of viewing cities goes back at least to Daniel Burnham's famous Chicago Plan of the early 1900s. Burnham recognized that Chicago was a metropolitan area composed of many disparate parts. However, what motivated his plan for the rejuvenation of the city was the idea that a comprehensive approach to development in the metropolis was the only way to stimulate the functionality of the city. To Burnham and his supporters, cities functioned on several levels. Urban areas provided society with virtually everything considered culturally valuable, from great works of art to towering monuments of culture and education. Cities also functioned as the central component of the engine that produced the industrial revolution. Healthy cities provided opportunities for immigrants in the smoke-belching factories of industrial America. They also served as the force for acculturation of ethnic residents, spinning them off as upwardly mobile and thoroughly assimilated middle-class Americans.

Critical to this process was the organizing power of the city itself. The force operated at the macro level and manifested itself in countless icons of urban life that became real and functional in their power. To look at the example of Chicago, inhabitants certainly resided in small districts or neighborhoods, but the primary organizing force for the urban society was the city itself. If the community's self-identity went no further than the neighborhood designation, then the city had failed. The Chicago identity should carry meaning and relevance in and of itself. It meant you loved the Lake Shore and Navy Pier. On weekends you went for strolls down Michigan Avenue or visited the Field Museum. You were a fan of the Bears or the Bulls or the Cubs or maybe even the White Sox. These icons of Chicago life carried meaning, and constituted the nature and identity of the city.

Clearly in this analysis of the self-identity of Tucson and Phoenix, the comprehensive, or metropolitan, approach will be the most useful. By 1980 both cities had grown to such an extent that residents could clearly be categorized as small-district residents. In Tucson, day-to-day life centered on Midtown, the Barrio, the Foothills, Casas Adobes, Oro Valley, South Tucson, or the far southwest side. In Phoenix, residents thought of themselves as belonging to

Glendale, Goodyear, Avondale, Tempe, Paradise Valley, Scottsdale, Carefree, or some other community. But for the purposes of this effort at arriving at an understanding of the cities' nature and identity, a broader focus is necessary. Admittedly, this approach constitutes a generalization that runs counter to a specific understanding of an individual's daily circumstances. Its validity rests in the notion that, if correctly and accurately configured, the generalization will apply to all residents of the city and will inform a general audience seeking an understanding of what it means to live in a desert city.

In both cities, urban life has taken on universal qualities of homogenized consumerism apparent throughout the United States, and so to get at an idea of the communities' identity, it is useful to look at what exists outside the developed region. By this I do not mean specifically outside the city limits. City leaders and residents made significant decisions about what exists outside the area of economic activity and residential inhabitance. In part this bipolar concept of urban life relates to the type of recreation residents desire, particularly if leisure pastimes require natural settings. It also characterizes the community itself in the way society often defines itself in terms of the Other.

Cities began self-consciously incorporating natural settings within the urban area in the mid-nineteenth century. Frederick Law Olmstead's career as a designer of city parks began with New York City's Central Park in 1858 and continued through the century. In 1893 he served as the chief landscape architect of the Columbian Exposition in Chicago and was one of the founders of the City Beautiful movement that influenced many plans for urban development and renewal. Many cities simultaneously developed areas of commercialized recreation within the residential and industrial areas of the city. These commercial entertainments spread with the increase in leisure time that ensued from industrialism's advance during the Gilded Age. City parks began competing with nickelodeons and movie theaters. Consumers traveled along tree-lined parkways to reach sparkling and garish amusement parks. All of these pathways and venues of recreation became part and parcel of the urban milieu.

Similar developments occurred in the cities of Tucson and Phoenix, with the particular manifestation of nature in the cities varying between pristine desert preserves and highly cultivated, lush city parks. City leaders in both places laid claim to a fundamental closeness to nature, with the desert as a primary element of this human-to-nature connection. The truth of these claims was questionable in earlier decades, given the extent of metropolitan sprawl in

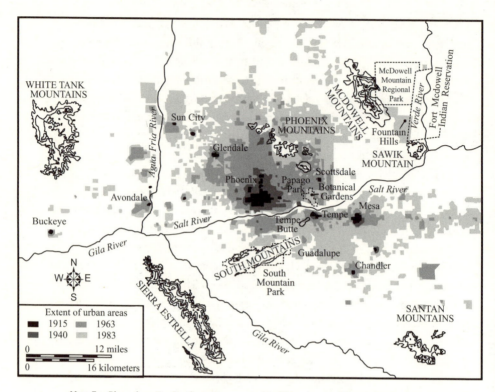

Map E.1. Phoenix 1983. By the 1980s, sprawl in Phoenix was filling in the open spaces east of the Phoenix Mountains. The effort to preserve natural desert areas had resulted in restrictions on development in the Phoenix Mountains and South Mountain.

both valleys, and remains questionable today. For the claims of nature's centrality to be true, desert preserves must be easily identifiable and accessible for the entire community, and the presence of nature must be expansive enough to provide for the desert escape. It can take the form of a city or county park or even be commercialized in its formulation by requiring an admission fee, but its natural qualities require a markedly separate existence from the developed urban region.

In Phoenix, desert landscapes exist in the form of parks and preserves that appear as islands of nature in an urban sea. Within the city itself natural landscapes have been so truncated that only vestiges remain. Phoenicians can still admire the visible markers of nature in their midst, for example, through the preserved hump of Camelback Mountain. I do not mean to suggest that this icon of nature is meaningless or of trivial significance. It remains an island of nature, however, protruding out of the ocean of development. Until about thirty years ago, the Phoenix Mountains constituted a sort of natural barrier, communicating to residents that just over the mountains, nature resided. But that came to an end in the postwar boom. The intervening space between Camelback and the next mountains to the east, the McDowell Mountains, began filling up with subdivisions and commercial development. The desert has become elusive in Phoenix, shrunk to insignificance within the urban area and increasingly remote in the lengthening distance to the boundary between the developed and natural landscape.

The Phoenix Mountain Preserve—including several separate preserve areas—represents the effort to set aside natural desert areas in a Krutch-like partial solution, but only the South Mountain section of the preserve encompasses sufficient space to represent desert landscapes in all of their fullness. The South Mountain park offers visitors more than one hundred miles of hiking trails through its 16,500 acres of foothills and steep slopes. The issue of encroachment exists, however, with the constant pressure of development pressing against the natural preserves. In many places subdivisions abut the fences surrounding the natural areas. Hiking up to one of the desert peaks provides a trek through desert settings and at the summit presents sweeping views of an urbanized landscape of rooftops, radio towers, snaking freeways, and the green smudge of urban golf courses.

As the challenge of protecting the vestige of the desert within the city increases in difficulty, likewise, the existence of a desert Other beyond the boundary of development also recedes into the distance. The next prospective natural barrier to development to the east, the McDowell Mountains, offers examples of both preservation and development.

Maricopa County proudly points to the McDowell Mountain Park as a natural preserve of 21,099 acres. The park includes trails for hiking, horseback riding, and mountain biking. The bikers particularly enjoy the three competitive loops added over recent years, which allow for races and large rallies. The seventeen hiking trails also provide venues for racers. Three of the hiking loops are labeled competitive. The park provides seventy-six camping sites, all developed with electrical and water hookups. The sites can accommodate recreational vehicles forty-five feet long.

As a natural preserve, the McDowell Mountain Park is impressive in its size but often appears preoccupied by its consumer-driven recreational uses. Nonetheless, the desert mountains within the park remain undeveloped, except for the occasional mark of a trail, and the sheer size of the park, bordered to the east by the Fort McDowell Indian Reservation and to the north by the Tonto National Forest, protects the area from the most egregious pressures of encroachment.

Also on the other side of the McDowell Mountains from Phoenix, just south of the park, is the upscale community of Fountain Hills. A promotional pamphlet describes the community, founded in the 1970s and incorporated in 1989: "Insulated from the rest of the metropolitan area by the McDowell Mountains, the community is characterized by uncongested streets winding through nature's hills and arroyos and clean, clearer air. Surrounding mountain views are ever changing and simply beautiful. A 1997 population of over 15,000 enjoys the benefits of master planning and sensitivity to the desert environment."[1]

Residents avail themselves of "three great golf courses," as well as a swimming/fitness facility and two community parks. And, of course, there is the namesake fountain. It operates from 9 a.m. to 9 p.m. "for 15 or 30 minutes on the hour, depending upon the season and the weather." It shoots up 560 feet, which makes it the tallest fountain in the world, according the Guinness Book of World Records. To lift the column of water up three times higher than Old Faithful requires multiple six-hundred-horsepower pumps. "During the day, the Fountain reflects the shifting shades of sunlight and it often shimmers with a rainbow. At night it sparkles with gold and silver lights." Promoters claim the fountain to be a "source of great pride for residents" and equally assume the "thrilling sight" to be an obvious allure for tourists and prospective residents.[2]

The fountain uses reclaimed irrigation water, the same type of water used to keep golf courses green in Arizona. Signs warn golfers using such facilities not to put their tees in their mouths. Using recycled water somewhat mitigates the blatant wastefulness. Whereas residents no doubt pride themselves on their sensitivity to the desert environment, the spewing fountain represents the continuum of conspicuous consumption of water in Phoenix that stretches back more than one hundred years. Fountain Hills developers used both the desert setting and the novelty of the fountain to create one of the most desirable communities in the Phoenix metropolitan area. Property values are sky high and the geographic and master plan restrictions on development are sure to keep property values exorbitant.

For the vast majority of Phoenicians, living in less affluent circumstances than are enjoyed by the residents of Fountain Hills, nature is something they visit but do not live in. An example of a commercialized nature preserve within the city is the Desert Botanical Garden in Papago Park. The garden is popular and attractive, but it is a 145-acre vestige of what was once an expansive desert landscape.[3]

Perhaps the most popular, and traditional, escape into nature in Phoenix is the drive to the Mogollon Rim and White Mountains of eastern Arizona. But this involves a complete escape from the desert, not an escape into the desert. To reach the cool high country of pine trees and lakes requires a drive of some significance, and on a Friday afternoon or evening you can see the stream of cars heading out of town.

The status of nature and desert landscape preservation in Tucson differs significantly from that in Phoenix.

Within the urban area, Tucsonans enjoy lush green parks, just as Phoenix residents do. A midtown example in Tucson is Randolph Park, site of a community swimming pool, championship tennis facility, two popular eighteen-hole golf courses, a baseball stadium, and the city zoo. Desert landscapes have little to do with the park and its activities. Like Phoenicians, Tucsonans can escape into a very nondesertlike nature by making the drive up to Mount Lemon in the Catalina Mountains. The drive takes you from the desert floor up into pine forests and cool mountain settings. Along the way the twisting drive takes you past many overlooks and trail heads and eventually delivers you to the ubiquitous ski area. A small village and residential area also perch on the mountain top. The commercial and residential development on the mountain intrudes into the natural setting, along with the radio towers protruding over the forested peaks, but overall the Catalina Mountains remain a prized, natural, albeit nondesert, component of the community.

Both cities contain similar types of commercialized natural recreation areas, and both cities include nature preserves of a more pristine sort. Tucson, however, has set aside natural desert landscapes, extending preservation far beyond the levels accomplished by its neighbor to the north. In extent and quality, the desert preserves in Tucson amount to a remarkable natural setting

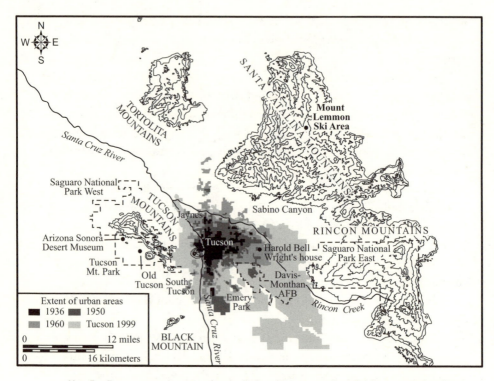

Map E.2. Tucson 1999. By 1999, the city limits of Tucson reached the Saguaro National Park east district and Tucson Mountain Park to the west. In addition, low-density development sprawled beyond the city limits to fill the basin up to the steep slopes of the surrounding mountains. Despite the advancing metropolitan circumstances, the extensive preservation of natural desert landscapes in Tucson maintained the community's image as the Old Pueblo.

that informs our understanding of the city's identity. An example of a popular escape into nature in Tucson is an easy trek to the west of the city that culminates at the Arizona-Sonora Desert Museum and the western district of the Saguaro National Park. The most likely route to the museum and park follows the major east-west artery of Speedway Boulevard. West Speedway travels through a typical urban landscape of neighborhoods, gas stations, and commercial strips. Approaching the Tucson Mountains, which form the western boundary of the Tucson Basin, West Speedway enters the foothills of the mountains and the low-density foothill suburbs. Ranch houses occupy lots ranging from a quarter of an acre or less to five acres or more. Architectural styles run the gamut from ecologically sensitive to outlandishly garish. Nearing the mountains, the road narrows and begins twisting in the approach to Gates Pass, the point of access through the mountains to the other side. Traffic slows to navigate the narrow turns, and suburban development ceases. West Speedway has delivered the traveler to a preserve of natural desert landscapes. It is Tucson Mountain Park, twenty thousand acres preserving the summit of the pass and the land on both sides of the summit—very valuable real estate indeed—as public land.

Beyond the summit is a vista of more desert landscape, with a small square of development in the near distance. The development is the theme park, movie set, and amusement area of Old Tucson. Originally constructed in 1938 for the filming of *Arizona*, the park still attracts both film crews and tourists seeking to walk back into the fabled western past and maybe see a movie star to boot.

Approaching the theme park and movie set, the road comes to a fork: the left branch leads to Old Tucson, the right to the Arizona-Sonora Desert Museum and the Saguaro National Park. Heading right, or north, the last miles of two-lane road traverse a preserved landscape of natural desert. Within the county preserve of Tucson Mountain Park is the Gilbert Ray Campground, which provides 130 recreational vehicle sites with electrical hookups. The campground represents the modest intrusion of commercialized recreation into the natural preserve. The other venue for recreation in Tucson Mountain Park is an archery, pistol, and rifle range. The Desert Museum also constitutes a developed section of the natural landscape, complete with a massive parking lot suitable for tour buses and auxiliary lots for those peak tourist days when the normal lots fill up. The museum's existence within the preserved landscape might offend preservation purists, and the developed sections of Old Tucson and the county-operated target range may diminish the natural escape into the desert, but I suspect most visitors, including permanent residents of Tucson, marvel at the open expanse and find the museum and other venues acceptable intrusions into the natural landscape: a partial solution.

This is likely because the county's preservation of desert landscapes is coupled with the 91,445 acres of Saguaro National Park. The west section of the park borders Tucson Mountain Park and the Desert Museum to the north, extending the preservation umbrella over most of the Tucson Mountains. Of course, campgrounds and other facilities, including roads and trails, intrude into the preserved landscape of the national park. But the intrusion is modest, and I suspect that most observers would marvel at the extent of natural desert areas preserved in Tucson just over the Tucson Mountains.

Not long ago, the open expanses existed to the west as far as the eye could see. There were indications of mine tailings in the distant mountains, and the dirt section roads and barbed-wire fences of the ranches marked the desert valley. But no subdivisions existed, and the view was clear. In more recent years, the sprawl in Tucson has proceeded beyond the mountains and now has started to encircle the natural settings of the county park, museum, and national park. It will not be long before housing areas completely fill in the next valley to the west, and then—perhaps when Tucson's population reaches 3 or 4 million— the subdivisions will be pressing firmly against the preservation boundary, just as Phoenix neighborhoods pressure the Phoenix Mountain Preserves today. In Tucson, however, it seems reasonable to assume that the extent of desert preservation—well over one hundred thousand acres—will survive the pressures of encroachment far into the future. The desert preserves in Tucson confirm the community's self-image as a desert-sensitive society.

Tucson's water conservation ethic supports much of this local self-congratulatory, ecologically sensitive self-image. The success of the Beat the Peak program, compared with the profligate use of water in Phoenix, allowed Tucsonans to consider themselves cutting edge and regionally superior in their careful use of the scarce resource. The fact remains, however, that water in Tucson is cheap and seemingly plentiful, which explains the optimism of planners and political leaders as they push for more and more immigration. The unanswered question is whether there is enough water in the valley for a Tucson population of 3 million residents, or 4 million, or 10 million.

Tucson's water conservation ethic largely arose out of the city's complete reliance on groundwater. The age-old system of wells and pumps provided sufficient water for the city to grow into a prosperous metropolis, but the limited underground source always seemed to threaten future development. Rising tantalizingly over the future horizon was the Central Arizona Project, which would deliver Colorado River water to the urban centers of Arizona. City leaders and planners in Tucson lusted after the new water source because it would bring to an end at last the pinched and limiting reliance on groundwater.

Colorado River water arrived in Tucson to much fanfare in 1990, but it took two more years of infrastructure development (including a water treatment plant) before the CAP water reached Tucson customers. The results were disastrous. Tucsonans had grown used to their fairly mild groundwater; CAP water proved to be much harsher. Traveling through a mostly open canal more than three hundred miles from Lake Havasu on the Colorado River (the water is lifted a total of twenty-nine hundred feet by the time it reaches Tucson), CAP water hardened through the normal process of evaporation and concentration of minerals during its travels. Many of the eighty-four thousand customers in Tucson who first received CAP water found that it ran orange out of their taps. The harsher water was leaching rust out of galvanized iron pipes. In the worst cases of rusted plumbing, pipes burst and Sheetrock walls melted. The water company persisted in delivering CAP water to Tucson residents for two years, vainly attempting to adjust the water chemistry to eliminate the residential catastrophes. Nothing seemed to work. By 1995 the city had ceased use of CAP water and resumed its total reliance on pumped groundwater.[4]

In contrast, Phoenix used CAP water without any noticeable problems. Perhaps the decades of experience in treating Salt River Project water provided the Phoenix water utility engineers with a clear advantage over their Tucson counterparts. The head of the water utility in Tucson, as well as the treatment plant manager, resigned as a result of the CAP disaster. Tucsonans reacted to the problem by launching a grassroots initiative in 1995. Opponents of the use of CAP water placed the Water Consumer Protection Act on the November 1995 ballot. Voters overwhelmingly approved the initiative, which virtually prohibited the use of CAP water. Tucson voters reaffirmed the act two years later in another initiative election, but relented in 1999 by voting to allow the water utility to experiment with mixing, blending, or otherwise finding some use for CAP water. Since then the Tucson Water Company has been slowly and cautiously introducing Colorado River water into the city system. A more careful and competent management of the water system has alleviated much of the political turmoil that initially greeted CAP water in Tucson. I am not suggesting that the issue of water supply or the manifestation of water politics in Tucson has reached a permanent situation of peace, but water in Tucson remains basically cheap for consumers and the overall supply derived from a combination of groundwater and CAP water allows city leaders to plan and project ever-increasing urban populations.

The conservation ethic remains, although the water supply comfort zone for consumers in Tucson seems to moderate any sense of urgency for increasing conservation. The positive comparisons remain, however. Tucsonans' use of water still compares quite favorably to the conspicuous and wasteful rates of water use in other desert cities, such as Phoenix and Las Vegas.

Tucsonans and Phoenicians typically live in the general urban and suburban circumstances dominated by our consumer-driven economy, and both cities have reached clear metropolitan status. Yet the identities of the two cities differ. Both are desert cities, but there are qualitative differences between them. Tucson has more of the desert to offer its visitors and residents but fewer jobs to offer newcomers. Phoenix has the economic might to satisfy new waves of immigrants but can offer those new residents less of the desert in the Valley of the Sun.

NOTES

Chapter 1: Two Rivers

1. Thomas Edwin Farish, "Southeastern Arizona, Its Varied Climate and Wonderful Resources," *Arizona Gazette*, 1889.

2. Jones and Stokes Associates, "Tres Rios, Arizona: Feasibility Study" (U.S. Army Corps of Engineers, Los Angeles District, South Pacific Division, 2000), iv-2; Christian E. Downum, "Between Desert and River: Hohokam Settlement and Land Use in the Los Robles Community," Anthropological Papers no. 57 (Tucson: University of Arizona, 1993), 16; Lee W. Arnold, "An Ecological Study of the Vertebrate Animals of the Mesquite Forest" (master's thesis, University of Arizona, 1940), 28–43, 49–53; J. J. Thornber, "Plant Acclimatization in Southern Arizona," *Plant World* 14 (January 1911): 1–9.

3. The quote is from Jack L. August, *Vision in the Desert: Carl Hayden and Hydropolitics in the American Southwest* (Fort Worth: Texas Christian University Press, 1999), 14. See also Geoffrey P. Mawn, "Promoters, Speculators, and the Selection of the Phoenix Townsite," *Arizona and the West* 19 (Fall 1977): 214–15; Robert J. Schmidli, *Climate of Phoenix, Arizona* (Phoenix: Weather Service Forecast Office, WR-177, December 1986), abridged online version by R. S. Cerveny, Office of Climatology, Arizona State University, December 1996, http://geography.asu.edu/cerveny/phxwx.htm; Amadeo M. Rea, *Once a River: Bird Life and Habitat Changes on the Middle Gila River* (Tucson: University of Arizona Press, 1983), 46, 53–69.

4. Measurements of watershed size are subject to interpretation. For example, regarding the Santa Cruz River's watershed, Parker cited 8,581 square miles, Charles Bowden claimed 8,990 square miles, and Julio Betancourt described the "total basin area" as 23,300 square kilometers (13,980 square miles). Regarding the Salt River's watershed, Powell cited 12,700 "at its mouth," while a report by the U.S. Army Corps of Engineers cited 13,700 square miles. Cable, Henry, and Doyle's report on the Salt River increased the corps' figure by 30 square miles, to 13,730. Julio Betancourt, "Tucson's Santa Cruz River and the Arroyo Legacy" (PhD diss., University of Arizona, 1990), 4; Charles Bowden, "Death of the Santa Cruz Calls for a Celebration," *Arizona Daily Star*, August 23, 1981; John T. C. Parker, "Channel Change on the Santa Cruz River, Pima County, Arizona, 1936–1986," Open-File Report 93-41, U.S. Geological Survey (hereafter USGS), December 1993, 1; Arthur Powell Davis, "Water Storage on Salt River, Arizona," Water-Supply and Irrigation Paper no. 73, USGS, 1903, 22; Jones and Stokes, "Tres Rios," ii-7; John S. Cable, Susan L. Henry, and David E. Doyel, eds., "City of Phoenix, Archaeology of the Original Townsite: Block 28-North," Central Phoenix Redevelopment Agency, City of Phoenix, November 1983, 25.

5. *Arizona Daily Star*, February 12, 1884; Davis, "Water Storage," 26–29.

6. John Field, Keith Katzer, Jim Lombard, and Jeanette Schuster, "A Geomorphic Survey of the Picacho and Northern Tucson Basins," in *The Northern Tucson Basin Survey: Research Directions and Background Studies*, Archaeological Series no. 182, ed. John H. Madsen, Paul R. Fish, and Suzanne K. Fish (Tucson: University of Arizona, Arizona State Museum, 1993), 36; Betancourt, "Arroyo Legacy," 33.

7. Walter R. Helmick, "The Santa Cruz River Terraces Near Tubac, Santa Cruz County, Arizona" (master's thesis, University of Arizona, 1986), 13.

8. M. Fenneman Nevin, *Physiography of Western United States* (New York: McGraw-Hill, 1931), 379–80.

9. Jon S. Czaplicki and James D. Mayberry, "An Archaeological Assessment of the Middle Santa Cruz River Basin, Rillito to Green Valley, Arizona, for the Proposed Tucson Aqueduct Phase B, Central Arizona Project," Archaeological Series no. 164 (Tucson: University of Arizona, Arizona State Museum, 1983), 7.

10. Parker, "Channel Change," 6.

11. Michael F. Logan, *The Lessening Stream: An Environmental History of the Santa Cruz River* (Tucson: University of Arizona Press, 2002), 209.

12. Ibid.

13. Joe Gelt, Jim Henderson, Kenneth Seasholes, Barbara Tellman, and Gary Woodard, "Water in the Tucson Area: Seeking Sustainability," Issue Paper no. 20 (Tucson: University of Arizona, College of Agriculture, Water Resources Research Center, 1999), 25.

14. Ibid., 17.

15. Logan, *Lessening Stream*, 217, 247–48.

16. William D. Sellers, "The Climate of Arizona," in *Arizona Climate*, ed. Christine R. Green and William D. Sellers, Institute of Atmospheric Physics (Tucson: University of Arizona Press, 1964), 11.

17. Cable, Henry, and Doyel, "City of Phoenix," 15.

18. Ibid., 26.

19. Ibid., 11.

20. Ibid., 19–20; B. W. Thomsen and J. J. Porcello, "Predevelopment Hydrology of the Salt River Indian Reservation, East Salt River Valley, Arizona," Water-Resources Investigations Report 91-4132, USGS, 1991.

21. Cable, Henry, and Doyel, "City of Phoenix," 22; Willis T. Lee, "The Underground Waters of Gila Valley, Arizona," Water-Supply and Irrigation Paper no. 14, series o, Underground Water, 25, USGS, 1904, 24–26.

22. Cable, Henry, and Doyel, "City of Phoenix," 38–41; E. Lendell Cockrum, *Mammals of the Southwest* (Tucson: University of Arizona Press, 1982), 7–8; Rea, *Once a River*, 103–6.

23. Paul Martin, "Pleistocene Overkill," *Natural History* 76 (December 1967): 32–38.

24. Czaplicki and Mayberry, "Archaeological Assessment," 8–9; Helmick, "Santa Cruz River Terraces," 7.

25. Bryan and MacNeish assume a human presence in the Southwest prior to 9500 BC, but other scholars suggest more recent habitation. Alan L. Bryan, *Paleo-American Prehistory*, Occasional Papers of the Idaho State University Museum no. 16 (Pocatello: Idaho

State University Press, 1965); Richard S. MacNeish, "Early Man in the New World," *American Scientist* 64 (1976): 316–27; Czaplicki and Mayberry, "Archaeological Assessment," 15–16.

26. F. W. Hodge, "Prehistoric Irrigation in Arizona," *American Anthropologist* 6 (July 1893): 323, 330.

27. For a discussion of the methodology behind population estimates, see Logan, *Lessening Stream*, 36–39; Paul R. Fish and Suzanne K. Fish, "Hohokam Political and Social Organization," in *Exploring the Hohokam*, ed. George J. Gummerman (Albuquerque: University of New Mexico Press, 1991), 165; Patricia L. Crown and W. James Judge, *Chaco and Hohokam: Prehistoric Regional Systems in the American Southwest* (Santa Fe, NM: School of American Research Press, 1991), 263, 303.

28. Barbara Tellman, Richard Yarde, and Mary G. Wallace, *Arizona's Changing Rivers: How People Have Affected the Rivers* (University of Arizona, College of Agriculture, Water Resources Research Center, Issue Paper 19, 1997), 11; Thomsen and Porcello, "Predevelopment Hydrology," 6.

29. William H. Doelle and Henry D. Wallace, "The Changing Role of the Tucson Basin in the Hohokam Regional System," in Gummerman, *Exploring the Hohokam*, 332–33; William H. Doelle, "Human Use of the Santa Cruz River in Prehistory" (paper presented at the American Society for Environmental History Conference, Tucson, Arizona, 1999).

30. For example, Thomsen and Porcello state, "Recent archaeological studies of the Hohokam irrigation system have recorded more than 300 miles of main canals, and 1,000 miles of smaller canals in the Salt River Valley." Thomsen and Porcello, "Predevelopment Hydrology," 6. The source for this assertion is Masse's statement: "Of the more than 500 kilometers of major canals and 1600 kilometers of smaller canals recorded, less than 10 kilometers remain intact." However, later in his study, Masse takes pains to explain that each canal had a "period of use" from AD 550 to 1850. For example, Masse explains that one particular canal "was constructed, remodeled twice and abandoned within the Hohokam Sedentary Period (A.D. 900 to 1150), most likely between A.D. 1100 and 1150." W. Bruce Masse, "Prehistoric Irrigation Systems in the Salt River Valley, Arizona," *Science* 214 (October 23, 1981): 408, 409.

31. Fish and Fish, "Hohokam Political and Social Organization," 157; Michael Meyer, *Water in the Hispanic Southwest* (Tucson: University of Arizona Press, 1984), 12; Suzanne K. Fish and Gary Naban, "Desert as Context: The Hohokam Environment," in Gummerman, *Exploring the Hohokam*, 49; Neal W. Ackerly, Jerry B. Howard, and Randall H. McGuire, *La Ciudad Canals: A Study of Hohokam Irrigation Systems at the Community Level*, 7 vols., Anthropological Field Studies no. 17 (Tempe: Arizona State University, 1985), 9–11; Fred L. Nials, David A. Gregory, and Donald A. Graybill, "Salt River Streamflow and Hohokam Irrigation Systems," in *The 1982–1984 Excavations at Las Colinas: Environment and Subsistence*, Archaeological Series no. 162, ed. Carol Ann Heathington and David A. Gregory, 1:70–74 (Tucson: University of Arizona Press, 1989).

32. Nials, Gregory, and Graybill, "Salt River Streamflow," 70–74; Doelle and Wallace, "Hohokam Regional System," 333; Betancourt, "Tucson's Santa Cruz River," 36.

Chapter 2: Dos Rios

1. Doelle and Wallace, "Hohokam Regional System," 334; Thomas E. Sheridan, *Landscapes of Fraud: Mission Tumacácori, the Baca Float, and the Betrayal of the O'odham* (Tucson: University of Arizona Press, 2006), 21–22.

2. James E. Officer, *Hispanic Arizona, 1536–1856* (Tucson: University of Arizona Press, 1987), 31.

3. John Francis Bannon, *The Spanish Borderlands Frontier, 1513–1821* (Albuquerque: University of New Mexico Press, 1974), 41, 79.

4. On early ranching, see Herbert Eugene Bolton, *Rim of Christendom: A Biography of Eusebio Francisco Kino, Pacific Coast Pioneer* (New York: Macmillan, 1936), 358, n. 2; Officer, *Hispanic Arizona*, 31–32; John L. Kessel, *Mission of Sorrows: Jesuit Guevavi and the Pimas, 1691–1767* (Tucson: University of Arizona Press, 1970), 51, n. 12; and John L. Kessel, "The Puzzling Presidio: San Felipe de Guevavi, alias Terrenate," *New Mexico Historical Review* 41 (January 1966): 22. For the reports on population, see Ernest J. Burrus, *Kino and Manje: Explorers of Sonora and Arizona; Their Vision of the Future, a Study of Their Expeditions and Plans, with an Appendix of Thirty Documents* (St. Louis, MO: Jesuit Historical Institute, 1971), 215–19. Manje's transcribed reports from the fourth expedition, November 2 to December 6, 1697, are on pp. 333–84 of Burrus's appendix.

5. Officer, *Hispanic Arizona*, 73.

6. Henry F. Dobyns, "Indian Extinction in the Middle Santa Cruz River Valley, Arizona," *New Mexico Historical Review* 38 (January 1963): 163–81.

7. Bannon, *Spanish Borderlands Frontier*, 70; Henry F. Dobyns, *Spanish Colonial Tucson: A Demographic History* (Tucson: University of Arizona Press, 1976), 32, 105, 139; Henry F. Dobyns, *Tubac through Four Centuries: An Historical Resume and Analysis* (Arizona State Parks Board, March 15, 1959, University of Arizona Library, microfilm no. 1045), 16–18, 32, 40–45, 99–106, 139; Dobyns, "Indian Extinction"; Meyer, *Water in the Hispanic Southwest*, 31, 41, 78–79; Bonaventure Oblasser, "Papagueria: The Domain of the Papagos," *Arizona Historical Review* 7 (April 1936): 6; Officer, *Hispanic Arizona*, 33–34.

8. Officer, *Hispanic Arizona*, 48, 51; Kieran McCarty, *A Spanish Frontier in the Enlightened Age: Franciscan Beginnings in Sonora and Arizona* (Washington, DC: Academy of American Franciscan History, 1981), 66, 51; Richard White, *It's Your Misfortune and None of My Own: A New History of the American West* (Norman: University of Oklahoma Press, 1991), 10, 12–14; Clark Wissler, *Indians of the United States* (New York: Doubleday, 1966), 224–28; Donald Emmet Worcester, "The Apache Indians of New Mexico in the Seventeenth Century" (master's thesis, University of California, Berkeley, 1940), 1, 19.

9. *Arizona Daily Star*, March 27, 2000; February 9, 2002.

10. Officer cites a fanega as equal to 3.2 bushels. Lt. Cave Johnson Couts described a fanega as 2.5 bushels in 1848. Officer, *Hispanic Arizona*, 119; Cave Johnson Couts, *Hepah, California! The Journal of Cave Johnson Couts, from Monterey, Nuevo Leon, Mexico to Los Angeles, California during the Year 1848–1849*, ed. Henry F. Dobyns (Tucson: Arizona Pioneers' Historical Society, 1961), 54–55.

11. Kieran McCarty, *Desert Documentary: The Spanish Years, 1767–1821*, Historical Monograph no. 4 (Tucson: Arizona Historical Society, 1976), 82–90.

12. Meyer, *Water in the Hispanic Southwest*, 56, 61.

13. McCarty, *Desert Documentary*, 85–87, 92.

14. Dobyns, *Spanish Colonial Tucson*, 79, 86–87; Officer, *Hispanic Arizona*, 63, 66.

15. David J. Weber, *The Taos Trappers: The Fur Trade in the Far Southwest, 1540–1846* (Norman: University of Oklahoma Press, 1970), 121, 123–24; Officer, *Hispanic Arizona*, 106; James O. Pattie, *The Personal Narrative of James O. Pattie*, ed. William H. Goetzmann (Philadelphia and New York: J. B. Lippincott, 1962).

16. Kieran McCarty, *Copper State Bulletin*, Arizona State Genealogical Society, 17 (Winter 1982): 93; Robert A. Potash, "Notes and Documents," *New Mexico Historical Review* 24 (October 1949), 332–35.

17. Henry W. Bigler, "Extracts from the Journal of Henry W. Bigler," *Utah Historical Quarterly* 5 (April 1932): 46–47; Robert S. Bliss, "The Journal of Robert S. Bliss," *Utah Historical Quarterly* 4 (July 1931): 79–80; Officer, *Hispanic Arizona*, 149.

18. Officer, *Hispanic Arizona*, 197–99.

19. Bliss, "Journal," 80–81; Bigler, "Extracts," 48–49; Officer, *Hispanic Arizona*, 197–99; Philip St. George Cooke, *The Conquest of New Mexico and California in 1846–1848* (New York: G. P. Putnam's Sons, 1878; reprinted Chicago: Rio Grande Press, 1964), 150; Frank Alfred Golder, *The March of the Mormon Battalion from Council Bluffs to California, Taken from the Journal of Henry Standage* (New York: Century, 1928), 195–96.

20. John E. Durivage, *Daily Picayune* (New Orleans), August 7, 1849.

21. Ralph P. Beiber, *Southern Trails to California in 1849* (Glendale, CA: Arthur H. Clarke, 1937), 5:319–20; Charles Edward Pancoast, *A Quaker Forty-Niner: The Adventures of Charles Edward Pancoast on the American Frontier*, ed. Anna Paschall Hannum (Philadelphia: University of Pennsylvania Press, 1930), 233; Officer, *Hispanic Arizona*, 229–30.

22. Durivage, *Daily Picayune*.

23. Officer, *Hispanic Arizona*, 231–34.

24. H. M. T. Powell, *Santa Fe Trail to California: The Journal and Drawings of H.M.T. Powell, 1849–1852*, ed. Douglas S. Watson (San Francisco: Book Club of California, 1931), 145–47; A. B. Clarke, *Travels in Mexico and California* (Boston: Wright and Hasty Printers, 1852), 81–82; Pancoast, *Quaker Forty-Niner*, 233.

25. Clarke, *Travels*, 81–86; Cornelius C. Cox, "From Texas to California in 1849," ed. Mabelle Eppard Martin, *Southwestern Historical Quarterly* 29 (October 1925): 144; Powell, *Santa Fe Trail*, 136; Pancoast, *Quaker Forty-Niner*, 233.

26. Hilario Gallego, "Reminiscences of an Arizona Pioneer—by Hilario Gallego," *Arizona Historical Review* 6 (January 1935): 78.

27. Carmen Lucero, "Reminiscences of Mrs. Carmen Lucero as Interpreted by Miss Maggy Brady to Mrs. Geo. F. Kitt, 1928." Typescript; two copies exist in the file, one containing red-pencil additions. Carmen Lucero File, L 935 Arizona Historical Society.

28. Officer, *Hispanic Arizona*, 283, 286–88; Thomas E. Sheridan, *Los Tucsonenses: The Mexican Community in Tucson, 1854–1941* (Tucson: University of Arizona Press, 1986), 30–31; Gallego, "Reminiscences," 78.

29. Phoenix Chamber of Commerce, *Resources of the Salt River Valley: Maricopa County, Arizona* (Special Collections, University of Arizona Library, 1891), 8.

Chapter 3: Indian Rings, Ditches, and Railroads

1. *A Historical and Biographical Record of the Territory of Arizona. Illustrated* (Chicago: McFarland and Poole, 1896), 259 (hereafter *Historical and Biographical Record*).

2. James H. Carleton, "Proclamation of James H. Carleton, Colonel First California Volunteers, Major Sixth U.S. Cavalry, at Tucson, Arizona, June 8, 1862," *War of the Rebellion Official Records of the Union and Confederate Armies*, series I, vol. 9 (Washington, DC: Government Printing Office, 1883), 561–62; Secretary Richard C. McCormick to President Abraham Lincoln, from Prescott, Arizona Territory, December 1, 1864, Record Group 59, Territorial Papers: Arizona, vol. 1; Jay J. Wagoner, *Arizona Territory, 1863–1912: A Political History* (Tucson: University of Arizona Press, 1970), 31–32, 55.

3. Wagoner, *Arizona Territory*, 55.

4. *Arizona Miner*, January 18, 1868; *Historical and Biographical Record*, 259; Wagoner, *Arizona Territory*, 28–31.

5. Officer, *Hispanic Arizona*, 287–88.

6. Sheridan, *Los Tucsonenses*, 63.

7. Charles D. Poston, *Building a State in Apache Land*, ed. John M. Meyers (Tempe, AZ: Aztec, 1963), 73–74, 80; Phocion R. Way, "Overland via 'Jackass Mail' in 1858: The Diary of Phocion R. Way," ed. William A. Duffen, *Arizona and the West* 2 (Spring–Winter 1960): 36; Waterman L. Ormsby, *The Butterfield Overland Mail, by Waterman L. Ormsby, Only Through Passenger on the First Westbound Stage*, ed. Lyle H. Wright and Josephine M. Bynum, a compilation of eight *New York Herald* articles published from September 26 to November 19, 1858 (San Marino, CA: Huntington Library, 1942); A. C. Green, *900 Miles on the Butterfield Trail* (Denton: University of North Texas Press, 1994), 14–15.

8. Thomas E. Sheridan, *Arizona: A History* (Tucson: University of Arizona Press, 1995), 105; Darlis Miller, *Soldiers and Settlers* (Albuquerque: University of New Mexico Press, 1989), 297.

9. For an explanation of the raids by Cochise, see Sheridan, *Arizona*, 67.

10. Miller, *Soldiers and Settlers*, 248–49.

11. Darlis Miller, "Civilians and Military Supply in the Southwest," *Journal of Arizona History* 23 (1982): 116; W. T. Sherman, "W.T. Sherman, General to General W.W. Belknap, Secretary of War, November 20, 1869," Executive Documents, 41st Cong., 2nd sess., 1869–70 (Washington, DC: Government Printing Office, 1870), Serial 1412, 2:30–31.

12. James Fowler Rusling, *Across America; or, The Great West and the Pacific Coast* (New York: Sheldon, 1874), 370.

13. Darlis Miller describes the freighting business as chaotic but not conspiratorial. As she summarizes (*Soldiers and Settlers*, 299), "In the fierce competition to obtain government contracts, firms sometimes employed questionable tactics." Maj. Gen. Schofield, "Report of Major General Schofield, Headquarters Military Division of the Pacific, San Francisco, Cali-

fornia, October 20, 1871," Executive Documents, 42nd Cong., 2nd. sess., 1871–72, vol. 2, part 1 (Washington, DC: Government Printing Office, 1872), Serial 1503, 66–69; George Crook, *General George Crook: His Autobiography*, ed. Martin F. Schnitt (Norman: University of Oklahoma Press, 1946), 183–84.

14. Miller, "Civilians and Military Supply," 115.

15. An article reporting on General Stoneman's report appears in the *Tucson Citizen*, April 15, 1871. James R. Hastings, "The Tragedy at Camp Grant in 1871," *Arizona and the West* 1 (Summer 1959): 150–52.

16. Officer, *Hispanic Arizona*, 290; J. Phillip Langellier, "Camp Grant Affair, 1871: Milestone in Federal Indian Policy?" *Military History of Texas and the Southwest* 15 (Summer 1979): 21–23; Oury's account appears in *Arizona Historical Review* 4 (April 1931): 15–20; *Arizona Miner*, May 6, 1871.

17. Schofield, "Report," 67.

18. Hastings, "Tragedy at Camp Grant," 158; Langellier, "Camp Grant Affair," 25; Don Schellie, *Vast Domain of Blood: The Story of the Camp Grant Massacre* (Los Angeles: Westernlore, 1968), 242–45.

19. *Arizona Miner*, December 9, 1871.

20. Crook, *Autobiography*, 183–84.

21. August V. Kautz, "August V. Kautz, Col. Eighth U.S. Infantry to the Assistant Adjutant-General, Military Division of the Pacific and Department of California, August 15, 1877," Executive Documents, 45th Cong., 2nd sess., 1877–78, vol. 1, part 2 (Washington, DC: Government Printing Office), Serial 1794, 143.

22. Ibid., 142, 143–46; Crook's criticism of Indian agents appears in Crook, *Autobiography*, 184–86.

23. Sheridan, *Arizona*, 88–90.

24. James E. Officer, *Arizona's Hispanic Perspective*, Arizona Academy, 8th Arizona Town Hall, May 1981 (research report prepared by University of Arizona, May 17–20, 1981), 79; Sheridan, *Los Tucsonenses*, 2, 88.

25. James M. Barney, *Tales of Old Arizona*, 3 vols. (Arizona Historical Foundation, n.d.), 2:15–16.

26. *Arizona Miner*, January 23, 30, 1889; *Historical and Biographical Record*, 263–64; Wagoner, *Arizona Territory*, 55, 117.

27. Dee Brown, "Geronimo, Part 1," *American History Illustrated* 15 (June 1980): 12–14.

28. *Arizona Miner*, September 3, 1870; Arthur Powell Davis, "Irrigation Near Phoenix, Arizona," Water-Supply and Irrigation Paper, no. 2, USGS, 1897, 51; Bradford Luckingham, "Urban Development in Arizona: The Rise of Phoenix," *Journal of Arizona History* 22 (Summer 1981): 197; Mawn, "Promoters, Speculators," 214–15.

29. Earl Zarbin, "The Swilling Legacy," Salt River Project, 1987 (reproduction of *Arizona Republic* articles by Zarbin published between August 13 and August 30, 1978, Arizona Collection, Hayden Library, Arizona State University), 6, 8; Mawn, "Promoters, Speculators," 210–11.

30. Zarbin, "Swilling Legacy," 6.

31. Ibid., 12; *Arizona Miner*, July 8, 1868.

32. Zarbin, "Swilling Legacy," 12.

33. Ibid.

34. *Arizona Miner*, May 2, 1868.

35. Mawn, "Promoters, Speculators," 215; *Arizona Miner*, August 27, 1870.

36. Zarbin explains the debate over who named the settlement Phoenix in "Swilling Legacy," 17–18. For example, G. Wesley Johnson, Jr., names Darrell Duppa as the founder who named the settlement Phoenix in "Directing Elites: Catalysts for Social Change," in *Phoenix in the Twentieth Century: Essays in Community History*, ed. G. Wesley Johnson, Jr. (Norman: University of Oklahoma Press, 1993), 13.

37. Ibid., 13–14.

38. Officer, *Arizona's Hispanic Perspective*, 62.

39. Davis, "Irrigation Near Phoenix," 49, 54–55.

40. Malcolm L. Comeaux, *Arizona: A Geography* (Boulder, CO: Westview, 1981), 208.

41. *Arizona Miner*, April 13, 1872.

42. Bradford Luckingham, *Minorities in Phoenix: A Profile of Mexican-American, Chinese American, and African American Communities, 1860–1992* (Tucson: University of Arizona Press, 1994), 18.

43. Officer, *Arizona's Hispanic Perspective*, 61–62.

44. Luckingham, *Minorities in Phoenix*, 18.

45. *Territorial Expositor*, May 9, 1879.

46. Luckingham, *Minorities in Phoenix*, 19.

47. Dee Brown, "Geronimo, Part 2," *American History Illustrated* 15 (July 1980): 41. Crook later recounted (*Autobiography*, 263) that Geronimo had "fled, full of mescal and lies."

48. Quoted in Officer, *Arizona's Hispanic Perspective*, 79–80.

49. Merwin L. Murphy, "W.J. Murphy and the Arizona Canal Company," *Journal of Arizona History* 23 (Summer 1982): 151–62.

50. Bradford Luckingham, *Phoenix: The History of a Southwestern Metropolis* (Tucson: University of Arizona Press, 1989), 132.

51. Johnson, "Directing Elites," 211.

52. Luckingham, *Phoenix*, 35; Karen Lynn Erhlich, "Arizona Territorial Capital Moves to Phoenix," *Arizona and the West* 23 (Fall 1981): 239–40; Margaret Finnerty, "Arizona Capital: The Politics of Relocation," *History Forum* 3 (Spring 1981): 29–30.

53. *Arizona Weekly Journal-Miner*, January 23, 30, 1889.

Chapter 4: The Duty of Water and Agrarian Rivalry

1. Warren Allison, "Allison Pioneer Days in Tucson," unpublished manuscript compiled by Elvira R. Odom, Allison Family Papers, Arizona Historical Society, MS 113, 16; *Arizona Daily Star*, January 16, 1892; May 1, 1902.

2. Davis, "Irrigation Near Phoenix," 54; Davis noted the claim of 150,000 acres, while the 1890 census recorded 61,888 acres of both developed and undeveloped land. Of the 61,888 acres, 13,126 were "unimproved," and 48,762 were "improved." U.S. Bureau of the

Census, *Census of the United States*, Eleventh, 1890, *Statistics of Agriculture*, 10:199 (hereafter *Statistics of Agriculture*).

3. *Statistics of Agriculture*, 199.

4. Davis, "Irrigation Near Phoenix," 49–54; Phoenix Chamber of Commerce, "Resources of the Salt River Valley," 28.

5. *Phoenix Herald*, October 1, 1880; *Arizona Gazette*, March 15, 1884; Karen L. Smith, "The Campaign for Water in Central Arizona," *Arizona and the West* 23 (Summer 1981): 128.

6. Davis, "Water Storage," 26–29.

7. *Arizona Daily Star*, "Irrigation Wells," April 27, 1893.

8. *Arizona Daily Star*, February 5, 1891.

9. *Arizona Daily Star*, "Water! Water!" July 10, 1902; *Arizona Daily Star*, "Develop the Underflow," July 30, 1902.

10. *Arizona Daily Star*, "Better than a Canal," February 5, 1891.

11. Smith, "Campaign for Water," 137–38, 140.

12. Ibid., 140–43.

13. Davis, "Water Storage," 32–34; Karen L. Smith, *The Magnificent Experiment: Building the Salt River Reclamation Project 1890–1917* (Tucson: University of Arizona Press, 1986), 31; "Water for Phoenix: Building of Roosevelt Dam," editorial, *Journal of Arizona History* 18 (Autumn 1977): 284; H. L. Meredith, "Reclamation in the Salt River Valley, 1902–1917," *Journal of the West* 7 (January 1968): 82, fn. 18.

14. Robert Follansbee, *A History of the Water Resources Branch of the United States Geological Survey to June 30, 1919* (internal manuscript printed and copied by USGS in 1939 with forward by Nathan C. Grover written in 1938), 35.

15. Ibid., 32–55.

16. Ibid., 57; *Arizona Daily Star*, February 12, 1884.

17. Follansbee, *History*, 64.

18. Todd A. Shallat, *Structures in the Stream: Water, Science, and the Rise of the U.S. Army Corps of Engineers* (Austin: University of Texas Press, 1994).

19. Follansbee, *History*, 69, 93.

20. Ibid., 169.

21. *Arizona Daily Star*, May 1, 1902.

22. Ibid.

23. Ibid., July 10, 1902.

24. See T. C. Chamberlain, "Requisites and Qualifying Conditions of Artesian Wells" (USGS Survey Annual Report, 1885), repr. in *Physical Hydrogeology*, ed. A. Allan Freeze and William Back, 297–307 (Stroudsburg, PA: Hutchinson Ross, 1983). Freeze and Back refer to Chamberlain's essay as being "generally recognized as the beginning of the science of hydrogeology in North America. In beautifully written prose, Chamberlain outlines the seven prerequisites for artesian flow and describes the hydrogeologic properties of water-bearing beds and confining beds" (291).

25. U.S. Bureau of the Census, *Census of the United States*, Twelfth, 1900, *Agriculture*, Part 2, *Crops and Irrigation*, 4:818.

26. Luckingham, *Phoenix*, 132.

27. William B. Alexander Papers, University of Arizona Library Special Collections, AZ 171; Smith, *Magnificent Experiment*, 92.

28. For references to artesian water in the Tucson Basin, see *Arizona Daily Star*, May 1, July 10, July 30, 1902. For descriptions of the Edwards Aquifer, see James F. Petersen, "San Antonio: An Environmental Crossroads on the Texas Spring Line," in *On the Border: An Environmental History of San Antonio*, ed. Char Miller, 28–29 (Pittsburgh, PA: University of Pittsburgh Press, 2001); Laura A. Wimberley, "Establishing 'Sole Source' Protection: The Edwards Aquifer and the Safe Drinking Water Act," in Miller, *On the Border*, 171.

29. *Arizona Daily Star*, May 1, July 10, July 30, 1902.

30. Gelt et al., "Water in the Tucson Area," 1, 25.

31. U.S. Bureau of the Census, *Census of the United States*, Fourteenth, 1920, *Irrigation and Drainage*, 7:113–14.

32. Comeaux, *Arizona*, 209, 211.

33. Luckingham, *Phoenix*, 135.

34. H. C. Schwalen and R. J. Shaw, *Groundwater Supplies of Santa Cruz Valley of Southern Arizona between Rillito Station and the International Boundary*, Agricultural Experiment Station Bulletin no. 288 (Tucson: University of Arizona, 1957), 75, 82–83.

35. Comeaux, *Arizona*, 211.

36. Gelt et al., "Water in the Tucson Area," 7; Karen L. Smith, "Community Growth and Water Policy," in Johnson, *Phoenix in the Twentieth Century*, 160–63.

37. Smith, "Community Growth," 158–59.

38. Luckingham, *Phoenix*, 28; Johnson, "Directing Elites," 17–19.

39. Comeaux, *Arizona*, 211; Richard E. Lynch, *Winfield Scott: A Biography of Scottsdale's Founder* (Scottsdale, AZ: City of Scottsdale, 1987), 120–21.

40. Johnson, "Directing Elites," 18–19; Sheridan, *Arizona*, 263.

41. Johnson, "Directing Elites," 19–20; Smith, "Campaign for Water," 137, 140–43.

Chapter 5: Where Winter Never Comes

1. William E. Smythe, *The Conquest of Arid America* (New York: Harper and Brothers, 1900), 238.

2. Ibid., 243–44.

3. Luckingham, *Minorities in Phoenix*, 18.

4. Phoenix Chamber of Commerce, "Resources of the Salt River Valley," 8.

5. *Phoenix Directory, 1892* (Phoenix: Bensel Directory Company, 1892, repr. 1971, University of Arizona Library, Special Collections), 19.

6. Luckingham, *Minorities in Phoenix*, 18.

7. *Phoenix City and Salt River Valley Directory, 1920* (Los Angeles: Arizona Directory Company, 1920), 3. The reference to Mexicans, Negroes, and foreigners was repeated in the 1921 directory, but by 1923 the reference was dropped: "Phoenix is a modern town of 35,000 of the best kind of people; schools that are the pride of citizens and admiration of vis-

itors . . ." *Phoenix City and Salt River Valley Directory, 1923* (Los Angeles: Arizona Directory Company, 1923), 3.

8. Officer, *Arizona's Hispanic Perspective*, 97.

9. G. W. Barter, *Directory of the City of Tucson, 1881* (San Francisco: H.S. Crocker, 1881, University of Arizona Library, Special Collections), 13.

10. Ibid., 39–40.

11. Sheridan, *Los Tucsonenses*, 184–86.

12. Andrew M. Honker, "A River Sometimes Runs Through It: A History of Salt River Flooding and Phoenix" (PhD diss., Arizona State University, 2002).

13. Billy M. Jones, *Health-Seekers in the Southwest, 1817–1900* (Norman: University of Oklahoma Press, 1967), 120; *Arizona Daily Star*, March 2, 1888.

14. Gaylord M. McGrath, "The Evolution of Resorts and Guest Ranches in Greater Phoenix," (unpublished manuscript, 1973, Arizona Collection MSM-132, Hayden Library, Arizona State University), 5; *Arizona Daily Star*, June 18, 1895.

15. J. George Hilzinger, *Treasure Land: A Story* (Tucson: Arizona Advancement Company, 1897, repr. Glorieta, NM: Rio Grande, 1969), 55–57.

16. Harold Bell Wright, "Why I Did Not Die," *American Magazine*, June 1924, 14–15; Lawrence V. Tagg, *Harold Bell Wright: Storyteller to America* (Tucson: Westernlore, 1986), 123–24 (a picture of Wright's camp on p. 124).

17. Dick Hall, "Ointment of Love: Oliver E. Comstock and Tucson's Tent City," *Journal of Arizona History* 19 (Summer 1978): 112.

18. Ibid., 112–13.

19. The 1911–1912 city directory estimated four thousand visitors, while the 1913 directory stated three thousand. *Arizona State Business Directory* (Denver: Gazetteer Publishing Company, 1912), 362; *Phoenix City and Salt River Valley Directory, 1913* (Los Angeles: Arizona Directory Company, 1913), 5.

20. McGrath, "Evolution of Resorts," 6.

21. Luckingham, *Phoenix*, 133; McGrath, "Evolution of Resorts," 6–8.

22. Luckingham stated 1924, McGrath stated 1926. Luckingham, *Phoenix*, 86; McGrath, "Evolution of Resorts," 9.

23. *Arizona Republican*, December 15, 1928.

24. Ibid., February 23, 1929.

25. McGrath, "Evolution of Resorts," 10; Luckingham, *Phoenix*, 86–87.

26. Susan Ey, "Room, Board, and Billiard Tables: The Early Hotels of Tucson, 1860–1900" (May 16, 1978, AHS ephemera file Tucson-Hotels-General, Arizona Historical Society, Tucson); Blake Brophy, "Tucson's Arizona Inn: The Continuum of Style," *Journal of Arizona History* 24 (Autumn 1983): 259; Kimmelman states that construction of the Santa Rita Hotel was completed in 1904. Alex Kimmelman, "Luring the Tourist to Tucson: Civic Promotion during the 1920s," *Journal of Arizona History* 28 (1987): 148; Mose Drachman, "L.H. Manning, City Builder," *Arizona Daily Star*, December 3, 1933.

27. "Westward Look Resort: Southwestern Hospitality since 1912" (promotional letter, mimeograph, n.d., in the possession of the author; hereafter "Westward Look").

28. *Arizona Daily Star*, November 23, 1928; Barbara Joan Ketchum, "A Critical Analysis of One of Tucson's Early Twentieth Century Hotels, the El Conquistador" (master's thesis, University of Arizona, 1985), 27; Kimmelman, "Luring the Tourist," 150.

29. Kimmelman, "Luring the Tourist," 150; Brophy, "Arizona Inn," 264.

30. Brophy, "Arizona Inn," 274–75.

31. Ibid., 255–82; Kimmelman, "Luring the Tourist," 135–54.

32. *Tucson Sunshine Climate Club, 1941* (brochure, Special Collections, University of Arizona Library).

33. *Arizona Graphic*, December 2, 1899.

34. Robert A. Trennert, "Phoenix and the Indians: 1867–1930," in Johnson, *Phoenix in the Twentieth Century*, 60–62.

35. *Arizona Republican*, February 22, 1896.

36. *Arizona Graphic*, October 7, 1899.

37. Ibid., December 9, 1899.

38. *Arizona Republican*, December 14, 1900.

39. Trennert, "Phoenix and the Indians," 62.

40. Kimmelman, "Luring the Tourist," 139–42.

41. *Tucson Citizen*, January 11, 1925; "Ed Echols (Mr. Rodeo) Tells of Birth of Tucson 'Fiesta'" (AHS ephemera file Rodeo-History, Arizona Historical Society, Tucson, n.d.).

42. Leighton Kramer, "La Fiesta de los Vagueros," *Progressive Arizona: A Magazine Illustrating Commercial, Industrial, Agricultural, Scenic Arizona* (Official Organ of the Automobile Club of Arizona), February 1926, 13; *Tucson Citizen*, January 15, 1925.

43. Kimmelman, "Luring the Tourist," 143.

44. *Progressive Arizona*, February 1926.

45. *Arizona Daily Star*, February 24, 1925. Ed Echols stated in his reminiscence that Shannon had been drunk, and the reference was picked up by Kimmelman and Sheridan, but the newspaper at the time made no such claim. Kimmelman, "Luring the Tourist," 146; Sheridan, *Arizona*, 243.

46. *Progressive Arizona*, February 1926; Sheridan, *Arizona*, 243.

47. Tagg, *Harold Bell Wright*, 120.

48. Ibid., 129.

49. Harold Bell Wright, *Mine with the Iron Door* (New York: D. Appleton, 1923), 4.

50. Tagg, *Harold Bell Wright*, 129.

51. Ibid., 127.

52. Jerome L. Rodnitzky, "Recapturing the West: The Dude Ranch in American Life," *Arizona and the West*, 10 (Summer 1968): 115.

53. "Westward Look"; Rodnitzky, "Recapturing the West," 118–19.

54. Douglas Kreutz, "The High Life: Foothills Living Part of the American Dream," *Arizona Daily Star*, July 12, 1987; Sheridan, *Arizona*, 242. In 1940 there were about forty dude ranches in the vicinity of Tucson, ranging from active ranches with modest guest accommodations to the most luxurious resort ranches. *Arizona Daily Star*, February 23, 1940. At the bottom of its magazine advertisements, for example, Rancho Linda Vista, a dude

ranch (and later an artists' commune) in Oracle, stated, "Absolutely no Tuberculars Accepted." Sheridan, *Arizona*, 240–41.

55. Sheridan, *Arizona*, 240–41.

56. Sheridan reports the club's formation in 1919, but the *Arizona Republican* reported 386 members in the club "in its first year" in 1923. The club's membership grew to 517 members in 1924 and 550 members in 1925. *Arizona Republican*, December 27, 1927.

57. Sheridan, *Arizona*, 240–41.

58. *Arizona Republican*, December 27, 1925; Bradford Luckingham, "The Promotion of Phoenix," in Johnson, *Phoenix in the Twentieth Century*, 86–87.

59. *Arizona Republican*, November 23, 1927; December 30, 1928; June 9, 1929.

60. *Arizona Daily Star*, November 23, 1928, 4; Ketchum, "El Conquistador," 27; The Valley of the Sun moniker was coined in 1934 by a Phoenix ad agency. Luckingham, *Phoenix*, 110.

61. *Arizona Republican*, February 23, 1929.

62. Tucson Chamber of Commerce, *Saguaro National Monument* (University of Arizona Library, Special Collections, 1933).

63. *Arizona Republican*, May 5, 22, 1921.

64. Luckingham, *Phoenix*, 110.

Chapter 6: Depression Proof

1. Luckingham, "Promotion of Phoenix," 86–87; Sheridan, *Arizona*, 240–41.

2. U.S. Bureau of the Census, *Census of the United States*, Sixteenth, 1940, *Census of Population*, 2:383 (hereafter *Population*, 1940). The Depression-proof quote is from Sheridan, *Arizona*, 242.

3. *Arizona Daily Star*, September 24, 1882; Lynn D. Baker, "Tucson Water History: A Reference Book," vol. 1 (unpublished manuscript, Tucson Water Department, August 13, 2000, University of Arizona Law Library Special Collections).

4. Betancourt, "Arroyo Legacy," 103; *Arizona Daily Star*, July 16, 1891.

5. Most references cite 1893 as the year of the water company's first well, although Gelt et al., "Water in the Tucson Area," gives 1889 as the year. This seems unlikely given the above-average rainfall in Tucson that year—more than eighteen inches—and a search of newspapers and water company records shows no reference to a well servicing the city system in 1889. *Arizona Daily Star*, March 3, 21, 31, 1893.

6. *Arizona Daily Star*, February 23, 1940; E. S. Davidson, *Geohydrology and Water Resources of the Tucson Basin, Arizona* (Water Supply Paper 1939-E, USGS, 1973).

7. City of Tucson, *Charter and Ordinances of the City of Tucson*, ed. Ben C. Hill (Tucson: City of Tucson, 1926), 288–89; *Arizona Daily Star*, February 13, 1923; Gelt et al., "Water in the Tucson Area," 8; Baker, "Tucson Water History," 13-4.

8. *Arizona Daily Star*, February 6, 1923.

9. Ibid., February 15, 1893.

10. Ibid., June 19, 1903.

11. Douglas E. Kupel, *Fuel for Growth: Water and Arizona's Urban Environment* (Tucson: University of Arizona Press, 2003), 105.

12. Solomon Warner, Manuscript Collection, Arizona Historical Society, MS 844.

13. Kupel, *Fuel for Growth*, 105–6.

14. *Arizona Daily Star*, November 15, 1932; January 11, 1934; July 24, 1935; August 2, 1938.

15. Ibid., July 24, 1935; August 1, 1938; Baker, "Tucson Water History," 134, 135.

16. Baker, "Tucson Water History," 132, 137.

17. Holzhauser says two miles; Condron says four miles. William Holzhauser, "Lake in the Catalinas Assured," *Tucson*, November 1934, 5; A. H. Condron, "What Sabino Canyon Means to Tucson," *Tucson*, April 1936, 12.

18. Holzhauser, "Lake in the Catalinas," 5.

19. Ibid., 17; Condron, "Sabino Canyon," 5, 12; see also David Wentworth Lazaroff, *Sabino Canyon: The Life of a Southwestern Oasis* (Tucson: University of Arizona Press, 1993), 98–99; Michael F. Logan, *Fighting Sprawl and City Hall: Resistance to Urban Growth in the Southwest* (Tucson: University of Arizona Press, 1995), 20.

20. Condron, "Sabino Canyon," 12.

21. *Arizona Republican*, September 21, December 3, 4, 1929.

22. Ibid., February 10, 11, 12, 1930.

23. Kupel, *Fuel for Growth*, 109; *Arizona Republican*, June 25, 26, 1930; Jay Edward Niebur, "The Social and Economic Effects of the Great Depression on Phoenix, Arizona, 1929–1934" (master's thesis, Arizona State University, 1967), 44–45, 47.

24. Kupel, *Fuel for Growth*, 110–11.

25. *Arizona Republican*, June 26, 1930.

26. Kupel, *Fuel for Growth*, 111–12.

27. Wenum explains that in 1951, "Officials in Phoenix were gravely concerned over the fact that the majority of fringe area residents disposed of sewerage in cesspools or outdoor toilets. With nearly 70,000 people living in the unincorporated fringe, Phoenix serviced only 739 connections outside the city limits. Inadequate disposal facilities in the densely populated fringe posed a serious threat to public health and to ground water resources in the valley." John D. Wenum, "Spatial Growth and the Central City: Problems, Potential, and the Case of Phoenix, Arizona" (PhD diss., Northwestern University, 1968), 119. For a general discussion of septic tank developments, see Adam Rome, *The Bulldozer in the Countryside: Suburban Sprawl and the Rise of American Environmentalism* (New York: Cambridge University Press, 2001), see particularly chap. 3, "Septic-Tank Suburbia: The Problem of Waste Disposal at the Metropolitan Fringe."

28. Wenum interviewed city officials involved in annexations and found that orderly growth, extension of urban services to fringe areas, and "enlargement of municipal tax base" to be the goals of proannexation forces. Wenum, "Spatial Growth," 93–94. See also Kupel, *Fuel for Growth*, 112–13.

29. *Arizona Republic*, August 19, 1933.

30. Ibid., October 19, December 8, 1933.

31. Ibid., October 19, December 8, 9, 19, 1933.

32. Ibid., August 28, 1934.

33. Ibid., August 30, 1934.

34. Ibid., August 30, October 19, 20, December 4, 9, 13, 1934.

35. Ibid., February 12, 16, March 17, 1935.

36. Ibid., March 17, 1935.

37. Ibid., May 12, 1935.

38. Kupel, *Fuel for Growth*, 115–16; *Arizona Republic*, August 4, 7, 1936; *Phoenix Gazette*, July 21, 1937.

39. Tagg, *Harold Bell Wright*, 137–39.

40. Arthur G. Horton, *An Economic, Political and Social Survey of Phoenix and the Valley of the Sun* (Tempe, AZ: Southside Progress, 1941), 145.

41. Ibid.

42. McGrath, "Evolution of Resorts," 13–14; Patricia Myers McElfresh, *Scottsdale: Jewel in the Desert* (Woodland Hills, CA: Windsor, 1984), 42; *Phoenix Gazette*, May 28, 1936.

43. McElfresh, *Scottsdale*, 27, 44.

44. Horton, "Survey of Phoenix," 145.

45. Horton, "Survey of Phoenix," 134–36; Luckingham, "Promotion of Phoenix," 87–88.

46. *Arizona Daily Star*, February 23, 1940.

47. Ibid.

48. Luckingham, *Phoenix*, 113; *Arizona Republic*, Nov. 17, 1940.

49. Tara A. Blanc, *An Oasis in the City: The History of the Desert Botanical Garden* (Phoenix: Heritage, 2000), 10–12.

Chapter 7: The Air-Conditioned Capital of the World

1. *Population, 1940*, 2:383.

2. *Arizona Daily Star*, August 6, September 24, 29, 1940; Charles H. Broman, *The Story of the Tucson Airport Authority, 1948–1966* (Tucson: Tucson Airport Authority, December 31, 1966, Special Collections, University of Arizona Library), 6; James E. Cook, "Making War in the Sunshine," *Arizona Republic*, December 3, 1978.

3. *Arizona Republic*, January 22, June 24, August 16, 1941.

4. Ibid., January 15, June 24, 1941.

5. *Arizona Daily Star*, September 2, 1945; Cook, "Making War."

6. C. L. Sonnichsen, *Tucson: The Life and Times of an American City* (Norman: University of Oklahoma Press, 1982), 272–73; Cook, "Making War."

7. Luckingham, *Phoenix*, 139–40.

8. Ibid., 140.

9. Ibid.; Cook, "Making War"; Susan M. Smith, "Litchfield Park and Vicinity" (master's thesis, University of Arizona, 1948), 94–101.

10. Sonnichsen, *Tucson*, 272. For the clunker label, see A. Scott Berg, *Lindbergh* (New York: G. P. Putnam's Sons, 1998), 446.

11. Tom McNight, "Manufacturing in Arizona," *University of California Publications in Geography* 8 (1962): 327–31.

12. *Arizona Republic*, July 24, 1935, April 12, 1936.

13. For an explanation of the various cooling technologies used in Arizona, see *Arizona Republic*, May 20, 1936.

14. *Arizona Republic*, November 17, 1940.

15. Ibid., May 20, 1936, November 17, 1940.

16. John Shirer, "The Motorola Research Laboratory in Phoenix," *Arizona Business and Economic Review* 2 (February 1953): 2; Phoenix organizations invested more time and money attracting people and business than did the other cities of the Southwest. During the 1950s the annual budget of the Phoenix Chamber of Commerce, for example, contained more funds for national advertising than similar organizations in the other cities. Some leaders in the other cities noticed this disadvantage and told their own booster organizations, calling for larger advertising budgets for their own chambers of commerce. See *Phoenix Action*, "Disinterested Outsiders Say Phoenix Best Publicized City in the U.S.," editorial, February 1950, 4–5; Luckingham, "Promotion of Phoenix," 89.

17. Shirer, "Motorola Research Laboratory," 3.

18. Daniel E. Noble, "Motorola Expands in Phoenix," *Arizona Business and Economic Review* 3 (June 1954): 1.

19. The legislature passed the tax reform on December 20, and Sperry-Rand announced its decision to move to Phoenix the next day, December 21, 1955. *Arizona Republic*, December 21, 22, 1955; Luckingham, "Urban Development," 224–28.

20. Luckingham, "Promotion of Phoenix," 90; *Arizona Republic*, December 10, 1955.

21. Luckingham, "Promotion of Phoenix," 90; McNight, "Manufacturing in Arizona," 336.

22. McNight, "Manufacturing in Arizona," 325, 331, 336.

23. Kupel, *Fuel for Growth*, 156–57.

24. At this juncture, analysis of the Phoenix leadership varies. Kupel considers the city's leaders to be well intentioned and basically competent. He gives them credit for engaging in long-range planning and taking the actions necessary to maintain the postwar boom. Smith, on the other hand, finds the city's leadership to be deficient. Ironically, city leaders pushed business expansion with zeal and generous resources but proved short sighted and penurious when it came to the management of the city's water system. Kupel, *Fuel for Growth*, 146–47; Smith, "Community Growth," 160, 162–63.

25. *Arizona Republic*, May 29, 30, 1946.

26. Ibid., May 29, 1946.

27. *Phoenix Gazette*, May 27, 28, 1946.

28. Smith, "Community Growth," 160–61; Kupel, *Fuel for Growth*, 140.

29. In one example of a stakeholder's concern, Pima Indians on the Gila River used extensive irrigation to cultivate crops. Such irrigation practices deposited minerals in the soil through the evaporation of the irrigation water. Over time, the minerals would reach levels of concentration that rendered the soil barren. The solution was simply to flush the minerals from the soil with water, which was routinely accomplished by the floods coming down the Salt River. If an upstream dam blocked the flood waters, then the minerals would build up and the farmers' land would become useless for cultivation.

30. Kupel, *Fuel for Growth*, 137–38, 140–46.

31. Smith, "Community Growth," 161; *Arizona Republic*, July 4, 5, 1951.

32. *Phoenix Republic*, May 30, 1946.

33. Smith, "Community Growth," 162; Kupel, *Fuel for Growth*, 158–59; *Phoenix Republic*, July 4, 5, 1951, January 1, 2, 1952.

34. Smith, "Community Growth," 161–62.

35. Ibid.

36. Kupel, *Fuel for Growth*, 161.

37. U.S. Bureau of the Census, *Census of the United States*, Sixteenth, 1940, 1:34, Seventeenth, 1950, 1:3.

Chapter 8: Leaving Tucson?

1. "Population, Housing and Employment Characteristics in Maryvale" (typescript, City of Phoenix Planning Department, n.d., Hayden Library, Arizona Documents, Arizona State University Library); "Maryvale Village: A Plan for Our Future" (City of Phoenix Planning Department, February 1985, Hayden Library, Arizona Documents, Arizona State University).

2. Land purchased for $250 in 1940 could be sold in 1980 for $25,000. Luckingham, *Phoenix*, 188; *Arizona Republic*, May 26,1980.

3. Luckingham, *Phoenix*, 191–93, 205–6; Anita Welch, "The Phoenix Mystique," *Phoenix*, March 1976, 44–45, 69.

4. Luckingham, *Phoenix*, 188–89.

5. Ibid., 187.

6. Luckingham, *Phoenix*, 191–93.

7. Wenum, "Spatial Growth," 129.

8. Luckingham, *Phoenix*, 194.

9. Luckingham understates the resistance to annexation, claiming a community consensus behind the city's expansion: "Unlike so many central cities elsewhere in the nation, the desert hub was not hemmed in by incorporated suburban communities. . . . A positive attitude remained regarding annexation as an appropriate tool to prevent overcrowding and other problems found in more compact cities." This was true after 1970, but glosses over the conflicts over annexations in the 1960s. Luckingham, *Phoenix*, 194.

10. Wenum, "Spatial Growth," 175–75.

11. Ibid., 174–76.

12. Ibid., 171–72.

13. Ibid., 172–73.

14. Kupel, *Fuel for Growth*, 163–64.

15. Frank Welsh, *How to Create a Water Crisis* (Boulder, CO: Johnson Books, 1985), 43.

16. Luckingham, *Phoenix*, 203–4; Doug MacEachern, "Agriculture: Essential Industry or Anachronistic Pursuit?" *Phoenix*, August 1980, C13–14.

17. Smith, "Community Growth," 163.

18. Luckingham, *Phoenix*, 188; *Phoenix*, "The Economy '76," August 1976, 77–78, 126.

19. Luckingham, *Phoenix*, 193–94.

20. Richard Newhall, "The Long Wait at the Intersection," Arizona, Sunday supplement, *Arizona Republic*, January 15, 1967.

21. Russell Pulliam, *Publisher, Gene Pulliam, the Last of the Newspaper Titans* (Ottawa, IL: Jameson Books, 1984), 285–86.

22. Luckingham, *Phoenix*, 199–200; Pulliam, *Publisher*, 286.

23. Luckingham, *Phoenix*, 200–201.

24. Luckingham, *Phoenix*, 182, 208–9; *Phoenix*, "Phoenix Mountain Preserve," editorial, August 1978, 49; Doug MacEachern, "Mountain Preserves: A Battle for Survival," *Phoenix*, August 1980, F-8–11.

25. Sonnichsen, *Tucson*, 284.

26. Weldon Heald and Phyllis Heald, "Tucson: Gracious Living in the Sun," *Arizona Highways*, February 1958, 12.

27. Hughes Aircraft Company, *Careers in the Sun* (Special Collections, University of Arizona Library).

28. Tucson Chamber of Commerce, *Tucson . . . a City, an Opportunity, a Way of Life* (Special Collections, University of Arizona Library, 1958).

29. Tucson Chamber of Commerce, *The Guest Informant, 1952–1953* (Special Collections, University of Arizona Library).

30. Ibid.

31. Kreutz, "High Life."

32. J. W. Murphey, J. W. Murphey Papers (Arizona Historical Society).

33. Kreutz, "High Life."

34. John D. Margolis, *Joseph Wood Krutch: A Writer's Life* (Knoxville: University of Tennessee Press, 1980); Sonnichsen, *Tucson*, 300; Logan, *Fighting Sprawl*, 79–83.

35. *Arizona Daily Star*, October 4, 1956; Joseph Wood Krutch, "Man's Mark on the Desert," in *If You Don't Mind My Saying So* (New York: William Sloane, 1964), 364.

36. Krutch, "Man's Mark," 361–67.

37. Ibid., 365.

38. Logan, *Lessening Stream*, 215–16.

39. William E. Martin, Helen M. Ingram, Nancy K. Laney, Adrian H. Griffin, *Saving Water in a Desert City* (Washington, DC: Resources for the Future, 1984), 16.

40. Ibid., 19.

41. Ibid., 20.

42. Ibid., 24; Logan, *Lessening Stream*, 216–17.

43. Logan, *Lessening Stream*, 24, 217–18.

Epilogue

1. Fountain Hills Chamber of Commerce and Arizona Office of Tourism, *The Tallest Fountain in the World Is at Fountain Hills, Arizona*, (pamphlet, Arizona Documents, Hayden Library, Arizona State University, 1997).

2. Ibid.

3. Blanc, *Oasis in the City*.

4. Gelt et al., "Water in the Tucson Area," 12–13.

BIBLIOGRAPHY

Ackerly, Neal W., Jerry B. Howard, and Randall H. McGuire. *La Ciudad Canals: A Study of Hohokam Irrigation Systems at the Community Level.* 7 vols. Anthropological Field Studies no. 17. Tempe: Arizona State University, 1985.

Alexander, William B. Alexander Papers. University of Arizona Library, Special Collections, AZ 171.

Allison, Warren. "Allison Pioneer Days in Tucson." Unpublished manuscript compiled by Elvira R. Odom. Allison Family Papers, Arizona Historical Society, MS 113.

Arizona State Business Directory, 1911–1912. Denver: Gazetteer Publishing Company, 1911–12.

Arnold, Lee W. "An Ecological Study of the Vertebrate Animals of the Mesquite Forest." Master's thesis, University of Arizona, 1940.

August, Jack L. *Vision in the Desert: Carl Hayden and Hydropolitics in the American Southwest.* Fort Worth: Texas Christian University Press, 1999.

Baker, Lynn D. "Tucson Water History: A Reference Book." Vol. 1. Unpublished manuscript. Tucson Water Department, August 13, 2000. University of Arizona Law Library Special Collections.

Bannon, John Francis. *The Spanish Borderlands Frontier, 1513–1821.* Albuquerque: University of New Mexico Press, 1974.

Barney, James M. *Tales of Old Arizona.* 3 vols. Arizona Historical Foundation, Arizona State University Library, n.d.

Barter, G. W. *Directory of the City of Tucson, 1881.* San Francisco: H.S. Crocker, 1881. University of Arizona Library, Special Collections.

Beiber, Ralph P. *Southern Trails to California in 1849.* Vol. 5. Glendale: Arthur H. Clarke Company, 1937.

Berg, A. Scott. *Lindbergh.* New York: G. P. Putnam's Sons, 1998.

Betancurt, Julio. "Tucson's Santa Cruz River and the Arroyo Legacy." Ph.D. diss., University of Arizona, 1990.

Bigler, Henry W. "Extracts from the Journal of Henry W. Bigler." *Utah Historical Quarterly* 5 (April 1932): 35–64.

Blanc, Tara A. *An Oasis in the City: The History of the Desert Botanical Garden.* Phoenix: Heritage, 2000.

Bliss, Robert S. "The Journal of Robert S. Bliss." *Utah Historical Quarterly* 4 (July 1931): 67–96.

Bolton, Herbert Eugene. *Rim of Christendom: A Biography of Eusebio Francisco Kino, Pacific Coast Pioneer.* New York: Macmillan, 1936.

Broman, Charles H. *The Story of the Tucson Airport Authority, 1948–1966.* Tucson: Tucson Airport Authority, December 31, 1966. Special Collections, University of Arizona Library.

Brophy, Blake. "Tucson's Arizona Inn: The Continuum of Style." *Journal of Arizona History* 24 (Autumn 1983): 255–82.

Brown, Dee. "Geronimo, Part 1." *American History Illustrated* 15 (June 1980): 12–20.

———. "Geronimo, Part 2." *American History Illustrated* 15 (July 1980): 36–45.

Bryan, Alan L. *Paleo-American Prehistory.* Occasional Papers of the Idaho State University Museum, no. 16. Pocatello: Idaho State University Press, 1965.

Burrus, Ernest J. *Kino and Manje: Explorers of Sonora and Arizona; Their Vision of the Future, A Study of Their Expeditions and Plans, with an Appendix of Thirty Documents.* St. Louis, MO: Jesuit Historical Institute, 1971.

Cable, John S., Susan L. Henry, and David E. Doyel, eds. "City of Phoenix, Archaeology of the Original Townsite: Block 28-North." Central Phoenix Redevelopment Agency, City of Phoenix, November 1983.

Carleton, James H. "Proclamation of James H. Carleton, Colonel First California Volunteers, Major Sixth U.S. Cavalry, at Tucson, Arizona, June 8, 1862." *War of the Rebellion Official Records of the Union and Confederate Armies,* series I, vol. 9, 561–62. Washington, DC: Government Printing Office, 1883.

Chamberlain, T. C. "Requisites and Qualifying Conditions of Artesian Wells." USGS Survey Annual Report, 1885. Reprinted in *Physical Hydrogeology,* edited by A. Allan Freeze and William Back, 297–307. Stroudsburg, PA: Hutchinson Ross, 1983.

Clarke, A. B. *Travels in Mexico and California.* Boston: Wright and Hasty Printers, 1852.

Cockrum, E. Lendell. *Mammals of the Southwest.* Tucson: University of Arizona Press, 1982.

Comeaux, Malcolm L. *Arizona: A Geography.* Boulder, CO: Westview Press, 1981.

Condro, A. H. "What Sabino Canyon Means to Tucson." *Tucson,* April 1936.

Cooke, Philip St. George. *The Conquest of New Mexico and California in 1846–1848.* New York: G. P. Putnam's Sons, 1878. Reprinted, Chicago: Rio Grande Press, 1964.

Couts, Cave Johnson. *Hepah, California! The Journal of Cave Johnson Couts, from Monterey, Nuevo Leon, Mexico to Los Angeles, California during the Year 1848–1849.* Edited by Henry F. Dobyns. Tucson: Arizona Pioneers' Historical Society, 1961.

Cox, Cornelius C. "From Texas to California in 1849." Edited by Mabelle Eppard Martin. *Southwestern Historical Quarterly* 29 (October 1925): 128–46.

Crook, George. *General George Crook: His Autobiography.* Edited by Martin F. Schnitt. Norman: University of Oklahoma Press, 1946.

Crown, Patricia L., and W. James Judge. *Chaco and Hohokam: Prehistoric Regional Systems in the American Southwest.* Santa Fe, NM: School of American Research Press, 1991.

Czaplicki, Jon, S., and James D. Mayberry. "An Archaeological Assessment of the Middle Santa Cruz River Basin, Rillito to Green Valley, Arizona, for the Proposed Tucson Aqueduct Phase B, Central Arizona Project." Archaeological Series no. 164. Tucson: University of Arizona, Arizona State Museum, 1983.

Davidson, E. S. *Geohydrology and Water Resources of the Tucson Basin, Arizona.* Water Supply Paper 1939-E. U.S.G.S., 1973.

Davis, Arthur Powell. "Irrigation Near Phoenix, Arizona." Water-Supply and Irrigation Papers, no. 2. U.S.G.S., 1897.

———. "Water Storage on Salt River, Arizona." Water-Supply and Irrigation Paper no. 73. U.S.G.S., 1903.

Dobyns, Henry F. "Indian Extinction in the Middle Santa Cruz River Valley, Arizona." *New Mexico Historical Review* 38 (January 1963): 163–81.

———. *Spanish Colonial Tucson: A Demographic History.* Tucson: University of Arizona Press, 1976.

———. *Tubac through Four Centuries: An Historical Resume and Analysis.* Arizona State Parks Board, March 15, 1959. University of Arizona Library microfilm no. 1045.

Doelle, William H. "Human Use of the Santa Cruz River in Prehistory." Paper presented at the American Society for Environmental History Conference, Tucson, Arizona, 1999.

Doelle, William H., and Henry D. Wallace. "The Changing Role of the Tucson Basin in the Hohokam Regional System." In Gummerman, *Exploring the Hohokam*, 279–346.

Downum, Christian E. "Between Desert and River: Hohokam Settlement and Land Use in the Los Robles Community." Anthropological Papers No. 7. Tucson: University of Arizona, 1993.

"Ed Echols (Mr. Rodeo) Tells of Birth of Tucson 'Fiesta.'" Rodeo-History ephemera file, Arizona Historical Society.

Erhlich, Karen Lynn. "Arizona Territorial Capital Moves to Phoenix." *Arizona and the West* 23 (Fall 1981): 239–40.

Ey, Susan. "Room, Board, and Billiard Tables: The Early Hotels of Tucson, 1860–1900," May 16, 1978. Tucson-Hotels-General ephemera file, Arizona Historical Society.

Field, John, Keith Katzer, Jim Lombard, and Jeanette Schuster. "A Geomorphic Survey of the Picacho and Northern Tucson Basins." In *The Northern Tucson Basin Survey: Research Directions and Background Studies*, Archaeological Series no. 182, edited by John H. Madsen, Paul R. Fish, and Suzanne K. Fish, 33–49. Tucson: University of Arizona, Arizona State Museum, 1993.

Finnerty, Maragret. "Arizona Capital: The Politics of Relocation," *History Forum* 23 (Spring 1981): 239–40.

Fish, Paul R., and Suzanne K. Fish. "Hohokam Political and Social Organization." In Gummerman, *Exploring the Hohokam*, 191–76.

Fish, Suzanne, and Gary Naban. "Desert as Context: The Hohokam Environment." In Gummerman, *Exploring the Hohokam*, 29–60.

Follansbee, Robert. *A History of the Water Resources Branch of the United States Geological Survey to June 30, 1919.* Internal manuscript printed and copied by U.S.G.S. in 1939. Forward by Nathan C. Grover written in 1938.

Fountain Hills Chamber of Commerce and Arizona Office of Tourism. *The Tallest Fountain in the World is at Fountain Hills, Arizona.* Pamphlet. 1997. Arizona Documents, Hayden Library, Arizona State University.

Gallego, Hilario. "Reminiscence of an Arizona Pioneer—by Hilario Gallego." Interviewed by Mrs. George F. Kitt and Charles Morgan Wood, Tucson, April 22, 1926. *Arizona Historical Review* 6 (January 1935): 78.

Gelt, Joe, Jim Henderson, Kenneth Seasholes, Barbara Tellman, and Gary Woodard. "Water in the Tucson Area: Seeking Sustainability." College of Agriculture, Water Resources Research Center, Issue Paper No. 20. University of Arizona, 1999.

Golder, Frank Alfred. *The March of the Mormon Battalion from Council Bluffs to California, Taken from the Journal of Henry Standage*. New York: Century, 1928.

Green, A. C. *900 Miles on the Butterfield Trail*. Denton: University of North Texas Press, 1994.

Gummerman, George J., ed. *Exploring the Hohokam*. Albuquerque: University of New Mexico Press, 1991.

Hall, Dick. "Ointment of Love: Oliver E. Comstock and Tucson's Tent City." *Journal of Arizona History* 19 (Summer 1978): 111–30.

Hastings, James R. "The Tragedy at Camp Grant in 1871." *Arizona and the West* 1 (Summer 1959): 150–52.

Heald, Weldon, and Phyllis Heald. "Tucson: Gracious Living in the Sun." *Arizona Highways*, February 1958.

Helmick, Walter R. "The Santa Cruz River Terraces Near Tubac, Santa Cruz County, Arizona." Master's thesis, University of Arizona, 1986.

Hilzinger, J. George. *Treasure Land: A Story*. Tucson: Arizona Advancement Company, 1897. Reprinted, Glorieta, NM: Rio Grande, 1969.

A Historical and Biographical Record of the Territory of Arizona, Illustrated. Chicago: McFarland and Poole, 1896.

Hodge, F.W. "Prehistoric Irrigation in Arizona." *American Anthropologist* 6 (July 1893): 323–30.

Holzhauser, William. "Lake in the Catalinas Assured." *Tucson*, November 1934.

Honker, Andrew M. "A River Sometimes Runs Through It: A History of Salt River Flooding and Phoenix." PhD diss., Arizona State University, 2002.

Horton, Arthur G. *An Economic, Political and Social Survey of Phoenix and the Valley of the Sun*. Tempe, AZ: Southside Progress, 1941.

Hughes Aircraft Company. *Careers in the Sun*. Special Collections, University of Arizona Library.

Johnson, G. Wesley, Jr. "Directing Elites: Catalysts for Social Change." In Johnson, *Phoenix in the Twentieth Century*, 13–32.

———, ed. *Phoenix in the Twentieth Century: Essays in Community History*. Norman: University of Oklahoma Press, 1993.

Jones, Billy M. *Health-Seekers in the Southwest, 1817–1900*. Norman: University of Oklahoma Press, 1967.

Jones and Stokes Associates. "Tres Rios, Arizona: Feasibility Study." U.S. Army Corps of Engineers, Los Angeles District, South Pacific Division, 2000.

Kautz, August V. "August V. Kautz, Col. Eighth U.S. Infantry to the Assistant Adjutant-General, Military Division of the Pacific and Department of California, August 15, 1877." *House Executive Documents*. Vol. 1, part 2, 1877–78, Serial 1794.

Kessell, John L. *Mission of Sorrows: Jesuit Guevavi and the Pimas, 1691–1767*. Tucson: University of Arizona Press, 1970.

————. "The Puzzling Presidio: San Felipe de Guevavi, alias Terrenate." *New Mexico Historical Review* 41 (January 1966): 21–46.

Ketchum, Barbara Joan. "A Critical Analysis of One of Tucson's Early Twentieth Century Hotels, the El Conquistador." Master's thesis, University of Arizona, 1985.

Kimmelman, Alex. "Luring the Tourist to Tucson: Civic Promotion during the 1920s." *Journal of Arizona History* 28 (1987): 135–54.

Kramer, Leighton. "La Fiesta de los Vagueros." *Progressive Arizona: A Magazine Illustrating Commercial, Industrial, Agricultural, Scenic Arizona*, Official Organ of the Automobile Club of Arizona, February 1926, 8–14.

Krutch, Joseph Wood. "Man's Mark on the Desert." In *If You Don't Mind My Saying So.* New York: William Sloane, 1964.

Kupel, Douglas E. *Fuel for Growth: Water and Arizona's Urban Environment.* Tucson: University of Arizona Press, 2003.

Langellier, J. Phillip. "Camp Grant Affair, 1871: Milestone in Federal Indian Policy?" *Military History of Texas and the Southwest* 15 (Summer 1979): 17–29.

Lazaroff, David Wentworth. *Sabino Canyon: The Life of a Southwestern Oasis.* Tucson: University of Arizona Press, 1993.

Lee, Willis T. "The Underground Waters of Gila Valley, Arizona." Water-Supply and Irrigation Paper No. 14, Series 0, Underground Water, 25. U.S.G.S., 1904.

Logan, Michael F. *Fighting Sprawl and City Hall: Resistance to Urban Growth in the Southwest.* Tucson, University of Arizona Press, 1995.

————. *The Lessening Stream: An Environmental History of the Santa Cruz River.* Tucson: University of Arizona Press, 2002.

Lucero, Carmen. "Reminiscences of Mrs. Carmen Lucero as Interpreted by Miss Maggy Brady to Mrs. Geo. F. Kitt, 1928." Typescript, two copies. Carmen Lucero File, L 935, Arizona Historical Society.

Luckingham, Bradford. *Minorities in Phoenix: A Profile of Mexican-American, Chinese American, and African American Communities, 1860–1992.* Tucson: University of Arizona Press, 1994.

————. *Phoenix: The History of a Southwestern Metropolis.* Tucson: University of Arizona Press, 1989.

————. "The Promotion of Phoenix." In Johnson, *Phoenix in the Twentieth Century*, 83–92.

————. "Urban Development in Arizona: The Rise of Phoenix." *Journal of Arizona History* 22 (Summer 1981): 197–234.

Lynch, Richard E. *Winfield Scott: A Biography of Scottsdale's Founder.* Scottsdale: City of Scottsdale, 1987.

MacEachern, Doug. "Agriculture: Essential Industry or Anachronistic Pursuit?" *Phoenix*, August 1980.

————. "Mountain Preserves: A Battle for Survival." *Phoenix*, August 1978.

MacNeish, Richard S. "Early Man in the New World." *American Scientist* 64 (1976): 316–27.

Margolis, John D. *Joseph Wood Krutch: A Writer's Life.* Knoxville: University of Tennessee Press, 1980.

Martin, Paul. "Pleistocene Overkill." *Natural History* 76 (December 1967): 32–38.

Martin, William E., Helen M. Ingram, Nancy K. Laney, and Adrian H. Griffin. *Saving Water in a Desert City.* Washington, DC: Resources for the Future, 1984.

"Maryvale Village: A Plan for Our Future." City of Phoenix Planning Department, February 1985. Arizona Documents, Hayden Library, Arizona State University.

Masse, W. Bruce. "Prehistoric Irrigation Systems in the Salt River Valley, Arizona." *Science* 214 (October 23, 1981): 408–9.

Mawn, Geoffrey P. "Promoters, Speculators, and the Selection of the Phoenix Townsite." *Arizona and the West* 19 (Fall 1977): 207–24.

McCarty, Kieran. *Copper State Bulletin.* Arizona State Genealogical Society 17 (Winter 1982): 91–93.

———. *Desert Documentary: The Spanish Years, 1767–1821.* Historical Monograph no. 4, Arizona Historical Society, 1976.

———. *A Spanish Frontier in the Enlightened Age: Franciscan Beginnings in Sonora and Arizona.* Washington, DC: Academy of American Franciscan History, 1981.

McCormick, Richard C. "Letter of Secretary Richard C. McCormick to President Abraham Lincoln from Prescott, Arizona Territory, Dec. 1, 1864." Record Group 59, Territorial Papers: Arizona, vol. 1, National Archives, Pacific Region–Laguna Niguel.

McElfresh, Patricia Myers. *Scottsdale: Jewel in the Desert.* Woodland Hills, CA: Windsor, sponsored by the Scottsdale Historical Society, 1984.

McGrath, Gaylord M. "The Evolution of Resorts and Guest Ranches in Greater Phoenix." Unpublished manuscript, 1973. Arizona Collection MSM-132. Hayden Library, Arizona State University.

McNight, Tom. "Manufacturing in Arizona." *University of California Publications in Geography* 8 (1962): 289–344.

Meredith, H. L. "Reclamation in the Salt River Valley, 1902–1917." *Journal of the West* 7 (January 1968): 76–83, 92.

Meyer, Michael. *Water in the Hispanic Southwest.* Tucson: University of Arizona Press, 1984.

Miller, Darlis. "Civilians and Military Supply in the Southwest." *Journal of Arizona History* 23 (1982): 115–38.

———. *Soldiers and Settlers.* Albuquerque: University of New Mexico Press, 1989.

Murphey, J.W. *J. W. Murphey Papers.* Arizona Historical Society.

Murphy, Merwin L. "W.J. Murphy and the Arizona Canal Company." *Journal of Arizona History* 23 (Summer 1982): 139–70.

Nevin, M. Fenneman. *Physiography of Western United States.* New York: McGraw-Hill, 1931.

Nials, Fred L., David A. Gregory, and Donald A. Graybill. "Salt River Streamflow and Hohokam Irrigation Systems." In *The 1982–1984 Excavations at Las Colonias; Environment and Subsistence,* Archaeological Series no. 162, 6 vols., edited by Carol Ann Heathington and David A. Gregory, 1:70–74. Tucson: University of Arizona, 1989.

Niebur, Jay Edward. "The Social and Economic Effects of the Great Depression on Phoenix, Arizona, 1929–1934." Master's thesis, Arizona State University, 1967.

Noble, Daniel E. "Motorola Expands in Phoenix." *Arizona Business and Economic Review* 3 (June 1954): 1–2.

Oblasser, Bonaventure. "Papagueria: The Domain of the Papagos." *Arizona Historical Review* 7 (April 1936): 6.

Officer, James, E. *Arizona's Hispanic Perspective.* Arizona Academy, 8th Arizona Town Hall, May 1981. "Research Report Prepared by University of Arizona, May 17–20, 1981."
———. *Hispanic Arizona, 1536–1856.* Tucson: University of Arizona Press, 1987.

Ormsby, Waterman L. *The Butterfield Overland Mail, by Waterman L. Ormsby, Only Through Passenger on the First Westbound Stage.* Edited by Lyle H. Wright and Josephine M. Bynum. San Marino, CA: Huntington Library, 1942.

Oury, William. *Arizona Historical Review* 4 (April 1931): 15–20.

Pancoast, Charles Edward. *A Quaker Forty-Niner: The Adventures of Charles Edward Pancoast on the American Frontier.* Edited by Anna Paschall Hannum. Philadelphia: University of Pennsylvania Press, 1930.

Parker, John T. C. "Channel Change on the Santa Cruz River, Pima County, Arizona, 1936–1986." Open-File Report 93-41, U.S.G.S., December 1993.

Pattie, James O. *The Personal Narrative of James O. Pattie.* Edited by William H. Goetzmann. Philadelphia and New York: J. Lippincott, 1962.

Peterson, James F. "San Antonio: An Environmental Crossroads on the Texas Spring Line." In *On the Border: An Environmental History of San Antonio,* edited by Char Miller, 17–37. Pittsburgh, PA: University of Pittsburgh Press, 2001.

Phoenix. "The Economy '76." Editorial. August 1976.
———. "Phoenix Mountain Preserve." Editorial. August 1978.

Phoenix Action. "Disinterested Outsiders Say Phoenix Best Publicized City in U.S." Editorial. February 1950.

Phoenix Chamber of Commerce. *Resources of the Salt River Valley: Maricopa County, Arizona.* 1891. Special Collections, University of Arizona Library.

Phoenix City and Salt River Valley Directory. Los Angeles: Arizona Directory Company, 1913, 1920, and 1923.

Phoenix Directory, 1882. Phoenix: Bensel Directory Company, 1892, reprinted 1971. University of Arizona Library, Special Collections.

"Population, Housing and Employment Characteristics in Maryvale." Typescript, no date. City of Phoenix Planning Department. Arizona Documents, Hayden Library, Arizona State University.

Poston, Charles D. *Building a State in Apache Land.* Edited by John M. Meyers. Tempe, AZ: Aztec, 1963.

Potash, Robert A. "Notes and Documents." *New Mexico Historical Review* 24 (October 1949): 332–35.

Powell, H. M. T. *Santa Fe Trail to California: The Journal and Drawings of H.M.T. Powell, 1849–1852.* Edited by Douglas S. Watson. San Francisco: Book Club of California, 1931.

Pulliam, Russell. *Publisher, Gene Pulliam, the Last of the Newspaper Titans.* Ottawa, IL: Jameson Books, 1984.

Rea, Amadeo M. *Once a River: Bird Life and Habitat Changes on the Middle Gila River.* Tucson: University of Arizona Press, 1983.

Rodnitzky, Jerome L. "Recapturing the West: The Dude Ranch in American Life." *Arizona and the West* 10 (Summer 1968): 111–26.

Rome, Adam. *The Bulldozer in the Countryside: Suburban Sprawl and the Rise of American Environmentalism.* New York: Cambridge University Press, 2001.

Rusling, James Fowler. *Across America; or, The Great West and the Pacific Coast.* New York: Sheldon, 1874.

Schellie, Don. *Vast Domain of Blood: The Story of the Camp Grant Massacre.* Los Angeles: Westernlore, 1968.

Schmidli, Robert, J. *Climate of Phoenix, Arizona.* Phoenix: Weather Service Forecast Office. WR-177, December 1986. Abridged on-line version by R.S. Cerveny, Office of Climatology, Arizona State University, December 1996. http://geography.asu.edu/cerveny/phxwx.htm.

Scholfield, Maj. Gen. John. "Report of Major General Schofield, Headquarters Military Division of the Pacific, San Francisco, California, October 20, 1871." Executive Documents, 42nd Cong., 2nd. sess., 1871–72, vol. 2, part 1, Serial 1503. Washington, DC: Government Printing Office, 1872.

Schwalen, H. C., and R. J. Shaw. *Groundwater Supplies of Santa Cruz Valley of Southern Arizona between Rillito Station and the International Boundary.* Agricultural Experiment Station Bulletin No. 288. Tucson: University of Arizona, 1957.

Sellers, William D. "The Climate of Arizona." In *Arizona Climate*, Institute of Atmospheric Physics, edited by Christine R. Green and William D. Sellers, 11–40. Tucson: University of Arizona Press, 1964.

Shallat, Todd A. *Structures in the Stream: Water, Science, and the Rise of the U.S. Army Corps of Engineers.* Austin: University of Texas Press, 1994.

Sheridan, Thomas E. *Arizona: A History.* Tucson: University of Arizona Press, 1995.

———. *Landscapes of Fraud: Mission Tumacácori, the Baca Float, and the Betrayal of the O'odham.* Tucson: University of Arizona Press, 2006.

———. *Los Tucsonenses: The Mexican Community in Tucson, 1854–1941.* Tucson: University of Arizona Press, 1986.

Sherman, W. T. "W.T. Sherman, General to General W.W. Belknap, Secretary of War, November 20, 1869." Executive Documents, 41st Cong., 2nd sess., 1869–70, vol. 2. Serial 1412. Washington, DC: Government Printing Office, 1870.

Shirer, John. "The Motorola Research Laboratory in Phoenix." *Arizona Business and Economic Review.* Bureau of Business Research, College of Business and Public Administration, University of Arizona 2 (February 1953): 1–4.

Smith, Karen L. "The Campaign for Water in Central Arizona." *Arizona and the West* 23 (Summer 1981): 127–48.

———. "Community Growth and Water Policy." In Johnson, *Phoenix in the Twentieth Century*, 155–63.

———. *The Magnificent Experiment: Building the Salt River Reclamation Project, 1890– 1917.* Tucson: University of Arizona Press, 1986.

Smith, Susan M. "Litchfield Park and Vicinity." Master's thesis, University of Arizona, 1948.

Smythe, William E. *The Conquest of Arid America*. New York: Harper and Brothers, 1900.

Sonnichsen, C. L. *Tucson: The Life and Times of an American City*. Norman: University of Oklahoma Press, 1982.

Tagg, Lawrence V. *Harold Bell Wright: Storyteller to America*. Tucson: Westernlore, 1986.

Tellman, Barbara, Richard Yarde, and Mary G. Wallace. *Arizona's Changing Rivers: How People Have Affected the Rivers*. Water Resources Research Center, Issue Paper 19. Tucson: College of Agriculture, University of Arizona, 1997.

Thomsen, B. W., and J. J. Porcello. "Predevelopment Hydrology of the Salt River Indian Reservation, East Salt River Valley, Arizona." Water-Resources Investigations Report 91-4132. U.S.G.S., 1991.

Thornber, J. J. "Plant Acclimatization in Southern Arizona." *Plant World* 14 (January 1911): 1–9.

Trennert, Robert A. "Phoenix and the Indians: 1867–1930." In Johnson, *Phoenix in the Twentieth Century*, 53–68.

Tucson, City of. *Charter and Ordinances of the City of Tucson*. Edited by Ben C. Hill. Tucson: City of Tucson, 1926.

Tucson Chamber of Commerce. *The Guest Informant, 1952–1953*. Special Collections, University of Arizona Library.

———. "Saguaro National Monument." Special Collections, University of Arizona Library, 1933.

———. *Tucson . . . a City, an Opportunity, a Way of Life*. 1958. Special Collections, University of Arizona Library.

Tucson Sunshine Climate Club, 1941. Brochure. Special Collections, University of Arizona Library.

U.S. Bureau of the Census. *Census of the United States*. Eleventh, 1890. Vol. 1, *Census of the Population*.

———. *Census of the United States*. Eleventh, 1890. Vol. 10, *Statistics of Agriculture*.

———. *Census of the United States*. Twelfth, 1900. Vols. 1 and 6, *Agriculture, Part 2, Crops and Irrigation*.

———. *Census of the United States*. Thirteenth, 1910. Vol. 2, *Census of the Population*.

———. *Census of the United States*. Fourteenth, 1920. Vols. 1 and 7, *Irrigation and Drainage*.

———. *Census of the United States*. Sixteenth, 1940. Vol. 2, *Census of the Population*.

———. *Census of the United States*. Seventeenth, 1950. Vol. 1, *Census of the Population*.

Wagoner, Jay J. *Arizona Territory, 1863–1912: A Political History*. Tucson: University of Arizona Press, 1970.

Warner, Solomon. Manuscript Collection. Arizona Historical Society, MS 844.

"Water for Phoenix: Building of Roosevelt Dam." Editorial. *Journal of Arizona History* 18 (Autumn 1977): 284.

Way, Phocion R. "Overland via 'Jackass Mail' in 1858: The Diary of Phocion R. Way." Edited by William A. Duffen. *Arizona and the West* 2 (Spring–Winter 1960): 35–53, 147–64, 279–92, 353–70.

Weber, David J. *The Taos Trappers: The Fur Trade in the Far Southwest, 1540–1846.* Norman: University of Oklahoma Press, 1970.

Welch, Anita. "The Phoenix Mystique." *Phoenix,* March 1976.

Welsh, Frank. *How to Create a Water Crisis.* Boulder, CO: Johnson Books, 1985.

Wenum, John D. "Spatial Growth and the Central City: Problems, Potential, and the Case of Phoenix, Arizona." PhD diss., Northwestern University, 1968.

"Westward Look Resort: Southwestern Hospitality since 1912." Promotional letter, mimeograph, no date, in the possession of the author.

White, Richard. *It's Your Misfortune and None of My Own: A New History of the American West.* Norman: University of Oklahoma Press, 1991.

Wimberley, Laura A. "Establishing 'Sole Source' Protection: The Edwards Aquifer and the Safe Drinking Water Act." In *On the Border: An Environmental History of San Antonio,* edited by Char Miller, 169–81. Pittsburgh, PA: University of Pittsburgh Press, 2001.

Wissler, Clark. *Indians of the United States.* New York: Doubleday, 1966.

Worcester, Donald Emmet. "The Apache Indians of New Mexico in the Seventeenth Century." Master's thesis, University of California, Berkeley, 1940.

Wright, Harold Bell. "Why I Did Not Die." *American Magazine,* June 1924.

Zarbin, Earl. "The Swilling Legacy." Salt River Project, 1987. Reproduction of *Arizona Republic* articles by Zarbin published between August 13 and August 30, 1978.

INDEX

air conditioning, 4, 95, 138, 144–45
AiResearch, 143, 148
A Mountain. *See* Sentinel Peak
Anglo settlements: and the Apaches, 40, 42; in Arizona, 4, 28, 34, 37, 39, 85, 144; in Florence, 66; in Phoenix, 52, 54, 88–89; in Tucson, 36, 39, 46, 50, 52
annexations: by Phoenix, 122, 163–65, 172, 182, 211n9; by Tucson, 117, 149, 150, 177, 182
Apaches: and Anglo settlements, 40, 42; concentration policy for, 44–45, 46, 47; and the Forty-niners, 34, 40; massacre at Camp Grant, 42–44; Mexican relations with, 30, 32–33; and Pima Indians, 26, 27; raids by, 39, 40, 42, 52; and Salt River valley development, 32, 36; Spanish relations with, 17, 26, 27–28, 30; and trappers, 31; and Tubac, 38; and Tucson, 28, 52, 59–60, 90, 96; U.S. Army's relations with, 41–42, 43, 44, 49, 56–57, 60. *See also* Camp Grant; Chiricahua Apaches; Geronimo; Indian Ring; Pinal Apaches; San Carlos Reservation
Arizona: as an American republic, 34–35; defense industries in, 141–42, 147; sovereignty established, 37, 39; state legislature, 133, 147, 166, 210n19; Supreme Court, 123; territorial capital of, 37–38; winter visitors to, 130. *See also* tourism; *individual city names*
Arizona (movie), 131, 191
Arizona Canal, 57, 64, 80, 81, 92, 156, 166
Arizona Groundwater Management Act, 166
Arizona-Sonora Desert Museum, 177, 178, 190, 191
Army Air Corps, 105, 138, 139, 140, 141
artesian water, 72–73, 76, 77, 203n24
Avondale, 78, 185

Barrio Libre, 87–88
Beat the Peak program, 180–81, 182, 192
Biltmore, 93, 94, 106
bond issues, for Horseshoe Dam, 153–54; in Phoenix, 119–20, 121, 122–24, 125, 132; in Tucson, 113, 116, 118, 126, 151
Buckeye, 58, 77
Bureau of Indian Affairs, 44, 45, 46, 120
Butte City, 53. *See also* Tempe

Camelback Inn, 128, 167
Camelback Mountain, as geological feature, 18, 81, 93, 106, 128; preservation of, 158, 171–72, 187
Camp Grant, 41–42, 42–44, 52
Camp Lowell, 40
Camp McDowell, 49
canals: by the Hohokam, 22, 23–24, 47, 49, 64, 197n30; and Phoenix, 57, 64, 66; by Pima Indians, 25; on the Salt River, 22, 57, 64, 69. *See also* Arizona

Canal; Consolidated Canal; Maricopa Canal; Mexican Ditch; Salt River Project; Salt River Valley Canal
Carleton, General James H., 37–38
Carrillo, Leopoldo, 46–47
Catalina Foothills Estates, 175–76
Catalina Mountains, 88, 90, 91, 103, 175, 189
Central Arizona Project (CAP), 156–57, 166, 192–93
Chamberlain, T. C., 73, 203n24
Chandler, 74, 92, 164
Chandler, Alexander J., 57–58, 74, 92
Chandler Ranch, 57, 92
Chiricahua Apaches, 45, 46, 59. *See also* Apaches; Cochise; Geronimo
Clum, John, 47, 55
Cochise, 40, 45. *See also* Apaches
Colorado River, 16, 20, 39, 120, 192, 193
concentration policy, 44–45, 46, 47. *See also* San Carlos Reservation
conservation: lack of in Phoenix, 155, 166, 167; in Tucson, 113–14, 151, 167, 192, 193–94. *See also* Beat the Peak program
Consolidated Canal, 92. *See also* Consolidated Canal Company
Consolidated Canal Company, 57, 74. *See also* Chandler, Alexander J.; Consolidated Canal
Cowboy and Indian Carnival, 96–97
Crook, General George, 41, 44, 56, 57, 59

Davis, Arthur Powell, 70, 73
Davis-Monthan Air Field, 138–39, 140, 141, 142, 148
Deer Valley Water Treatment Plant, 165–66
Depression. *See* Great Depression
Desert Botanical Garden, 133, 189
Dude Ranchers Association, 102, 104
dude ranches, 89, 99, 102–4, 129, 206n54
Duppa, Darrell, 53, 202n36

El Conquistador, 94–95, 105, 141
El Pueblito, 26. *See also* San Agustín

Federal Emergency Relief Administration (FERA), 118
federal reclamation, 12, 64, 66–67, 68, 70, 82. *See also* Reclamation Act of 1902; Salt River Project
Fiesta de los Vaqueros, 98–99, 130
Florence, 1, 58, 66–67
Fort Huachuca, 99, 139
Fort McDowell Indian Reservation, 120, 182, 188
Fort Whipple, 37, 38
Forty-niners, 33–34
Fountain Hills, 188–89
Fowler, Benjamin, 82–83
Fulton, James C., 72, 73